Email & Dark Web Investigations: Tracking Leaks & Breaches

Algoryth Ryker

Emails are the backbone of modern communication, but they also serve as a goldmine of intelligence. From tracking cybercriminals to exposing phishing campaigns and uncovering leaked data, email OSINT plays a pivotal role in digital investigations. Meanwhile, the dark web—the shadowy underbelly of the internet—acts as a marketplace for stolen credentials, ransomware services, and illicit transactions.

This book, Email & Dark Web Investigations: Tracking Leaks & Breaches, bridges the gap between these two critical domains. It equips investigators, cybersecurity professionals, and OSINT analysts with the skills to trace email origins, analyze metadata, monitor data breaches, and navigate the dark web legally and ethically.

By the end of this book, you'll be able to:

✓ Investigate email senders, headers, and authentication records.

✓ Track email breaches and leaks across the surface web and dark web.

✓ Analyze phishing campaigns and scam tactics.

✓ Investigate ransomware groups and threat actors.

✓ Trace cryptocurrency transactions linked to cybercrime.

✓ De-anonymize dark web users and track online footprints.

Let's dive deep into the digital shadows and uncover intelligence where others can't.

Chapter Breakdown

1. Introduction to Email Investigations

- The role of emails in OSINT and cyber investigations.
- Understanding how email systems work (SMTP, POP3, IMAP).
- Identifying common threats: spoofing, phishing, and breaches.
- Tools and techniques for gathering intelligence from emails.
- How email investigations help track cybercriminals.
- Case Study: How an email address led to a major cyber arrest.

2. Tracking Email Origins & Headers

- Understanding email headers and metadata.
- How to extract sender IP addresses and mail server details.

- Analyzing SPF, DKIM, and DMARC records for email authentication.
- Detecting email forwarding, spoofing, and redirection tactics.
- **Case Study**: Exposing a fake CEO email scam.

3. Email Breach & Leak Investigations

- How emails end up in data breaches and why it matters.
- Investigating leaks using "Have I Been Pwned" and breach databases.
- Tracking stolen credentials and reused passwords.
- Investigating email use across dark web marketplaces.
- **Case Study**: Tracking a hacked corporate email account.

4. Investigating Phishing Attacks & Scam Emails

- Understanding phishing campaigns and common attack vectors.
- Analyzing suspicious links, attachments, and fraudulent emails.
- Reverse-engineering phishing domains and attack infrastructure.
- Tracking phishing kit sellers on the dark web.
- **Case Study**: Investigating a global phishing operation.

5. Using Data Breach Databases & Leak Sites

- The role of paste sites, breach dumps, and leak forums.
- Searching for compromised credentials and PII.
- Investigating "combolists" and corporate breaches.
- Monitoring for future leaks using open-source tools.
- **Case Study**: How a data breach exposed millions of users.

6. Dark Web Basics: Accessing & Investigating

- What the dark web really is—myths vs. reality.
- How Tor, I2P, and other anonymity networks function.
- OSINT techniques for monitoring dark web activities legally.
- Exploring dark web search engines and intelligence tools.
- **Case Study**: A law enforcement dark web takedown.

7. Marketplaces & Criminal Forums on the Dark Web

- Evolution of dark web marketplaces and their role in cybercrime.
- How stolen data is bought, sold, and traded.

- Investigating cybercrime forums and vendor reputations.
- Identifying connections between different illicit marketplaces.
- **Case Study**: Tracking an illegal marketplace's operators.

8. Cryptocurrency Tracking in the Dark Web

- How cryptocurrencies facilitate anonymity in cybercrime.
- Using blockchain explorers to track Bitcoin transactions.
- Identifying money laundering techniques on the dark web.
- Investigating ransomware and extortion payments.
- **Case Study**: Unmasking a dark web drug dealer through crypto analysis.

9. OSINT on Ransomware Groups & Threat Actors

- Understanding how ransomware groups operate.
- Investigating ransomware victim data leaks and extortion tactics.
- Tracking communications between attackers and victims.
- Analyzing Ransomware-as-a-Service (RaaS) models.
- **Case Study**: How OSINT helped disrupt a ransomware group.

10. De-anonymizing Dark Web Users

- How cybercriminals attempt to remain anonymous.
- Identifying behavioral patterns and OPSEC failures.
- Cross-referencing dark web identities with surface web data.
- Using linguistic analysis and writing style profiling.
- **Case Study**: How a simple mistake unmasked a dark web vendor.

11. Case Study: Investigating a Dark Web Operation

- Discovery of a suspicious dark web marketplace.
- Gathering intelligence and identifying key actors.
- Cross-referencing dark web data with surface web OSINT.
- Analyzing financial transactions and hidden clues.
- Coordinating with law enforcement and cybersecurity teams.
- **Final Outcome**: Lessons learned from the investigation.

12. Ethical & Legal Concerns in Dark Web OSINT

- Legal risks of investigating the dark web.

- Jurisdictional challenges in cybercrime cases.
- Ethics of engaging with dark web forums and actors.
- How to safely collect and report dark web intelligence.
- The future of OSINT in combating dark web crime.
- **Case Study**: When OSINT crossed legal and ethical boundaries.

Final Thoughts

In the world of cyber investigations, email intelligence and dark web OSINT are crucial for tracking digital threats, exposing scams, and protecting businesses and individuals. The ability to trace email origins, monitor data breaches, analyze ransomware groups, and uncover hidden dark web activities can make the difference between stopping a cybercriminal or letting them operate unchecked.

By the time you finish this book, you'll have the skills to:

✓ Investigate email senders, leaks, and phishing campaigns.

✓ Analyze cybercriminal networks operating on the dark web.

✓ Track cryptocurrency transactions linked to cybercrime.

✓ De-anonymize hidden actors using OSINT techniques.

✓ Navigate legal and ethical challenges in cyber investigations.

With cybercrime evolving every day, mastering email and dark web OSINT is no longer an option—it's a necessity.

Let's get started. 🚀

1. Introduction to Email Investigations

In this chapter, we will delve into the crucial world of email investigations, a cornerstone of modern OSINT (Open Source Intelligence) operations. With email being one of the most widely used communication channels, it often serves as a gateway for cybercriminal activities, data breaches, and unauthorized leaks. We will explore the techniques and tools used to trace email origins, identify fraudulent activities, and connect digital footprints to uncover hidden networks and potential threats. Whether you're looking into a single suspicious email or mapping out a larger breach, mastering the art of email investigations is an essential skill in tracking down elusive cybercriminals and protecting sensitive information.

1.1 The Role of Emails in OSINT & Cyber Investigations

Emails have long been an essential communication tool for both personal and professional use, but they also serve as a powerful tool for cyber investigators in the realm of Open Source Intelligence (OSINT). In the digital age, emails are integral to cybercrime, cyber espionage, data breaches, and many forms of illicit online activities. As such, understanding the role of emails in OSINT and cyber investigations is crucial for investigators seeking to uncover hidden information, identify perpetrators, and protect sensitive data.

At its core, OSINT involves the gathering of publicly available information from open sources—whether that be from the internet, social media platforms, or even public records—to build a comprehensive understanding of a subject. In this context, emails play a pivotal role in OSINT investigations because they are an often overlooked but highly valuable source of digital footprints. Emails serve as critical communication channels that can lead investigators to uncovering identities, tracing cybercriminal activities, and mapping out networks of individuals involved in illegal operations. The following sections will explore the key ways in which emails contribute to OSINT and cyber investigations, focusing on email forensics, tracing digital footprints, uncovering connections, and understanding the evolving threats associated with email-based crimes.

1. Email as a Digital Fingerprint

One of the primary roles of email in OSINT and cyber investigations is as a form of a "digital fingerprint." When investigating potential cybercrimes, the email address used in communications, whether as part of a phishing scam, malware distribution, or as a source of a data breach, can reveal a lot about the individual or group responsible. By tracking email addresses and analyzing the metadata associated with those emails, investigators can uncover hidden connections to criminal organizations, identify patterns of attack, and find links to other online identities.

Email addresses are often the primary point of contact in cybercrime and online fraud. For example, during a phishing attack, the attacker uses a fake email address to impersonate a trusted entity, such as a bank or government agency, in order to deceive the victim into revealing sensitive information. By tracing this email address, an investigator can search for other similar phishing campaigns, identify the sender's domain, and find other instances where this address has been used. Forensic analysis of these patterns can lead to the identification of networks of cybercriminals who share similar tactics, techniques, and procedures (TTPs).

Furthermore, the metadata embedded in every email—such as the sender's IP address, the routing details of the message, and the timestamp—can be crucial in tracking the origin of an email. By following these leads, investigators can trace the path an email took across the internet, identifying the exact locations and servers involved. Even if the sender attempts to mask their identity using methods such as VPNs or Tor, investigators can still detect and piece together valuable data through header analysis and traffic correlation techniques.

2. Email forensics and Header Analysis

Email forensics is a branch of cyber forensics that focuses on recovering and analyzing email data in order to identify critical evidence of cybercrime. By examining the structure of email headers, investigators can glean essential information about the route an email took to reach the recipient's inbox, the server used to send it, and the originating IP address. This information is especially important when investigating criminal activities such as spam campaigns, phishing attempts, or unauthorized data breaches.

Email headers provide insights into the authentication and routing of the email. For example, email protocols like SPF (Sender Policy Framework), DKIM (DomainKeys Identified Mail), and DMARC (Domain-based Message Authentication, Reporting, and Conformance) are used to authenticate whether an email is from a legitimate source or if it has been spoofed. Investigators can scrutinize these headers to determine whether an email is legitimate or whether it was fabricated using malicious intent. Spoofing—where attackers forge the sender's email address to appear legitimate—is a common tactic used by cybercriminals, especially in phishing campaigns. By analyzing these headers, investigators can expose fraudulent emails, trace them back to the originating server, and even pinpoint the geographic location from which they were sent.

In addition to the technical analysis of email headers, investigators can also examine the content of emails themselves. Malicious emails often contain signs that can point to cybercrime, such as suspicious attachments, links to fake websites, or the inclusion of stolen credentials. By cross-referencing email content with known patterns from previous cybercrime campaigns, investigators can quickly identify and assess the threat posed by these emails.

3. Investigating Email-Based Data Breaches

Data breaches, particularly those involving email accounts, are a significant concern in the world of cybercrime and cybersecurity. In many cases, cybercriminals gain unauthorized access to email accounts in order to steal sensitive information, which they may later use for identity theft, financial fraud, or corporate espionage. Investigating these email-based breaches is an essential aspect of OSINT and cyber investigations.

Emails are often the entry point for larger breaches, whether through phishing attacks, weak passwords, or exploiting known vulnerabilities. Once a breach occurs, stolen email addresses and credentials are frequently sold on the dark web, where they can be used to commit a variety of cybercrimes. Investigators can track down these compromised email addresses by searching breach databases and leak sites, cross-referencing the exposed email information with known patterns, and tracing back the origin of the breach.

Tools like Have I Been Pwned allow investigators to quickly check whether an email address has been part of a known breach, providing valuable intelligence on the extent of the breach and which services or accounts have been compromised. In some cases, investigators may be able to trace the source of the breach and identify the perpetrators, especially when the breach involves a phishing campaign or other targeted attack.

4. Email in Phishing and Social Engineering

Phishing remains one of the most widespread and dangerous cybercrimes, with email being the primary method for carrying out these attacks. Cybercriminals often use email as a tool to carry out social engineering attacks, which manipulate victims into divulging confidential information such as passwords, banking details, or other personal data. Understanding the role of email in phishing attacks is essential for investigators looking to disrupt these activities.

Phishing emails often involve fraudulent websites or links that mimic legitimate entities, such as banks, email service providers, or government organizations. Investigators can analyze these fraudulent websites and email addresses to uncover the criminals behind the phishing campaign. By performing OSINT on the email addresses involved in the phishing attempt, investigators can identify the patterns used by cybercriminals, track the origin of the attack, and ultimately prevent future incidents. Moreover, a comprehensive analysis of phishing emails, including the IP addresses, sender domains, and attached files, can help investigators link multiple phishing campaigns together, uncovering larger criminal networks.

5. Leveraging Email Intelligence in Cyber Investigations

Finally, emails play an important role in the broader context of cyber investigations. OSINT investigators often use email intelligence to piece together complex criminal activities, track individuals, and uncover the broader scope of cybercrime operations. By analyzing email communications between cybercriminals, investigators can gain insight into their strategies, partners, and even their intentions.

Email intelligence also plays a significant role in preventing future cyberattacks. By understanding the tactics used by attackers to infiltrate systems through email, investigators can proactively identify vulnerabilities and strengthen defense measures. Furthermore, by monitoring email traffic and analyzing metadata in real time, investigators can detect early signs of cyber threats, allowing for rapid response to potential attacks.

Emails are much more than just a tool for communication; they are a critical source of intelligence in OSINT and cyber investigations. From tracing the origin of suspicious emails and uncovering email-based data breaches to identifying phishing campaigns and social engineering attempts, emails provide invaluable insights into the digital world of cybercrime. By leveraging email forensics and investigating the trail of evidence left behind in email communications, OSINT investigators can expose hidden networks, track down cybercriminals, and protect individuals and organizations from the ever-growing threats in the digital age.

1.2 Understanding Email Infrastructure: SMTP, POP3 & IMAP

Email communication is a fundamental part of digital interaction, serving both personal and professional needs. However, for investigators, cybersecurity professionals, and OSINT analysts, understanding the technical backbone of email infrastructure is crucial. The way emails are sent, received, and stored can provide valuable insights into cyber investigations, especially when tracing malicious activities, tracking phishing attempts, or uncovering email-based fraud.

Three primary protocols govern how email functions over the internet: Simple Mail Transfer Protocol (SMTP), Post Office Protocol v3 (POP3), and Internet Message Access Protocol (IMAP). Each of these protocols plays a distinct role in handling email communications, and understanding their differences helps investigators extract useful intelligence. This chapter will delve into the mechanics of these protocols, their significance in email investigations, and how cybercriminals exploit them.

1. The Role of SMTP in Sending Emails

SMTP (Simple Mail Transfer Protocol) is the standard protocol used for sending emails across networks. It operates on port 25 (traditional), 587 (secured submission), and 465 (legacy SSL/TLS encryption). SMTP is responsible for relaying messages between mail servers and ensuring that emails reach their intended recipients.

When a user sends an email, the SMTP server of their email provider processes the request and attempts to deliver the message. The process follows these key steps:

- **Connection Establishment** – The sender's email client connects to an SMTP server, authenticates the user, and initiates the email transaction.
- **Email Transmission** – The email is sent from the sender's email server to the recipient's email server, passing through one or more intermediary servers.
- **Email Delivery or Failure** – The recipient's mail server either accepts the email for delivery or rejects it due to policy violations, authentication failures, or blacklisting.

SMTP in Cyber Investigations

Since SMTP leaves behind a detailed digital footprint, investigators can extract valuable metadata from email headers, including:

- The originating IP address of the sender
- The route the email took across different mail servers
- The timestamps of when the email was sent and received
- Information about possible spoofing or phishing attempts

Attackers often manipulate SMTP headers to hide their true identity or make their emails appear legitimate. Email spoofing—where a sender forges the "From" field to appear as a trusted source—is a common trick used in phishing campaigns. Investigators use SPF (Sender Policy Framework), DKIM (DomainKeys Identified Mail), and DMARC (Domain-based Message Authentication, Reporting & Conformance) records to verify if an email's origin is legitimate.

Additionally, compromised SMTP servers are frequently used to distribute spam and malware. Cybercriminals often exploit open relay SMTP servers, which allow anyone to send emails without authentication, to distribute mass phishing emails or spam campaigns. Tracking SMTP relay paths can help analysts determine whether an email originated from a legitimate corporate server or a hijacked machine controlled by attackers.

2. POP3: Retrieving Emails from a Server

POP3 (Post Office Protocol v3) is an email protocol used for retrieving messages from a mail server. Unlike SMTP, which focuses on sending, POP3 allows email clients to download messages to a local device and then remove them from the server. It typically operates on port 110 (unencrypted) and 995 (SSL/TLS encrypted).

The POP3 process follows these steps:

- The email client connects to the mail server and authenticates using a username and password.
- The server transfers all new emails to the client.
- Emails are then deleted from the server (depending on the settings).

POP3 in Cyber Investigations

While POP3 is simple and efficient, it presents both advantages and challenges in cyber investigations:

- **Forensic Recovery**: Because emails are downloaded and often removed from the server, investigators may need access to the local email client (e.g., Outlook, Thunderbird) to retrieve deleted messages.
- **Tracing Deleted Emails**: If a user deletes an email on their device, recovery depends on whether backups exist. Digital forensics tools can sometimes recover deleted emails from local storage.
- **Account Hijacking**: Many cybercriminals use POP3-based access to compromise email accounts, retrieve sensitive information, and then erase traces of their activity by deleting emails from the server.

One common investigation scenario involves business email compromise (BEC) attacks, where attackers gain access to corporate email accounts and extract sensitive data. If an organization uses POP3, emails may not be stored on the server, making real-time monitoring difficult. Cybercriminals exploit this limitation by downloading emails and deleting them before IT teams can react.

To counteract this, many modern email services have moved away from POP3 in favor of IMAP, which retains emails on the server, allowing for better forensic analysis and account recovery options.

3. IMAP: A Modern Approach to Email Retrieval

IMAP (Internet Message Access Protocol) is a more advanced protocol compared to POP3, designed for retrieving and managing emails across multiple devices while keeping them stored on the server. It operates on port 143 (unencrypted) and 993 (SSL/TLS encrypted).

Unlike POP3, IMAP offers:

- **Server-Side Storage** – Emails remain on the server, allowing access from multiple devices.
- **Selective Synchronization** – Users can download only the headers of emails and retrieve full messages when needed.
- **Folder Management** – Users can organize emails into folders, mark messages as read/unread, and use search functions.

IMAP in Cyber Investigations

IMAP's server-side storage is highly beneficial for digital forensic investigations, as emails remain accessible even if the local device is compromised or wiped. Investigators can:

- **Recover Deleted Emails**: Since emails remain on the server, deleted messages may be recoverable for a certain period, depending on retention policies.
- **Monitor Ongoing Threats**: IMAP access logs on email servers provide detailed information on login attempts, IP addresses, and potential unauthorized access.
- **Detect Compromised Accounts**: Cybercriminals often use IMAP to access victim email accounts without triggering alerts, as they can read and move messages without downloading them permanently.

One common attack technique involves credential stuffing, where attackers use previously leaked email-password combinations to log into IMAP-enabled accounts and extract sensitive emails. Organizations that fail to enforce strong password policies or multi-factor authentication (MFA) are particularly vulnerable.

4. Comparative Analysis: SMTP vs. POP3 vs. IMAP

Feature	SMTP (Sending)	POP3 (Retrieval)	IMAP (Retrieval & Management)
Primary Function	Sends emails	Downloads emails	Synchronizes emails across devices
Port Numbers	25, 587, 465	110, 995	143, 993
Email Storage	Not stored	Downloaded & deleted from server	Stored on server
Access from Multiple Devices	N/A	No	Yes
Common Vulnerabilities	Spoofing, open relay abuse	Data loss from local deletion	Credential stuffing, unauthorized access

Understanding SMTP, POP3, and IMAP is crucial for OSINT analysts and cyber investigators, as these protocols form the foundation of email communication. SMTP provides a wealth of metadata useful for tracking email origins, while POP3 and IMAP govern how emails are stored and accessed. Cybercriminals frequently exploit weaknesses in these protocols to conduct phishing attacks, account takeovers, and data exfiltration.

By mastering these protocols and their forensic applications, investigators can uncover hidden digital footprints, trace malicious activities, and strengthen cybersecurity defenses against evolving email-based threats.

1.3 Common Threats: Spoofing, Phishing & Breaches

Emails are one of the most widely used communication tools in the digital age, but they are also a primary vector for cyber threats. Cybercriminals frequently exploit vulnerabilities in email systems to deceive users, steal sensitive information, and launch large-scale data breaches. Understanding the most common threats—email spoofing, phishing attacks, and data breaches—is essential for investigators, cybersecurity professionals, and OSINT analysts.

This chapter explores how these threats work, the techniques used by attackers, and the investigative methods that can help detect and mitigate risks.

1. Email Spoofing: Forging Identities for Fraud and Misinformation

What is Email Spoofing?

Email spoofing is a technique used by attackers to forge the "From" field of an email to make it appear as though it was sent by a trusted source. This tactic is often used in phishing attacks, business email compromise (BEC), misinformation campaigns, and spam distribution.

How Email Spoofing Works

Email protocols, particularly SMTP (Simple Mail Transfer Protocol), do not inherently verify sender authenticity. This allows attackers to manipulate email headers to make an email appear as though it originated from a legitimate source. Spoofed emails can be used to:

- Impersonate trusted individuals (e.g., CEOs, IT departments, government agencies)
- Trick victims into revealing sensitive data or transferring funds
- Spread misinformation or conduct social engineering attacks

Real-World Example: CEO Fraud (Business Email Compromise)

A cybercriminal spoofs the email address of a company's CEO and sends a request to the finance department, instructing them to wire a large sum of money to an external account. Since the email appears to come from the CEO's address, the employee may comply without verifying the authenticity of the request.

How to Investigate and Detect Spoofed Emails

- **Analyze Email Headers** – Check the Return-Path, Received-SPF, and DKIM-Signature fields to determine whether the sender's address has been forged.
- **Verify SPF, DKIM, and DMARC Records** – These authentication mechanisms help verify whether an email was actually sent from the claimed domain.

- **Compare Email Metadata** – The originating IP address in the headers can reveal discrepancies between the sender's real location and their claimed identity.
- **Check WHOIS Data for Domains** – If a spoofed domain is used, a WHOIS lookup can provide details about its registration and potential malicious intent.

2. Phishing Attacks: Deceptive Emails for Credential Theft

What is Phishing?

Phishing is a social engineering attack that tricks victims into revealing sensitive information, such as login credentials, credit card numbers, or personal data. Attackers typically send fraudulent emails that appear to be from legitimate sources (e.g., banks, tech companies, government agencies), urging recipients to take action.

Common Types of Phishing Attacks

- **Spear Phishing** – A targeted attack against a specific individual or organization, often using personal information to appear more convincing.
- **Whaling** – A phishing attack aimed at high-profile executives or decision-makers within an organization.
- **Clone Phishing** – Attackers copy a legitimate email, modify links or attachments, and resend it to victims.
- **Vishing & Smishing** – Voice phishing (vishing) and SMS phishing (smishing) use phone calls or text messages instead of emails to deceive victims.

How Phishing Attacks Work

- Attackers send emails that contain links to fake login pages designed to harvest credentials.
- Some phishing emails contain malicious attachments (e.g., PDFs, Word documents with macros) that execute malware upon opening.
- Other phishing attempts use urgency tactics, such as fake security alerts or account suspension warnings, to pressure users into acting quickly.

Real-World Example: PayPal Phishing Scam

An attacker sends an email claiming to be from PayPal, warning the recipient that their account has been locked due to "suspicious activity." The email contains a fake login link that redirects victims to a fraudulent PayPal website where they unknowingly enter their credentials, giving the attacker full access to their accounts.

How to Investigate and Detect Phishing Emails

- **Inspect Links Before Clicking** – Hover over links to see if they redirect to suspicious domains.
- **Analyze Email Headers** – Verify the sender's domain and check SPF, DKIM, and DMARC authentication results.
- **Check for Grammar and Formatting Issues** – Many phishing emails contain spelling errors, generic greetings, and unusual formatting.

Use OSINT Tools to Analyze Phishing Domains

- **VirusTotal** – Scan suspicious links and attachments for malware.
- **PhishTank** – Check if a URL has been reported as a phishing site.
- **WHOIS Lookup** – Identify the registrant details of a suspicious domain.

3. Email Breaches: Data Leaks & Credential Exposure

What is an Email Breach?

An email breach occurs when a database containing email addresses, passwords, or personal information is compromised and exposed to unauthorized parties. These breaches often result from hacks, database leaks, or insider threats.

How Email Breaches Happen

- **Credential Dumping** – Attackers steal large databases of email credentials from websites with weak security and post them on the dark web.
- **Data Leaks** – Poorly secured cloud storage, such as misconfigured AWS S3 buckets or unprotected databases, can lead to massive email leaks.
- **Third-Party Breaches** – Users who reuse passwords across multiple platforms are at risk if one of those platforms is breached.

Real-World Example: The LinkedIn Data Breach

In 2012, LinkedIn suffered a massive data breach, exposing over 117 million email-password combinations. These credentials were later sold on the dark web, leading to a surge in credential stuffing attacks—where attackers use stolen passwords to gain unauthorized access to other accounts.

How Cybercriminals Exploit Email Breaches

- **Credential Stuffing** – Using stolen credentials to access other accounts where users have reused passwords.
- **Business Email Compromise (BEC)** – Attackers hijack corporate email accounts to conduct fraud or intercept financial transactions.
- **Extortion Scams** – Cybercriminals send emails claiming to have hacked a victim's account, using leaked passwords as "proof" to demand ransom payments.
- How to Investigate and Respond to Email Breaches

Check if an Email is Breached

Use OSINT tools like Have I Been Pwned or DeHashed to check if an email address has appeared in breach databases.

Analyze Dark Web Leak Sites

Investigate dark web forums and marketplaces where breached email credentials are traded.

Investigate the Scope of the Breach

Determine whether leaked credentials have been used in further attacks (e.g., credential stuffing, account takeovers).

Encourage Security Measures

Users should reset passwords, enable multi-factor authentication (MFA), and avoid reusing passwords across platforms.

Email-based attacks—whether through spoofing, phishing, or breaches—pose significant risks to individuals and organizations. By understanding how these threats work, investigators can detect fraudulent emails, trace their origins, and mitigate potential damage.

From analyzing email headers to verifying breached credentials on the dark web, OSINT techniques play a crucial role in investigating email-related cybercrimes. As attackers continuously refine their tactics, staying informed about evolving threats and leveraging forensic analysis tools are essential steps in combating email fraud and data breaches.

1.4 Tools & Techniques for Email Intelligence Gathering

Email intelligence gathering is a critical skill for OSINT analysts, cybersecurity professionals, and investigators. By analyzing email metadata, headers, domain records, and potential breaches, analysts can uncover valuable insights about senders, recipients, and hidden cyber threats.

This chapter explores the essential tools and techniques used in email intelligence gathering, covering everything from email header analysis to dark web investigations.

1. Extracting & Analyzing Email Headers

What Are Email Headers?

Email headers contain metadata that reveals crucial details about an email's origin, transmission path, and potential signs of spoofing. While email clients display only the body of an email, the header contains:

- Sender's IP address
- Mail server hops and timestamps
- Email authentication results (SPF, DKIM, DMARC)
- Reply-to addresses and possible anomalies

How to Extract Email Headers

Each email service provides a method to view email headers:

- **Gmail** – Open an email → Click the three-dot menu → "Show original"

- **Outlook** – Open an email → Click "File" → "Properties" → Look under "Internet headers"

- **Yahoo Mail** – Open an email → Click "More" → "View raw message"

Tools for Email Header Analysis

Tool	Function	Website
MXToolbox	Analyzes email headers and checks mail server configurations	mxtoolbox.com
Email Header Analyzer (Google Admin Toolbox)	Extracts detailed routing information	toolbox.googleapps.com
WhatIsMyIP Email Header Analyzer	Traces sender IP and email route	whatismyip.com

Key Investigation Steps

- **Check SPF, DKIM, and DMARC Status** – Validate if the email is from a legitimate source or if it's spoofed.
- **Extract the Sending IP Address** – Identify the originating server's IP and perform a geolocation lookup.
- **Analyze the Route (Received Fields)** – Detect anomalies in email transmission paths.
- **Inspect Email Redirections** – Some phishing emails redirect through multiple servers to obscure their origins.

2. Investigating Email Domains & Server Infrastructure

Why Investigate Email Domains?

Cybercriminals often use fraudulent domains to impersonate trusted organizations. OSINT analysts can uncover valuable intelligence by analyzing:

- Domain registration details (WHOIS lookup)
- Mail server and DNS records
- Historical domain activity

Tools for Domain Analysis

Tool	Function	Website
Whois Lookup	Retrieves domain registration details	whois.domaintools.com
SpyOnWeb	Shows related domains & websites linked to an email domain	spyonweb.com
MXToolbox (MX Lookup)	Analyzes mail server (MX) records	mxtoolbox.com/MXLookup
ViewDNS.info	Identifies connected IPs and domain relationships	viewdns.info

Key Investigation Steps

- **Perform a WHOIS Lookup** – Check when and where a domain was registered.
- **Check MX (Mail Exchange) Records** – Validate if the domain is configured for legitimate email traffic.
- **Look for Related Domains** – Identify malicious infrastructure linked to cybercrime campaigns.
- **Check Domain Blacklists** – See if the domain is flagged for phishing or spamming.

3. Investigating Email Breaches & Leaks

Why Investigate Email Breaches?

Leaked credentials can be used in:

- Credential stuffing attacks (using stolen passwords to access multiple accounts)
- Identity theft & fraud
- Business email compromise (BEC)

Tools for Email Breach Investigation

Tool	Function	Website
Have I Been Pwned	Checks if an email has been in data breaches	haveibeenpwned.com
DeHashed	Searches leaked emails, usernames, and passwords	dehashed.com
LeakCheck	Finds breached credentials & leaked email databases	leakcheck.io
IntelX	Searches dark web leaks & paste sites	intelx.io

Key Investigation Steps

- **Search for Breached Credentials** – Identify if the target email appears in leak databases.
- **Analyze Past Breaches** – Determine when and where the email was leaked.
- **Investigate Dark Web Forums** – Check if the email is associated with hacked data markets.
- **Monitor for Credential Reuse** – Attackers often use leaked credentials for further cyberattacks.

4. Investigating Phishing Emails & Malicious Attachments

Why Investigate Phishing Emails?

Phishing is one of the most effective social engineering tactics. Analyzing phishing emails helps:

- Identify attacker infrastructure
- Trace malicious links and payloads
- Find connections to larger cybercrime networks

Tools for Phishing Analysis

Tool	Function	Website
PhishTank	Checks if a URL is a known phishing site	phishtank.com
VirusTotal	Scans email attachments and links for malware	virustotal.com
URLScan.io	Analyzes suspicious URLs and website behavior	urlscan.io
Any.Run	Runs email attachments in a sandbox environment	any.run

Key Investigation Steps

- **Extract Links from the Email** – Identify if they redirect to phishing pages.
- **Analyze Malicious Attachments** – Scan for malware, trojans, or ransomware payloads.
- **Track IP Addresses** – Investigate the origin of phishing emails.
- **Search for Similar Attacks** – Cybercriminals often reuse domains and infrastructure.

5. Dark Web & Cryptocurrency Investigations

Why Investigate Dark Web Email Activity?

Many cybercriminals buy, sell, and trade stolen emails on dark web marketplaces. Investigating these transactions can:

- Identify compromised accounts
- Trace ransomware campaigns
- Uncover cybercrime networks

Tools for Dark Web Email Investigations

Tool	Function	Website
DarkTracer	Monitors leaked credentials on dark web sites	darktracer.com
DarkSearch	Search engine for dark web marketplaces	darksearch.io
OnionSearch	Finds email leaks in .onion sites	onionsearchengine.com

Email intelligence gathering is a powerful OSINT skill that reveals insights into cybercrime, fraud, and breaches. By analyzing email headers, domain records, breaches, phishing emails, and dark web leaks, investigators can track cybercriminals, prevent fraud, and strengthen security measures.

Mastering these techniques and tools is essential for any digital investigator in the modern age of cybersecurity threats.

1.5 How Email Investigations Help Track Cybercriminals

Email investigations are a powerful tool for tracking cybercriminals, uncovering fraud, and preventing cyberattacks. Since email is a primary communication method used in phishing, business email compromise (BEC), ransomware, and dark web transactions, investigators can extract valuable intelligence by analyzing email metadata, domains, and sender behavior.

By leveraging OSINT techniques, law enforcement, cybersecurity professionals, and threat intelligence analysts can identify cybercriminals, trace their infrastructure, and even de-anonymize actors operating on the dark web. This chapter explores how email investigations aid in tracking cybercriminals and disrupting their operations.

1. Identifying the True Source of an Email

Why Is Identifying the Source Important?

Cybercriminals often use fake sender identities, spoofed addresses, or disposable email accounts. However, advanced email header analysis and metadata extraction can reveal the real sender's IP address, mail server, or even geolocation.

Key Investigation Techniques

Email Header Analysis

- Extract the Received and X-Originating-IP fields to determine the true sender's IP address.
- Use MXToolbox or Google Admin Toolbox to analyze email headers.

Tracing IP Addresses

1. Perform a WHOIS lookup on the originating IP to determine the hosting provider and possible location.
2. Use IPinfo.io or ViewDNS.info to get ISP and geolocation details.

Checking SPF, DKIM & DMARC

- If an email fails authentication checks, it may indicate spoofing or a malicious source.
- Use DMARC Analyzer or MXToolbox SPF Checker to verify legitimacy.

Real-World Example: Phishing Email from a Fake CEO

A finance employee receives an email from "ceo@company.com" requesting a wire transfer. By analyzing the email headers, investigators find that the originating IP belongs to a VPN provider in Russia, exposing the attacker's deception.

2. Investigating Domains & Email Infrastructure

Why Investigate Email Domains?

Many cybercriminals register fake domains that resemble legitimate companies (e.g., paypall-support.com instead of paypal.com). Investigating these domains can expose malicious infrastructure, phishing sites, and criminal networks.

Key Investigation Techniques

WHOIS Lookup for Domain Registration Details

- Identify when and where a domain was registered.
- Use Whois.domaintools.com to find registrant details.

Checking Mail Server (MX) Records

- Find out which mail servers handle emails for a domain.
- Use MXToolbox MX Lookup to analyze mail configurations.

Investigating Domain History

- View past ownership and changes using Wayback Machine or ViewDNS.info.

Real-World Example: Fake Banking Email Scam

A phishing email claims to be from "support@secure-bank-login.com." A WHOIS lookup reveals that the domain was registered only two weeks ago by an anonymous user, raising red flags.

3. Tracking Cybercriminals Through Email Breaches

Why Investigate Leaked Email Credentials?

Cybercriminals often reuse emails and passwords across multiple platforms. Analyzing breached email data can:

- Link criminals to past cyber activities.
- Reveal compromised accounts used in scams.
- Expose connections between different threat actors.

Key Investigation Techniques

Checking if an Email is Breached

Use Have I Been Pwned or DeHashed to see if an email appears in known data breaches.

Searching Dark Web Leak Sites

Use DarkTracer or IntelX to find leaked credentials.

Cross-Referencing Leaked Passwords

If a cybercriminal's email has leaked passwords, investigators can use this to track their other accounts.

Real-World Example: Dark Web Marketplace Admin Unmasked

A hacker running a dark web forum used an anonymous email for registration. A breach search revealed the same email was previously used for a personal PayPal account, leading to their real-world identity.

4. Following the Money: Tracking Email-Based Fraud & Ransomware Payments

How Emails Reveal Financial Crimes

Many cybercriminals use emails to request payments via:

- Cryptocurrency (Bitcoin, Monero, etc.)
- Gift cards and prepaid cards
- Bank wire fraud (BEC scams)

By tracking email conversations, investigators can uncover Bitcoin wallets, transaction patterns, and links to money laundering networks.

Key Investigation Techniques

Extracting Bitcoin Wallets from Emails

Search email contents for Bitcoin addresses and track them on Blockchair or BTCExplorer.

Identifying Financial Accounts in Emails

Look for bank details, PayPal accounts, or Venmo links mentioned in scam emails.

Monitoring Dark Web Transactions

Use Chainalysis or Elliptic to trace Bitcoin transactions linked to cybercrime.

Real-World Example: Ransomware Email Investigation

A victim receives a ransomware demand email instructing them to send 0.5 BTC to a wallet address. Investigators track the Bitcoin transaction flow, leading to an exchange account that reveals the attacker's real identity.

5. Linking Email Activity to Dark Web Identities

Why Investigate Dark Web Email Usage?

Many cybercriminals operate on dark web forums, marketplaces, and hacking communities, using emails for:

- Buying and selling stolen data
- Communicating with ransomware victims
- Registering accounts on illegal markets
- Key Investigation Techniques

Searching Dark Web Marketplaces for Emails

Use DarkSearch.io or OnionSearchEngine to find mentions of an email on the dark web.

Analyzing PGP Keys Linked to Emails

Some dark web criminals use PGP encryption to secure communications. Investigators can search for their PGP key fingerprints to identify linked accounts.

Tracking Vendor Activity on Marketplaces

Cybercriminals selling stolen emails or hacking tools often reuse their handles across multiple platforms.

Real-World Example: Cybercriminal Caught via Dark Web Email Reuse

An investigator found an email address linked to stolen credit card sales on a dark web forum. A search revealed the same email was used to register a public GitHub account, leading to the suspect's real name and social media profiles.

6. De-Anonymizing Cybercriminals Through Email Correlations

How Cybercriminals Make Mistakes

Even the most careful cybercriminals sometimes make small errors, such as:

- Using the same email on multiple platforms
- Registering domains with real names
- Forgetting to use anonymous VPNs

By correlating these mistakes, investigators can unmask real identities.

Key Investigation Techniques

Reverse Searching Emails

Use Pipl or That's Them to find social media and account registrations linked to an email.

Finding Alternate Email Variants

Check if a cybercriminal used similar usernames on different services.

Social Engineering & Undercover OSINT

Engaging with cybercriminals under an alias can help gather intelligence.

Real-World Example: Anonymous Hacker Exposed

A hacker using "anon_h4x0r@tormail.net" registered a website with a backup email linked to their real identity. A simple search connected the hacker to their personal Facebook account.

Email investigations are a crucial weapon in tracking cybercriminals. From analyzing email headers to tracing financial fraud and unmasking dark web criminals, OSINT techniques provide powerful insights that can disrupt cybercrime operations.

By combining technical analysis, database searches, and human intelligence (HUMINT), investigators can turn an anonymous email into a real-world identity, ultimately helping law enforcement and cybersecurity teams take down digital threats.

1.6 Case Study: How an Email Address Led to a Major Cyber Arrest

Cybercriminals often take extensive precautions to remain anonymous—using VPNs, the Tor network, burner phones, and encrypted messaging apps. However, even the most sophisticated threat actors can make small mistakes, and investigators can use OSINT techniques to track them down.

This case study follows a real-world investigation where a single email address became the key to unmasking a high-profile cybercriminal, leading to their arrest. It highlights the email OSINT techniques, tools, and analytical steps that played a crucial role in the takedown.

The Cybercriminal: "AlphaSupreme" – A Dark Web Kingpin

In early 2021, an anonymous cybercriminal operating under the alias "AlphaSupreme" emerged as a major figure on the dark web. This individual was involved in:

- Selling stolen credit card data & financial records
- Operating a ransomware-as-a-service (RaaS) operation
- Providing phishing kits to cybercriminals
- Running a dark web marketplace for illicit goods

Authorities had been monitoring dark web forums and Telegram groups where "AlphaSupreme" was active, but his identity remained unknown. Investigators knew they needed a lead—somewhere this cybercriminal had slipped up.

Step 1: Identifying an Email Address from Dark Web Forums

Investigators combed through multiple dark web forums where AlphaSupreme was active, searching for any email addresses associated with his accounts. On one forum, a breakthrough appeared:

In an old post from 2019, "AlphaSupreme" had provided a contact email for business inquiries:

"supremealpha@tormail.net"

Tormail was a dark web email provider commonly used by cybercriminals. However, while the service itself was designed for anonymity, the email address itself could still be traced using OSINT techniques.

Step 2: Checking for Data Breaches & Leaks

The next step was to check whether "supremealpha@tormail.net" had been exposed in any data breaches. Investigators used:

- Have I Been Pwned
- DeHashed
- IntelX

A hit came back—the email appeared in a 2017 database leak from a hacked gaming forum. Shockingly, the cybercriminal had used the same Tormail email to sign up for an online gaming website years earlier.

But there was more—the database also contained a backup email address:

"johnwalker1988@gmail.com"

This was a significant lead. If AlphaSupreme had reused an email address tied to his real-world identity, it could provide a direct link between his online persona and his actual name.

Step 3: Reverse Searching the Secondary Email

Investigators then conducted a reverse email search on "johnwalker1988@gmail.com" using:

- Pipl
- That's Them
- Social media lookups

This email was linked to an old LinkedIn profile for a John Walker, a cybersecurity consultant from London. Further checks showed this email was also tied to:

- A personal Facebook account with pictures
- A GitHub profile where he contributed to security-related repositories
- A domain name registered under his real name

This was the moment of confirmation. "John Walker" had left a digital footprint tying his personal identity to the dark web alias "AlphaSupreme."

Step 4: Tracking Bitcoin Transactions from Email Communications

Many dark web criminals rely on cryptocurrency payments, and "AlphaSupreme" was no different. Investigators reviewed past ransomware demand emails attributed to him, searching for Bitcoin wallet addresses.

- Several Bitcoin addresses were found in phishing scam emails linked to his dark web activities.
- Using Blockchair and Chainalysis, authorities traced Bitcoin transactions from these wallets.
- The transactions led to a known cryptocurrency exchange that required KYC (Know Your Customer) verification.

Upon issuing a subpoena to the exchange, authorities obtained KYC details—which were registered under none other than John Walker's real-world identity.

Step 5: Surveillance & Arrest

With this overwhelming evidence, law enforcement placed John Walker under surveillance. Despite using VPNs and privacy-focused tools, his past mistakes had created a clear chain of digital breadcrumbs leading straight to him.

Authorities arrested Walker in August 2021. After searching his residence, they found:

- A server hosting a dark web marketplace
- Over 500 stolen credit cards
- Ransomware deployment scripts

Bitcoin wallets containing over $2 million in cryptocurrency

During his trial, prosecutors presented the key piece of evidence—his Tormail email address, which he had linked to his real identity years before.

Lessons from the Case: Key Takeaways for Investigators

This case demonstrates how a single email address can be the weak link in a cybercriminal's anonymity. Investigators successfully used OSINT techniques to de-anonymize a major dark web operator, leading to their arrest.

Key OSINT Techniques Used:

Dark Web Email Extraction

Searching hacker forums and marketplaces for email addresses.

Data Breach Analysis

Checking if the email appeared in past leaks using Have I Been Pwned & DeHashed.

Reverse Email Lookup

Finding connected accounts via Pipl, That's Them, and social media.

Domain & WHOIS Investigation

Checking if the email was used to register domains.

Cryptocurrency Tracking

Analyzing Bitcoin transactions using Blockchair and Chainalysis.

Common Mistakes Cybercriminals Make:

✓ Reusing the same email address across different services
✓ Using a secondary email that can be linked back to them
✓ Failing to maintain strict OPSEC over many years
✓ Registering cryptocurrency accounts with real-world details

Conclusion: The Power of Email Intelligence

This case proves that email investigations are one of the most powerful OSINT techniques available. Even when cybercriminals use Tor, VPNs, and encrypted messaging, small mistakes—such as reusing an email—can expose their real identity.

For investigators, tracking email addresses, analyzing breaches, and linking accounts across platforms remains a key method for identifying and arresting cybercriminals.

In the digital age, an email address is more than just a communication tool—it's a fingerprint.

2. Tracking Email Origins & Headers

In this chapter, we'll explore the process of tracking the origin of emails through their headers, which often contain a wealth of hidden information. Email headers can reveal the path an email took across the internet, providing critical clues about its true origin, sender, and routing details. By analyzing these headers, investigators can uncover the source IP address, email servers used, timestamps, and potential signs of manipulation or spoofing. We will break down how to read and interpret email headers, identify red flags, and use this data to trace back the email to its rightful source, helping to detect phishing attacks, unauthorized access, or potential leaks. Mastery of email header analysis is key to uncovering the truth behind a seemingly innocent message.

2.1 Understanding Email Headers & Their Structure

Email headers are a crucial component of email investigations, providing valuable metadata about the email's journey from sender to recipient. By analyzing headers, investigators can uncover the true source of an email, detect spoofing attempts, and track cybercriminal activity. This section breaks down email header structure, how to interpret key fields, and techniques for using header analysis in OSINT investigations.

1. What Are Email Headers?

An email header is a block of metadata included in every email message. Unlike the email's body, which contains the actual message, the header contains routing and authentication details about the email's origin, path, and authentication status.

When an email is sent, it passes through multiple mail servers (SMTP relays) before reaching the recipient. Each server adds a line to the email header, creating a traceable log of the email's journey.

Investigators analyze these headers to determine:

- Who really sent the email?
- Did the sender spoof their email address?
- What mail servers handled the email?
- What was the originating IP address?

By examining headers, OSINT professionals and cybersecurity analysts can verify if an email is legitimate or malicious and track cybercriminals back to their source.

2. Accessing Email Headers

How to View Email Headers in Different Email Clients

To analyze an email header, you must first extract it from your email client. Here's how:

- **Gmail**: Open the email → Click the three dots (⋮) → Select "Show original"
- **Outlook**: Open the email → Click File → Properties → Check the "Internet Headers" section
- **Yahoo Mail**: Open the email → Click More → View raw message
- **Apple Mail**: Open the email → Click View → Message → All Headers

Once accessed, the email header appears as a block of text containing multiple lines of metadata.

3. Key Components of an Email Header

1. Received Headers (Email Routing Information)

Example:

Received: from mail.sender.com (192.168.1.10) by mail.receiver.com with SMTP; Tue, 13 Feb 2025 12:34:56 -0500
The Received field logs each mail server the email passed through.
The IP address (192.168.1.10) reveals the sender's originating server.
The timestamp shows when the email was processed.

💡 **Use Case:**

Investigators can extract the first "Received" line (closest to the sender) to trace the true origin of the email.

2. From (Sender's Email Address – Can Be Spoofed)

Example:

From: "Amazon Support" <support@amazon.com>
This field shows the sender's email address, but it can be faked (spoofed).
Verification is needed using SPF, DKIM, and DMARC checks.

💡 Use Case:

If an email appears to be from Amazon, but the "Received" headers indicate an IP from Russia, it may be a phishing attempt.

3. Return-Path (Where Bounced Emails Go)

Example:

Return-Path: <spammer@fraudulent-site.com>
This field shows the actual return email address, which is often different from the "From" address in spoofed emails.
Attackers sometimes forget to hide their real return-path, revealing their identity.

💡 Use Case:

If an email claims to be from Microsoft (support@microsoft.com), but the Return-Path is "hacker@malicious.com", it's a phishing attempt.

4. Message-ID (Unique Email Identifier)

Example:

Message-ID: <12345.abc@mail.google.com>
A unique identifier assigned to every email by the sending mail server.
The domain in the Message-ID can reveal the true sending server.

💡 Use Case:

If a phishing email claims to be from "paypal.com", but the Message-ID is from a free mail provider (gmail.com), it is likely fraudulent.

5. SPF, DKIM, and DMARC Authentication Results

Example:

Received-SPF: fail (sender IP is not authorized)
Authentication-Results: dmarc=fail
SPF (Sender Policy Framework): Checks if the email server is allowed to send emails for the domain.
DKIM (DomainKeys Identified Mail): Ensures the email was not altered during transit.
DMARC (Domain-based Message Authentication, Reporting & Conformance): Prevents email spoofing by verifying SPF and DKIM.

💡 Use Case:

If an email from paypal.com has an SPF fail, it means it wasn't sent from PayPal's real servers—indicating spoofing.

6. X-Originating-IP (The True Sender's IP Address)

Example:

X-Originating-IP: [203.0.113.45]
Some email providers include the true sender's IP in this field.
This IP can be geolocated to find the attacker's location.

💡 Use Case:

If a scam email claims to be from New York, but the X-Originating-IP traces to Nigeria, it's a scam.

4. How to Analyze Email Headers for OSINT Investigations

Step 1: Extract and Format the Header

- Use an Email Header Analyzer to format and highlight key details:
- MXToolbox Email Header Analyzer
- Google Admin Toolbox MessageHeader

Step 2: Identify the True Source of the Email

- Look for the earliest "Received" line to find the sender's IP.
- Perform a WHOIS lookup on the IP using:
- Whois.domaintools.com

- ViewDNS.info

Step 3: Check for Spoofing & Authentication Failures

Look for SPF, DKIM, and DMARC results.
If SPF fails, the sender is not authorized to send emails for the domain.

Step 4: Trace the Email Back to a Cybercriminal

Reverse search the Return-Path email on:

- Pipl
- That's Them
- IntelX

If an IP is linked to a hosting provider or VPN, check if it's used in known attacks.

5. Real-World Case Study: How Email Headers Exposed a Phishing Scam

A company's CFO received an email from their "CEO" requesting an urgent $100,000 wire transfer. The email appeared legitimate, but a header analysis revealed:

✓ **From Address**: "ceo@company.com" (Looked Real)

✗ **Return-Path**: "attacker@hacker.com" (Spoofed)

✗ **X-Originating-IP**: 45.123.67.89 (Traced to a Russian VPN)

✗ SPF/DKIM Failed

🔎 **Outcome**: The email was a Business Email Compromise (BEC) scam. The headers exposed the attacker's true location, leading to further investigation.

Understanding email headers is a crucial skill for OSINT professionals, cybersecurity analysts, and law enforcement. By analyzing routing information, authentication results, and hidden metadata, investigators can detect phishing, track cybercriminals, and prevent fraud.

In the next section, we'll explore advanced techniques for extracting and analyzing email headers using OSINT tools.

2.2 How to Extract Metadata from Email Headers

Extracting metadata from email headers is a crucial step in email investigations, fraud detection, and cybercrime tracking. Email headers contain hidden information about the sender, recipient, mail servers, and security authentication, which can help verify legitimacy, detect spoofing, and trace cybercriminals.

This section will guide you through:

✅ How to access email headers from different email clients

✅ How to extract key metadata fields

✅ Tools for analyzing email headers

✅ Real-world use cases for OSINT investigations

1. Accessing Email Headers from Different Email Clients

To extract metadata, you first need to access the full email header. Here's how to do it in common email services:

✉ **Gmail**

- Open the email
- Click the three-dot menu (⋮) in the top-right corner
- Select "Show original"
- The full header appears in a new tab—click "Copy to clipboard"

✉ **Microsoft Outlook (Desktop App)**

- Open the email
- Click File → Properties
- Scroll down to the "Internet Headers" section

✉ **Outlook.com / Hotmail**

- Open the email
- Click the three dots (⋮) → View message source

✉ Yahoo Mail

- Open the email
- Click More → View raw message

✉ Apple Mail (Mac)

- Open the email
- Click View → Message → All Headers

Once you have the email header, copy the raw text for further analysis.

2. Key Metadata Fields to Extract from Email Headers

When analyzing email headers, the most important metadata fields include:

1⃣ Received Headers (Email Routing Information)

Example:

Received: from mail.sender.com (192.168.1.10) by mail.receiver.com with SMTP;
  Tue, 19 Feb 2025 12:34:56 -0500

✅ **Reveals**: The actual mail servers involved in sending the email.
✅ **How to use**: The first "Received" line (from bottom-up) shows the originating IP address of the sender.

2⃣ From (Sender's Email Address) – Can Be Spoofed

Example:

From: "Amazon Support" <support@amazon.com>

⚠ **Warning**: The "From" address can be spoofed, meaning it may appear legitimate even if it's fake.

3⃣ Return-Path (Actual Reply-To Email)

Example:

Return-Path: <hacker@fraudulent-domain.com>

✅ **Reveals**: Where bounced emails go.
✅ **How to use**: If the "Return-Path" differs from the "From" address, it might be a phishing attempt.

4️⃣ Message-ID (Unique Email Identifier)

Example:

Message-ID: <12345abc@mail.google.com>

✅ **Reveals**: The mail server that sent the email.
✅ **How to use**: If a "paypal.com" email has a Message-ID from gmail.com, it's likely spoofed.

5️⃣ X-Originating-IP (Sender's Real IP Address)

Example:

X-Originating-IP: [203.0.113.45]

✅ **Reveals**: The sender's true IP address.
✅ **How to use**: Use IP lookup tools (e.g., WhoIs, IPinfo.io) to geolocate the sender.

6️⃣ SPF, DKIM, DMARC (Email Authentication Results)

Example:

Received-SPF: fail (sender IP is not authorized)
Authentication-Results: dmarc=fail

✅ **Reveals**: Whether the email was sent from an authorized server.
✅ **How to use**: If SPF or DMARC fails, it means the email is likely spoofed.

3. Tools for Extracting and Analyzing Email Metadata

Instead of manually reading headers, use automated tools to extract key metadata:

📌 **Email Header Analysis Tools**

☑ **Google Admin Toolbox (MessageHeader Analyzer)** – toolbox.googleapps.com
☑ **MXToolbox Email Header Analyzer** – mxtoolbox.com
☑ **IPinfo.io** – ipinfo.io (for geolocating IP addresses)
☑ **Whois Lookup** – whois.domaintools.com

📌 **Online Data Breach & OSINT Lookups**

☑ **Have I Been Pwned?** – haveibeenpwned.com (Check if an email appears in breaches)
☑ **DeHashed** – dehashed.com (Find related leaked accounts)
☑ **IntelX** – intelx.io (Advanced OSINT lookups)

4. Real-World Use Cases of Email Header Analysis

☑ Case 1: Tracing a Phishing Email

An executive receives an urgent email from "CEO@company.com" asking for a wire transfer. The email looks legitimate but header analysis reveals:

🖥 **Received**: The email came from IP: 195.133.12.89 (Russia)
🖥 **SPF/DKIM Failed**: The sender is not authorized to send from "company.com"
🖥 **Return-Path**: hacker@fraudulentbank.com

🔍 **Conclusion**: A Business Email Compromise (BEC) attack was prevented.

☑ Case 2: Identifying a Cybercriminal's IP Address

A hacker sends a ransomware demand via email. The email claims to be from "support@bank.com", but the X-Originating-IP field reveals 203.0.113.45.

🔍 **OSINT Investigation:**

1️⃣ **IP Lookup (IPinfo.io):** Shows the IP is in Nigeria.

2️⃣ **WHOIS Lookup:** The IP belongs to an ISP known for hosting cybercrime.

3️⃣ **Data Breach Check:** The sender's email appears in a dark web leak.

☐ **Outcome:** The attacker was identified and their network was shut down.

5. Step-by-Step Guide: Investigating an Email Using OSINT\

🔍 **Step 1: Extract the Header** – Copy the raw email header from Gmail, Outlook, Yahoo, etc.

🔍 **Step 2: Use an Email Header Analyzer** – Google Admin Toolbox or MXToolbox

🔍 **Step 3: Check the First "Received" Line** – Identify the originating IP address

🔍 **Step 4: Perform an IP Lookup** – Use IPinfo.io or Whois Lookup

🔍 **Step 5: Verify SPF, DKIM, DMARC** – Look for authentication failures

🔍 **Step 6: Cross-check Email in Data Breaches** – Use Have I Been Pwned

🔍 **Step 7: Search for the Email Address in OSINT Databases** – Use DeHashed or IntelX

🚀 **Final Result:** You now have the sender's true location, ISP details, and potential links to past cybercrimes.

Email headers store crucial metadata that can expose scammers, cybercriminals, and phishing attacks. By using OSINT techniques and specialized tools, investigators can trace emails back to their true source, detect spoofing, and prevent fraud.

2.3 Identifying Sender IP Addresses & Mail Servers

Email investigations rely heavily on extracting sender IP addresses and mail server details from email headers. These elements help OSINT analysts, cybersecurity professionals, and law enforcement track the true origin of emails—whether in phishing attacks, cyber fraud, or hacking attempts.

This chapter will cover:

✓ How to locate the sender's IP address in an email header

✓ How to identify the mail servers used in email transmission

✓ Tools for tracing IPs and mail servers

✓ Real-world examples of tracking cybercriminals through email analysis

1. Understanding How Email Travels: The Role of Mail Servers

Every time an email is sent, it moves through multiple mail transfer agents (MTAs) before reaching its destination. Each mail server handling the email adds a "Received" header, allowing analysts to reconstruct the email's path.

📌 The Three Key Email Protocols Involved

1️⃣ **SMTP** (Simple Mail Transfer Protocol): Sends email from sender to recipient.

2️⃣ **IMAP** (Internet Message Access Protocol): Retrieves emails for reading.

3️⃣ **POP3** (Post Office Protocol 3): Downloads emails from a server.

💡 Why This Matters:

- SMTP logs every mail server an email passes through.
- The earliest "Received" header (bottom-most) contains the sender's original IP.

2. Finding the Sender's IP Address in Email Headers

The sender's IP address is often found in the "Received" and "X-Originating-IP" fields. Let's analyze an actual email header:

Example Email Header (Simplified)

Received: from mail.sender.com (192.168.1.10) by mail.receiver.com with SMTP;
Tue, 19 Feb 2025 12:34:56 -0500

Received: from attackerpc (45.133.21.78) by mail.sender.com;
  Tue, 19 Feb 2025 12:33:00 -0500

X-Originating-IP: [45.133.21.78]

From: "PayPal Support" <support@paypal.com>

Steps to Extract the Sender's IP

1️⃣ Find the First "Received" Header (starting from the bottom up)

- This is the first mail server that received the email from the sender.
- IP Address Found: 45.133.21.78

2️⃣ Check for an "X-Originating-IP" Field

- Some email providers include the sender's actual IP here.
- IP Address Found: 45.133.21.78

3️⃣ Verify the IP Address Using Online Tools

- **IPinfo.io** → Geolocate the IP
- **Whois Lookup** → Find ISP details
- **AbuseIPDB** → Check if the IP is linked to spam/scams

3. Identifying Mail Servers in an Email Header

Mail servers process emails between the sender and recipient. They can reveal hacked email servers, malicious domains, and unauthorized relays used by attackers.

Key Mail Server Fields in Headers

📌 **Received**: Shows the email's path through mail servers
📌 **Return-Path**: The actual reply-to address
📌 **Message-ID**: Reveals the true sending domain
📌 **SPF/DKIM/DMARC**: Authentication results to detect spoofing

How to Extract Mail Server Information

1️⃣ Identify the Sending Mail Server

Find the last "Received" header (bottom-most). Example:

Received: from smtp.mailserver.com (192.168.1.10) by mail.receiver.com

✅ Mail Server: smtp.mailserver.com

✅ IP Address: 192.168.1.10

2️⃣ Verify the Mail Server's Legitimacy

Use MXToolbox (mxtoolbox.com):

- Perform an MX Lookup to check if the domain's mail servers match the header.
- Check if the IP appears in blacklists (Spamhaus, AbuseIPDB, etc.).

3️⃣ Check SPF, DKIM, and DMARC Records

If these fail, the email was not sent from an authorized server and is likely spoofed.

4. Tools for Tracing Email IPs & Mail Servers

🔎 IP Tracking & Geolocation Tools

✅ **IPinfo.io** – ipinfo.io → Geolocate IPs

✅ **Whois Lookup** – whois.domaintools.com → Find ISP details

✅ **AbuseIPDB** – abuseipdb.com → Check if an IP is linked to fraud

🔎 Mail Server Analysis Tools

✅ **MXToolbox** – mxtoolbox.com → Analyze mail servers & blacklist status

✅ **Google Admin Toolbox** – toolbox.googleapps.com → Verify email authenticity

✅ **DNSDumpster** – dnsdumpster.com → Find related domains & subdomains

5. Real-World OSINT Use Cases

✅ Case 1: Tracing a Business Email Compromise (BEC) Attack

A company's CFO receives an email from "CEO@company.com" requesting a wire transfer. Header analysis reveals:

🔒 **Received**: The email came from 195.133.12.89 (Russia)
🔒 **Mail Server**: smtp.fakecompany.com (not the real domain)
🔒 **SPF/DKIM Failed**: The sender is not authorized

🔍 OSINT Action:

- IP lookup shows the sender is using a VPN from Russia.
- MXToolbox scan reveals the mail server is blacklisted for phishing.
- WHOIS lookup finds that the fraudulent mail server was recently registered under an unknown name.

☐ **Outcome**: The finance team stopped the transfer, preventing a $250,000 loss.

✅ Case 2: Unmasking a Phishing Campaign

A phishing email claims to be from PayPal, asking users to reset their passwords. Header analysis shows:

🔒 **From**: "support@paypal.com" (Looks legit)
🔒 **Received**: Mail server is hosted in Nigeria, not PayPal's real server
🔒 **X-Originating-IP**: 41.217.203.99 (Nigeria)
🔒 **SPF Check**: FAIL (Not an authorized PayPal server)

🔍 OSINT Action:

- IPinfo.io lookup reveals the scammer's ISP in Nigeria.
- DNSDumpster shows that the domain was registered one week ago.
- PhishTank database confirms that the domain was flagged for phishing.

☐ **Outcome**: Security teams reported the phishing domain, leading to its takedown.

6. Step-by-Step: How to Investigate an Email's Origin

🚀 **Step 1**: Extract the email header (Gmail, Outlook, Yahoo, etc.)

🚀 **Step 2:** Locate the first "Received" header (bottom-most) to find the sender's IP

🚀 **Step 3**: Use Whois/IPinfo to geolocate the IP and check its ISP

🚀 **Step 4**: Verify the mail server using MXToolbox

🚀 **Step 5:** Check SPF, DKIM, DMARC for authentication failures

🚀 **Step 6**: Cross-check the email sender domain in phishing blacklists

☐ **Final Outcome**: The investigation reveals whether the email is legitimate, spoofed, or part of a cybercrime operation.

By extracting IP addresses and mail server metadata, OSINT analysts can track cybercriminals, prevent fraud, and verify email authenticity. The next section will explore advanced techniques for tracing emails in breach investigations. 🚀

2.4 Analyzing SPF, DKIM & DMARC Records for Email Authentication

Email authentication protocols—SPF (Sender Policy Framework), DKIM (DomainKeys Identified Mail), and DMARC (Domain-based Message Authentication, Reporting, and Conformance)—are essential in verifying whether an email is legitimate or spoofed. OSINT analysts and cybersecurity professionals rely on these records to identify phishing attempts, track email fraud, and trace cybercriminals.

This chapter will cover:

✅ What SPF, DKIM, and DMARC do and how they work

✅ How to extract and analyze these records from email headers

✅ Tools for checking email authentication records

✅ Real-world use cases in cyber investigations

1. Why SPF, DKIM, and DMARC Matter in OSINT & Cybersecurity

Attackers often spoof email addresses to impersonate trusted entities like banks, corporations, or government agencies. Without proper authentication checks, these forged emails can bypass spam filters and trick users into clicking malicious links or sharing sensitive information.

💡 How SPF, DKIM & DMARC help stop email fraud:

- SPF verifies that the email came from an authorized mail server.
- DKIM ensures the email was not altered during transmission.
- DMARC enforces policies on SPF/DKIM failures and provides reporting.

By analyzing these records, investigators can determine whether an email is legitimate or part of a phishing attack.

2. Understanding SPF (Sender Policy Framework)

SPF is an email authentication method that specifies which mail servers are allowed to send emails on behalf of a domain. It prevents attackers from sending spoofed emails using fake domains.

📌 How SPF Works

1️⃣ The recipient's email server checks the sender's domain SPF record (stored in DNS).
2️⃣ If the sending server's IP is listed in the SPF record → ✅ PASS
3️⃣ If the IP is not authorized → ❌ FAIL (Email may be spoofed)

📌 Example SPF Record (TXT Record in DNS)

v=spf1 ip4:192.168.1.1 ip4:203.0.113.5 include:_spf.google.com -all

📌 Breakdown:

- v=spf1 → SPF version 1

- ip4:192.168.1.1 → Only this IP is authorized to send emails

- include:_spf.google.com → Google's mail servers are also authorized

- -all → Reject emails from unauthorized servers

🔎 How to Extract SPF from an Email Header

Look for the "Received-SPF" field in the email header:

- **Received-SPF**: fail (domain of attacker.com does not designate 203.0.113.5 as permitted sender)

✅ **SPF Pass** → The email came from an authorized server.

❌ **SPF Fail** → Possible spoofing attempt.

🔲 SPF Lookup Tools

- **MXToolbox SPF Lookup** → https://mxtoolbox.com/SPFRecordLookup.aspx
- **Google Admin Toolbox SPF Checker** → https://toolbox.googleapps.com/apps/checkmx/

3. Understanding DKIM (DomainKeys Identified Mail)

DKIM helps verify email integrity by digitally signing the email with a cryptographic key. This ensures the message was not altered in transit and confirms that it originated from the specified domain.

📌 How DKIM Works

1️⃣ The sender's mail server adds a DKIM signature to the email header.

2️⃣ The recipient's mail server retrieves the sender's public key from DNS.

3️⃣ The signature is verified against the email's content.

✅ **Pass** → Email is authentic.

❌ **Fail** → Email may have been altered or spoofed.

📌 Example DKIM Signature in an Email Header

DKIM-Signature: v=1; a=rsa-sha256; d=example.com; s=key1;

- h=from:subject:date;
- bh=abcdef1234567890==;
- b=MIIBIjANBgkqh…

📌 **Breakdown:**

- **d=example.com** → The domain signing the email.
- **s=key1** → The DKIM selector (used to retrieve the key from DNS).
- **b=MIIBIjAN**... → The cryptographic signature.

🔎 **How to Check DKIM Authentication in an Email Header**

Look for "Authentication-Results" in the email header:

Authentication-Results: dkim=pass header.d=paypal.com

✅ **DKIM Pass** → The email is authentic and wasn't altered.

❌ **DKIM Fail** → Possible email spoofing or tampering.

🛠️ **DKIM Lookup Tools**

- **Google Admin Toolbox DKIM Checker** → https://toolbox.googleapps.com
- **MXToolbox DKIM Lookup** → https://mxtoolbox.com/DKIMLookup.aspx

4. Understanding DMARC (Domain-based Message Authentication, Reporting & Conformance)

DMARC enforces policies on SPF and DKIM failures to prevent spoofing attacks. It also provides email activity reports to the domain owner.

📌 **How DMARC Works**

1️⃣ The sender's domain publishes a DMARC record in DNS.

2️⃣ If SPF or DKIM fails, DMARC enforces one of three policies:

- p=none → No action (only monitoring).
- p=quarantine → Send suspicious emails to spam.
- p=reject → Block the email entirely.

📌 Example DMARC Record (TXT Record in DNS)

v=DMARC1; p=reject; rua=mailto:reports@example.com; sp=quarantine

📌 Breakdown:

- p=reject → Block emails that fail SPF/DKIM.
- rua=mailto:reports@example.com → Send reports to this address.
- sp=quarantine → Subdomains follow a "quarantine" policy.

🔎 How to Check DMARC Authentication in an Email Header

Look for "Authentication-Results" in the email header:

Authentication-Results: dmarc=fail policy.reject

✅ **DMARC Pass** → The email meets authentication policies.

✖ **DMARC Fail** → The email was likely spoofed.

☐☐ DMARC Lookup Tools

- **DMARC Analyzer** → https://dmarcanalyzer.com
- **MXToolbox DMARC Lookup** → https://mxtoolbox.com/DMARCLookup.aspx

5. Real-World Use Cases

✅ Case 1: Preventing a CEO Fraud Attack

A CFO receives an urgent email from CEO@company.com requesting a wire transfer. Header analysis reveals:

🔏 **SPF Failed**: The email did not come from company.com's mail servers.

🔏 **DKIM Failed**: The signature did not match the sender's domain.

🔏 **DMARC Policy**: p=reject blocked the email.

🔍 **OSINT Outcome**: Attack prevented; no money lost.

Analyzing SPF, DKIM, and DMARC is essential for detecting email fraud, phishing, and cybercrime. OSINT investigators can use these records to verify whether an email is genuine or part of an attack.

2.5 Tracking Email Forwarding, Redirects & Spoofing Techniques

Email forwarding, redirection, and spoofing are common techniques used by both legitimate organizations and cybercriminals. While forwarding and redirection help in managing emails efficiently, attackers exploit these features to conceal their identities, execute phishing attacks, and bypass security measures. Spoofing, on the other hand, is a technique used to impersonate a trusted sender to deceive recipients.

In this chapter, we will cover:

✅ How email forwarding and redirection work

✅ How attackers use these methods for phishing and fraud

✅ Techniques to detect email spoofing and forgery

✅ Tools and methods to track suspicious email activity

1. Understanding Email Forwarding & Redirection

Email forwarding and redirection allow emails to be automatically routed from one inbox to another. This can be configured at:

📌 **Server-Level Forwarding** – Configured at the email provider's server (e.g., Gmail, Outlook).

📌 **Client-Level Forwarding** – Set up within an email client like Microsoft Outlook or Thunderbird.

📌 **How Cybercriminals Exploit Forwarding & Redirection**

1️⃣ **Auto-Forwarding Rules** – Attackers who compromise an account often create forwarding rules to exfiltrate sensitive emails.

2️⃣ **Hidden Email Redirects** – Some email providers allow redirecting emails without notifying the recipient.

3️⃣ **Phishing via Email Redirection** – Malicious emails redirect users to spoofed login pages.

4️⃣ **Business Email Compromise (BEC)** – Attackers set up rules that forward financial transaction emails to their own accounts.

🔎 **How to Detect Suspicious Forwarding & Redirection**

✅ **Check Auto-Forwarding Rules** – Review settings in email accounts (Gmail, Outlook, etc.).

✅ **Analyze Email Headers** – Look for "X-Forwarded-For" or "Resent-From" fields in headers.

✅ **Use DMARC Reports** – DMARC logs can show unauthorized email activity.

✅ **Monitor Login Activity** – If a compromised email account is forwarding messages, check for unusual login locations.

2. Detecting Email Spoofing

Email spoofing occurs when an attacker fakes the "From" address to appear as a trusted sender. This is commonly used in:

🚨 Phishing attacks (e.g., fake PayPal or bank emails)
🚨 CEO fraud / Business Email Compromise (BEC)
🚨 Scam emails asking for money or personal information

📌 **Common Email Spoofing Techniques**

◆ **Simple Display Name Spoofing** – Changing the sender's display name (e.g., "Amazon Support" hacker@email.com)

◆ **SMTP Spoofing** – Modifying email headers to fake the "From" address.

◆ **Compromised Email Accounts** – Using a real hacked email account to send malicious emails.

◆ **Lookalike Domains** – Using domains like paypa1.com (instead of paypal.com).

🔎 How to Detect Email Spoofing

✅ **Check SPF, DKIM, and DMARC Records** – If SPF or DKIM fails, the email is likely spoofed.

✅ **Inspect the Email Header** – Look for mismatched Return-Path, From, and Reply-To fields.

✅ **Analyze the "Received" Headers** – If the email claims to be from amazon.com, but the server IP is from Russia, it's likely spoofed.

✅ **Look for Hidden Encoding** – Some phishing emails use Unicode characters to disguise domain names (e.g., аpple.com instead of apple.com).

🗄 Tools for Detecting Spoofed Emails

- **Google Admin Toolbox** (https://toolbox.googleapps.com) – Checks SPF, DKIM, DMARC results.
- **MXToolbox Email Header Analyzer** (https://mxtoolbox.com/EmailHeaders.aspx) – Decodes email headers.
- **IPinfo.io** (https://ipinfo.io) – Traces sender IPs.

3. Investigating Email Forwarding & Redirection in Headers

To track forwarded or redirected emails, investigators analyze email headers for key fields such as:

📌 **"X-Forwarded-For"** – Shows if the email was forwarded through multiple addresses.

📌 **"Resent-From" / "Resent-To"** – Indicates an email redirected by another user or service.

📌 **"Return-Path" vs. "From" Address** – If these don't match, it's a sign of spoofing or email redirection.

📌 Example Email Header with Forwarding

Received: from mail.google.com (mail.google.com [209.85.220.41])

```
    by smtp.server.com (Postfix) with ESMTPS id 3CDE12345
X-Forwarded-For: user1@gmail.com, user2@company.com
Resent-From: forwarded@example.com
Return-Path: hacker@attacker.com
From: "PayPal Support" <support@paypal.com>
```

🔏 Red Flags in This Header:

X-Forwarded-For: The email was forwarded from multiple accounts.
Resent-From: It was redirected by a different user.
Return-Path vs. From Mismatch: The email pretends to be from PayPal but was actually sent from "attacker.com".

🔲 Tools to Analyze Email Forwarding & Redirection

- **MXToolbox Email Header Analyzer** – https://mxtoolbox.com/EmailHeaders.aspx
- **Header Analysis with Google Admin Toolbox** – https://toolbox.googleapps.com
- **IP Geolocation Tools** – https://ipinfo.io

4. Real-World OSINT Cases: Tracking Email Forwarding & Spoofing

✅ Case 1: Catching a CEO Fraud Scam

A finance manager receives an email from CEO@company.com, asking for an urgent wire transfer. Upon analysis:

🔏 **SPF Fail** – The email did not come from an authorized server.
🔏 **X-Forwarded-For Detected** – The email was routed through a hacked vendor's email account.
🔏 **Reply-To Mismatch** – The reply address was ceo@fake-company.com.

🔎 **Outcome**: The fraud attempt was detected, and the finance team blocked the transfer.

✅ Case 2: Tracking a Phishing Campaign

A university IT team investigates multiple reports of fake Microsoft login emails. The email headers reveal:

📸 **DKIM Fail** – The sender forged the email signature.

📸 **Hidden Forwarding Rule** – A compromised staff email was auto-forwarding emails to an attacker.

📸 **IP Trace** – The sender's IP belonged to a VPN exit node in Nigeria.

🔎 **Outcome**: The IT team removed the forwarding rule, reset credentials, and reported the phishing attack.

Tracking email forwarding, redirection, and spoofing is essential for OSINT analysts, cybersecurity professionals, and law enforcement. Attackers exploit these techniques to steal information, impersonate trusted sources, and evade detection.

🚀 **Key Takeaways:**

✓ Analyze email headers for "X-Forwarded-For", "Resent-From", and mismatched sender addresses.

✓ Use SPF, DKIM, and DMARC to detect spoofing.

✓ Monitor auto-forwarding rules in compromised accounts.

✓ Use OSINT tools like MXToolbox, Google Admin Toolbox, and IP lookup services.

2.6 Case Study: Exposing a Fake CEO Email Scam

In this case study, we will analyze a real-world CEO fraud attack—a sophisticated scam where cybercriminals impersonate company executives to manipulate employees into transferring funds or sharing sensitive information. We'll break down how OSINT techniques and email forensic analysis helped uncover the scam, track the attackers, and prevent financial loss.

1. The Incident: Suspicious Email from the CEO

A finance manager at a multinational company received an urgent email from the CEO instructing them to wire $250,000 to a new bank account for a confidential acquisition deal. The email had the CEO's full name, signature, and corporate branding, making it look legitimate.

📌 **Email details:**

From: CEO@company.com
To: Finance.manager@company.com
Subject: Urgent: Confidential Wire Transfer Instructions

Message:

"Please process the attached payment as soon as possible. This is highly confidential and time-sensitive. Let me know once it's done."

🔍 **Red Flags Noticed by the Finance Team:**

☑ The email was unexpected and mentioned urgency & secrecy—common in fraud attempts.

☑ The tone felt slightly different from the CEO's usual emails.

☑ The attached invoice was a poorly formatted PDF with an unfamiliar beneficiary.

2. Initial OSINT Analysis: Examining the Email Header

Before taking action, the company's IT security team performed email forensic analysis on the email header.

Extracting the Email Header

Using Gmail, Outlook, or any email client, the IT team extracted the full email header and analyzed the following fields:

📌 **Key Header Fields (Excerpt):**

Return-Path: <ceo@company.co>
Received: from mail.example.com ([103.87.12.56])
    by companymailserver.com with ESMTPS
Received-SPF: FAIL (domain of company.co does not designate 103.87.12.56 as a permitted sender)
Authentication-Results: dkim=fail (signature mismatch)
Reply-To: hacker@secure-transfers.net

From: "John Smith - CEO" <ceo@company.com>

🚨 Findings from the Email Header:

● **Return-Path Mismatch** → The real return path was ceo@company.co (a fake domain).

● **SPF Failed** → The sending IP (103.87.12.56) was not authorized to send emails for company.com.

● **DKIM Failed** → The email signature was forged, meaning it didn't originate from the company's official email system.

● **Reply-To Address** → It pointed to hacker@secure-transfers.net, a domain unrelated to the company.

📌 The sender spoofed the CEO's email address and used a lookalike domain (company.co instead of company.com).
📌 The email authentication failed (SPF & DKIM mismatches).
📌 The actual email was sent from an IP address in Nigeria, not the company's mail servers.

3. Deep OSINT Investigation: Tracing the Attacker

After confirming the fraud attempt, the security team used OSINT techniques to gather more intelligence on the attacker.

Step 1: Checking the Fake Domain (company.co)

Using Whois Lookup, they found:

🔎 **Domain**: company.co
🔎 **Registrar**: Namecheap
🔎 **Created**: 5 days ago
🔎 **Owner**: Private registration (hidden)

🚨 **Red Flag**: The domain was recently registered, which is common in fraud cases.

✅ OSINT Tools Used:

- **Whois Lookup**: https://who.is
- **DomainTools**: https://whois.domaintools.com

Step 2: Investigating the Sender's IP Address (103.87.12.56)

The IT team checked the sender's IP address using OSINT tools.

🔎 IP Geolocation Results:

- **Location**: Lagos, Nigeria
- **ISP**: A small hosting provider known for abuse reports
- **Blacklisted**?: ✅ Yes, found in Spamhaus & AbuseIPDB databases

🚨 **Red Flag**: The IP was associated with past phishing campaigns.

✅ OSINT Tools Used:

- **IPinfo.io**: https://ipinfo.io
- **AbuseIPDB**: https://www.abuseipdb.com

Step 3: Investigating the Fake Reply-To Email (secure-transfers.net)

Since the attacker used hacker@secure-transfers.net as the reply email, the team checked that domain.

🔎 Domain Analysis (secure-transfers.net)

- **Whois Lookup**: Registered anonymously 2 months ago.
- **MX Records**: Used a free email provider (ProtonMail).
- **Google Search**: Found reports linking it to past scams.

🚨 **Red Flag**: The domain was linked to previous fraud attempts.

✅ OSINT Tools Used:

- **MXToolbox**: https://mxtoolbox.com
- **Google Dorking**: site:secure-transfers.net

4. The Security Response & Outcome

Once the fraud attempt was confirmed, the security team:

✅ Warned all employees to ignore similar emails.

✅ Blocked the attacker's IP and domain at the firewall.

✅ Reported the scammer's domain (secure-transfers.net) to abuse services.

✅ Enabled DMARC enforcement (p=reject) to prevent future spoofing.

✅ Filed a report with law enforcement & anti-cybercrime agencies.

🚨 **Potential Loss Prevented: $250,000**

5. Lessons Learned & Prevention Strategies

◆ **Enable DMARC Policy (p=reject)** – Ensures that emails failing authentication are blocked.

◆ **Train Employees** – Teach staff to recognize urgent & suspicious emails.

◆ **Verify Transactions by Phone** – Always confirm wire transfers via voice verification.

◆ **Monitor New Domains Imitating Your Company** – Use tools like DNSTwist to find typo-squatting domains.

◆ **Implement Email Security Tools** – Use services like Proofpoint or Mimecast to filter spoofed emails.

✅ Recommended Tools for Preventing CEO Fraud Attacks:

- **DMARC Analyzer** – https://dmarcanalyzer.com
- **AbuseIPDB (IP reputation check)** – https://www.abuseipdb.com
- **MXToolbox (Email header analysis)** – https://mxtoolbox.com
- **DNSTwist (Typosquatting detection)** – https://dnstwist.it

This case study highlights how email header analysis, OSINT techniques, and proper security controls helped expose and prevent a CEO fraud attack. Cybercriminals constantly evolve their tactics, so organizations must remain vigilant.

3. Email Breach & Leak Investigations

In this chapter, we will focus on investigating email breaches and leaks, a growing concern in the digital landscape. As organizations and individuals increasingly rely on email for communication, it becomes a prime target for cybercriminals and malicious insiders looking to exploit sensitive data. We will examine various types of breaches, from compromised email accounts to large-scale data leaks, and explore the methods used to identify when and how these incidents occur. Additionally, we will discuss how to trace breached email addresses, identify exposed credentials, and determine the potential impact of leaks on both individuals and organizations. By understanding the nuances of email-related breaches, investigators can quickly mitigate damage and prevent further unauthorized access, while also contributing to a broader understanding of cyber threats.

3.1 How & Why Emails End Up in Data Breaches

Email addresses are among the most frequently exposed data points in cyber breaches. Whether through hacked databases, phishing attacks, or corporate leaks, email credentials often fall into the hands of cybercriminals. Once exposed, they can be used for identity theft, phishing campaigns, account takeovers, and even dark web sales.

In this chapter, we will explore:

✓ Common ways emails are breached

✓ Why cybercriminals target emails

✓ What happens after an email breach

✓ Real-world examples of major email leaks

1. Common Ways Emails Are Breached

There are multiple ways email addresses end up in public or private breach databases. Some of the most common causes include:

1.1 Data Breaches from Hacked Companies

Large companies store millions of email addresses in customer accounts. If their security is compromised, these emails (along with passwords and personal details) are stolen.

● **Example:**

The 2013 Yahoo! Breach exposed 3 billion email accounts, making it one of the largest breaches in history.

1.2 Phishing Attacks

Cybercriminals trick users into entering their credentials on fake login pages. Once an email and password are captured, attackers use them for further exploitation.

● **Example:**

Google Docs Phishing (2017): Attackers sent fake Google Docs links, stealing thousands of Gmail credentials.

1.3 Credential Stuffing Attacks

Many users reuse passwords. Attackers use previously leaked email/password combinations and try them on other platforms (e.g., banking, social media).

● **Example:**

The Collection #1 Data Dump (2019) contained 773 million unique email addresses and 21 million passwords, enabling mass credential stuffing.

1.4 Malware & Keyloggers

Some malware captures keystrokes, stealing email credentials when users log in. Others directly extract stored passwords from browsers.

● **Example:**

Emotet Malware (2020): One of the most widespread banking trojans, it collected email credentials for further exploitation.

1.5 Insider Threats & Corporate Leaks

Disgruntled employees or compromised insiders can leak customer email lists to cybercriminals. Some sell these on dark web markets.

● **Example:**

Twitter Insider Hack (2020): Employees were bribed to give attackers access to VIP accounts, exposing private email addresses.

2. Why Cybercriminals Target Emails

Email addresses are valuable assets for hackers. Here's why:

2.1 Identity Theft & Account Takeovers

📌 Compromised emails allow access to personal accounts, which may store financial information.
📌 Many users use their email address as a username for multiple platforms.
📌 Attackers can use email addresses to reset passwords for bank accounts or cryptocurrency wallets.

2.2 Spam & Phishing Campaigns

📌 Stolen email lists are used to send mass phishing emails.
📌 Attackers impersonate trusted companies (banks, PayPal, Microsoft) to steal additional credentials.
📌 Email addresses in breaches often appear in future phishing attacks.

2.3 Selling Emails on the Dark Web

📌 There is a thriving black market for email addresses.
📌 Some databases bundle emails with passwords for hacking purposes.
📌 Prices vary based on domain reputation (e.g., corporate emails are worth more than personal Gmail accounts).

2.4 Social Engineering & Targeted Attacks

📌 Cybercriminals use breached emails for spear phishing—targeting specific individuals.
📌 CEO fraud and business email compromise (BEC) scams rely on authentic-looking email addresses.
📌 Government and corporate emails are used for espionage & intelligence gathering.

3. What Happens After an Email Breach?

Once an email is exposed in a breach, it follows a cycle in the cybercriminal underground:

Step 1: Initial Leak on Hacking Forums

📌 Attackers dump stolen emails on hacking forums or Telegram channels.

⬤ Example:

The Facebook Data Leak (2021) saw 533 million emails and phone numbers dumped for free.

Step 2: Dark Web & Private Market Sales

📌 Cybercriminals package email lists into "combo lists" (email + password pairs).
📌 These lists are sold on dark web markets.
📌 High-value corporate emails are auctioned to cybercrime groups.

⬤ Example:

The "Cit0day Breach Market" sold over 23,000 hacked databases with emails/passwords.

Step 3: Credential Stuffing & Secondary Exploitation

📌 Cybercriminals test stolen credentials on multiple sites (Netflix, PayPal, banking).
📌 If passwords match, attackers steal money or sensitive data.

⬤ Example:

The Disney+ Credential Stuffing Attack (2019)—many users' accounts were hacked due to reused passwords.

Step 4: Phishing & Targeted Attacks

📌 Leaked emails are used to send malware, ransomware, or phishing emails.
📌 Attackers impersonate trusted senders to trick victims.

● **Example:**

The LinkedIn Data Leak (2021) saw 500 million emails used in job offer phishing scams.

4. Real-World Examples of Major Email Breaches

Breach	Year	Number of Emails Leaked	Cause
Yahoo! Breach	2013	3 Billion	Hacked Database
Facebook Leak	2021	533 Million	Public Database Scraping
LinkedIn Leak	2021	500 Million	Scraped Public Data
Adobe Breach	2013	153 Million	Hacked Database
MySpace Breach	2016	360 Million	Old User Credentials Stolen
Collection #1	2019	773 Million	Data Dump from Multiple Breaches

5. How to Check If Your Email Has Been Breached

🔍 Use these tools to check if your email is exposed:

✅ **Have I Been Pwned?** – Checks email leaks in known data breaches.
✅ **DeHashed** – Advanced search for leaked credentials.
✅ **LeakCheck** – Looks up breached email/password combos.

Emails are one of the most targeted assets in cybercrime. Attackers use phishing, hacking, and dark web sales to exploit leaked credentials. Understanding how breaches happen helps users and organizations take steps to protect their email accounts.

3.2 Using "Have I Been Pwned" & Other Leak Databases

When an email address is leaked in a data breach, it often ends up in public or private breach databases. Cybercriminals use these databases for phishing attacks, credential stuffing, identity theft, and more. However, cybersecurity researchers, ethical hackers, and investigators can also use these databases to track compromised accounts, analyze breaches, and protect users from cyber threats.

In this chapter, we'll cover:

✓ How "Have I Been Pwned" (HIBP) helps identify breached emails.

✓ Other leak databases used for OSINT investigations.

✓ How to analyze leaked credentials safely.

✓ Ethical & legal considerations when using breach data.

1. What Is "Have I Been Pwned"?

Have I Been Pwned (HIBP) is a free online service created by cybersecurity expert Troy Hunt. It allows users to check if their email or password has been leaked in a data breach.

◆ Key Features:

✓☐ Checks if an email is in a known breach.
✓☐ Provides details about the breached service (e.g., LinkedIn, Adobe).
✓☐ Offers "Notify Me" alerts for future breaches.
✓☐ Provides a secure way to check password leaks (Pwned Passwords).

◆ Why It's Useful for Investigators:

✓☐ Helps identify compromised emails in security audits.
✓☐ Tracks how cybercriminals obtain credentials.
✓☐ Provides insight into large-scale breaches.
✓☐ Aids in threat intelligence & OSINT research.

2. How to Use "Have I Been Pwned" for Email Breach Investigations

Step 1: Checking if an Email Is Breached

1☐ Go to https://haveibeenpwned.com/
2☐ Enter an email address.
3☐ Click "Pwned?"

🔎 Results:

✅ **Green (No Breach)** → Email is safe (not in HIBP's database).

✕ **Red (Pwned!)** → Email was found in breaches.

📌 **Example Output:**

Oh no — pwned!

Your email appeared in the following breaches:

- **LinkedIn (2021)** – Emails & hashed passwords leaked
- **Adobe (2013)** – 153 million accounts exposed
- **Collection #1 (2019)** – 773 million records leaked

Step 2: Analyzing the Breach Details

📌 **What to check?**

✓☐ Which company was breached? (Was it a major leak like LinkedIn?)
✓☐ What data was exposed? (Email, password, phone, address?)
✓☐ Is the password still in use? (Force a reset if necessary.)
✓☐ Has the email been in multiple breaches? (Higher risk for phishing attacks.)

Step 3: Checking for Leaked Passwords

◆ **Use the Pwned Passwords tool on HIBP:**

- Go to https://haveibeenpwned.com/Passwords
- Enter a password (⚠☐ DO NOT enter real passwords you currently use)
- HIBP will check if the password has appeared in past breaches.

📌 **Example Output:**

- This password has been seen 1,236,745 times in data breaches.
- You should NEVER use this password!

3. Other Leak Databases for OSINT Investigations

While HIBP is the most popular breach-checking tool, other databases provide more detailed breach information, including passwords, hashed credentials, and dark web leaks.

3.1 DeHashed (https://www.dehashed.com)

◆ Advanced OSINT tool for searching breached emails, usernames, passwords, and IP addresses.
◆ Allows wildcard & Boolean searches (e.g., searching for parts of emails).
◆ Requires an account, and some searches require a paid subscription.

📌 Example Use Case:

An investigator searching for "johndoe@gmail.com" might find:

- Leaked passwords from multiple breaches.
- Associated usernames from dark web leaks.
- Phone numbers linked to the email.

3.2 LeakCheck (https://leakcheck.io)

◆ Similar to DeHashed but provides real-time breach alerts.
◆ Shows passwords in plaintext or hashed form.
◆ Paid accounts can access full breach details.

📌 Example Use Case:

A cybersecurity analyst monitoring leaked credentials finds a compromised company email and forces a password reset before attackers can use it.

3.3 Snusbase (https://snusbase.com)

◆ Focuses on searching breach databases with emails, usernames, or IPs.
◆ Provides hashed & plaintext passwords for known breaches.
◆ Paid service, but widely used by OSINT professionals.

📌 Example Use Case:

A penetration tester finds that an employee at a bank reused their password from a 2018 MyFitnessPal breach, creating a security risk.

4. How Cybercriminals Use These Databases

● Credential Stuffing Attacks

- Attackers use leaked email/password combos to log into accounts on different platforms.
- **Example**: An email from the Dropbox breach is used to access a PayPal account.

● Phishing & Social Engineering

- Cybercriminals send targeted phishing emails based on leaked credentials.
- **Example**: A user whose email was in the LinkedIn leak gets fake job offers with malware.

● Dark Web Market Sales

- Hackers sell bulk email/password lists for profit.
- Some accounts (e.g., banking, corporate) sell for higher prices.

5. Ethical & Legal Considerations

While using breach databases for OSINT investigations is legal in most cases, there are some important rules to follow:

✅ What You Can Do:

✓☐ Use HIBP or other databases to check your own email & accounts.
✓☐ Use OSINT tools to protect clients, employees, or your organization.
✓☐ Report breached accounts to affected users.

🚫 What You Should NOT Do:

✗ Search for random people's emails (violates privacy laws).

✗ Use leaked credentials for unauthorized access (illegal hacking).

✘ Share breach data publicly (may violate GDPR & data protection laws).

📌 **Important Laws to Consider:**

- **GDPR (Europe):** Leaked data cannot be stored or shared without permission.
- **Computer Fraud & Abuse Act (USA):** Unauthorized access to breach data is a federal crime.
- **Data Protection Laws (Various Countries):** Accessing or distributing breach data without permission may be illegal.

6. How to Protect Your Email from Future Breaches

◆ **Enable Two-Factor Authentication (2FA):** Even if a password is leaked, 2FA prevents unauthorized access.

◆ **Use Unique Passwords for Every Site**: Prevents credential stuffing.

◆ **Monitor Email Breach Alerts**: Use HIBP notifications to stay informed.

◆ **Check If Your Passwords Are Leaked**: Use HIBP's Pwned Passwords.

◆ **Consider a Password Manager**: Generates & stores secure passwords.

Email breaches are a major cybersecurity risk, but tools like HIBP, DeHashed, and LeakCheck help track and mitigate damage. By using OSINT techniques responsibly, investigators can identify leaked credentials, protect users, and prevent cybercrime.

3.3 Investigating Stolen Credentials & Their Sources

Stolen credentials—compromised usernames, passwords, and email addresses—are at the core of modern cybercrime. These credentials are used for account takeovers, financial fraud, identity theft, and phishing attacks. Once stolen, they often end up on hacking forums, data leak sites, dark web markets, and private Telegram groups.

For OSINT analysts, cybersecurity professionals, and law enforcement, investigating stolen credentials can help:

✓ Track cybercriminals and their methods

✓ Identify the sources of major data breaches

✓ Understand how stolen credentials are bought, sold, and misused

✅ Prevent future attacks by detecting exposed data early

In this chapter, we'll explore:

- How credentials are stolen
- Where they are traded or leaked
- Techniques for investigating stolen credentials
- Legal & ethical considerations

1. How Credentials Are Stolen

Stolen credentials originate from various attack vectors, including:

1.1 Data Breaches & Database Dumps

◆ Large-scale breaches expose millions of login credentials.

◆ Hackers extract email-password pairs and sell them on the dark web.

◆ Some breaches leak full PII (Personally Identifiable Information), increasing the risk of identity theft.

⬤ **Example:**

- The Adobe Breach (2013) exposed 153 million user credentials.
- The Collection #1 Dump (2019) contained 773 million email-password pairs.

1.2 Phishing Attacks

◆ Cybercriminals send fake emails mimicking banks, social media platforms, or IT services.

◆ Victims unknowingly enter their credentials into a malicious login page.

◆ Stolen credentials are automatically logged and used for fraud.

⬤ **Example:**

- The Google Docs Phishing Attack (2017) tricked thousands of users into logging into a fake Google login page.

1.3 Malware & Keyloggers

- Malware-infected devices silently capture keystrokes and steal login credentials.
- Some malware extracts saved passwords from browsers.
- Advanced malware sends credentials directly to C2 (Command and Control) servers operated by hackers.

● Example:

- Emotet Malware (2020) was one of the most widespread credential-stealing trojans.

1.4 Credential Stuffing & Password Spraying

- Attackers use previously leaked credentials and test them on multiple websites.
- Credential Stuffing: If a user reuses passwords, attackers gain access to multiple accounts.
- Password Spraying: Attackers try common passwords (e.g., "123456", "Password1") across many accounts.

● Example:

- The Disney+ Credential Stuffing Attack (2019) resulted in thousands of hacked accounts due to reused passwords.

1.5 Insider Threats & Corporate Leaks

- Employees steal and sell company credentials.
- Some employees leak corporate login details on hacker forums or dark web markets.

● Example:

- In 2020, Twitter employees were bribed to provide access to VIP accounts.

2. Where Stolen Credentials Are Traded

Stolen credentials are sold, shared, or leaked through various online platforms:

2.1 Dark Web Marketplaces

- Darknet markets host credential dumps for sale.

- Hackers sell premium streaming, banking, and corporate accounts.
- Some marketplaces use cryptocurrency payments for anonymity.

● **Example:**

- The Genesis Market specialized in selling "fingerprints"—stolen cookies and login credentials for bypassing 2FA.

2.2 Hacking Forums & Telegram Groups

- Public hacking forums provide free or premium credential dumps.
- Some Telegram groups share real-time breach alerts with cracked credentials.

● **Example:**

- The "Cit0day Breach Market" sold over 23,000 hacked databases before it was shut down.

2.3 Paste Sites (Pastebin, Ghostbin, Doxbin)

- Hackers use paste sites to dump stolen credentials.
- Many credentials appear in plaintext or hashed formats.

● **Example:**

- Pastebin was frequently used to leak login credentials and API keys.

3. Investigating Stolen Credentials: OSINT Techniques

3.1 Searching Breach Databases

- Use Have I Been Pwned (HIBP) or DeHashed to check if an email/password was leaked.

◆ **Tools:**

✓ **Have I Been Pwned** – Checks for email leaks.
✓ **DeHashed** – Searches breached credentials.

✅ **LeakCheck** – Provides detailed credential breach data.

3.2 Monitoring Dark Web Markets & Forums

◆ Investigators can monitor dark web sites for credential sales.
◆ Use Tor browsers and dark web monitoring tools.
◆ Clearnet mirrors of hacking forums sometimes provide leads.

◆ **Tools:**

✅ **Onion Search Engine** – Searches dark web pages.
✅ **DarkOwl** – Dark web intelligence platform.
✅ **IntSights** – Dark web monitoring for enterprises.

3.3 Extracting Password Hashes & Cracking Techniques

◆ Some credential leaks contain hashed passwords instead of plaintext.
◆ Investigators use tools like John the Ripper or Hashcat to analyze hashes.

◆ **Tools:**

✅ **John the Ripper** – Fast password hash cracking tool.
✅ **Hashcat** – GPU-based password recovery and analysis.
✅ **CrackStation** – Online hash lookup.

3.4 Tracking Stolen Credentials in Use

◆ If an email is compromised, check for unauthorized logins using:

- Google Account Security Checkup
- Microsoft Account Activity
- Apple ID Login History

◆ Use Have I Been Pwned's Pwned Passwords to check if a password is already leaked.

4. Legal & Ethical Considerations

◆ Is it legal to access breach databases?

✓ Checking your own email is legal.

✓ Using OSINT tools to protect organizations is ethical.

✗ Searching for random individuals' credentials may violate privacy laws.

✗ Accessing or using stolen credentials is illegal under most cybersecurity laws.

📌 **Key Laws to Consider:**

- **GDPR (Europe):** Prohibits unauthorized use of personal data.
- **Computer Fraud & Abuse Act (USA):** Criminalizes unauthorized access to data.
- **Data Protection Laws (UK, Canada, Australia, etc.):** Regulate the handling of leaked credentials.

5. How to Protect Against Credential Theft

◆ **Enable Two-Factor Authentication (2FA):** Even if credentials are stolen, 2FA prevents unauthorized logins.

◆ **Use Unique Passwords**: Avoid reusing passwords across multiple sites.

◆ **Monitor for Breaches**: Use Have I Been Pwned's notification service.

◆ **Regularly Change Passwords**: Especially if your email appears in any breach database.

◆ **Use a Password Manager**: Generates and stores secure passwords.

Investigating stolen credentials is a critical aspect of cybersecurity and OSINT. By analyzing how credentials are stolen, where they are leaked, and how they are used, investigators can prevent cybercriminal activity and strengthen digital security.

3.4 Identifying Reused Passwords & Security Risks

Password reuse is one of the most common and dangerous cybersecurity risks. When users recycle the same password across multiple platforms, a single data breach can expose multiple accounts to unauthorized access. Cybercriminals exploit reused passwords in credential stuffing, phishing, and account takeover (ATO) attacks to gain control over email, banking, and corporate accounts.

For OSINT analysts, cybersecurity professionals, and investigators, identifying reused passwords is essential to:

✅ Assess security risks for individuals and organizations

✅ Detect compromised accounts before attackers exploit them

✅ Mitigate the impact of password breaches

✅ Educate users and businesses on secure password practices

In this chapter, we'll cover:

- How and why users reuse passwords
- Techniques for detecting password reuse
- How cybercriminals exploit reused passwords
- Tools for investigating leaked credentials
- Best practices for mitigating password reuse risks

1. Why Do People Reuse Passwords?

Despite constant warnings from security experts, many users still recycle passwords across multiple accounts. Some common reasons include:

◆ **Convenience**: Memorizing unique passwords for each account is difficult.

◆ **Lack of Awareness**: Users underestimate the risk of password reuse.

◆ **Trust in a Single Strong Password**: Some believe a complex password is enough, even if used everywhere.

◆ **Password Fatigue**: Managing too many credentials without a password manager is overwhelming.

◆ **Corporate Culture**: Employees often reuse work passwords across personal accounts.

⬤ **Example:**

A user with the email johndoe@gmail.com has the password "Summer2023!" for their:

✓☐ Email account (Gmail)

✓☐ Social media (Facebook, Instagram, Twitter)

✓☐ Streaming service (Netflix)

✓☐ Banking login

If one of these platforms suffers a breach, attackers can use the same password to access multiple accounts.

2. How Cybercriminals Exploit Reused Passwords

2.1 Credential Stuffing Attacks

◆ Attackers use automation tools to test stolen username-password pairs on multiple platforms.
◆ Large-scale credential stuffing campaigns target banking, shopping, and email accounts.

● **Example:**

The Disney+ Credential Stuffing Attack (2019) led to thousands of hacked accounts within days of the service's launch. Attackers used passwords from previous breaches to log in to Disney+ accounts.

2.2 Password Spraying Attacks

◆ Instead of testing unique stolen credentials, attackers try common passwords across many accounts.
◆ Uses low login attempts per account to avoid detection.

● **Example:**

Hackers attempt passwords like "Welcome123" or "Password1" across thousands of email addresses.

2.3 Business Email Compromise (BEC)

◆ Attackers use reused corporate passwords to gain access to business email accounts.
◆ Compromised emails are used for fraud, phishing, and wire transfer scams.

● **Example:**

A LinkedIn data breach exposes an employee's email and password. If the employee reuses the same password for their corporate email, attackers can access sensitive business communications.

3. Identifying Reused Passwords in OSINT Investigations

3.1 Searching Breach Databases for Reused Credentials

Investigators can check if an email or password has been leaked using breach databases.

- **Have I Been Pwned (HIBP)** – Searches for breached emails & passwords.
- **DeHashed** – Finds credentials linked to an email or username.
- **Snusbase** – Analyzes leaked data for password reuse patterns.
- **LeakCheck** – Checks password reuse across multiple breaches.

● **Example:**

If the email "johndoe@gmail.com" appears in multiple breaches with the same password, this indicates password reuse across different platforms.

3.2 Extracting & Cracking Password Hashes

If a breach dump includes hashed passwords, OSINT analysts can attempt to recover plaintext passwords and check for reuse.

- **John the Ripper** – A tool for cracking password hashes.
- **Hashcat** – GPU-based password hash recovery.
- **CrackStation** – Online password hash lookup.

● **Example:**

An investigator finds that MD5 hash "5f4dcc3b5aa765d61d8327deb882cf99" corresponds to the plaintext password "password", revealing a weak reused credential.

3.3 Monitoring Dark Web for Reused Passwords

- Dark web marketplaces sell stolen credentials from previous breaches.
- Investigators monitor forums and Telegram groups for reused password dumps.
- Dark web tools can help identify leaked corporate credentials.

◆ Tools for Dark Web OSINT:

✓ **DarkOwl** – Tracks stolen credentials.
✓ **Onion Search Engine** – Searches leaked passwords.
✓ **IntSights** – Dark web intelligence monitoring.

● Example:

A bank's leaked credentials appear in a dark web forum. If employees reuse these passwords for other internal systems, attackers can escalate privileges.

4. Case Study: The Impact of Password Reuse

Case: The LinkedIn Data Breach & Its Domino Effect

◆ What Happened?

In 2012, LinkedIn suffered a breach that exposed 6.5 million hashed passwords. In 2016, the full 167 million records were leaked online, including email addresses and plaintext passwords.

◆ How Password Reuse Made It Worse:

- Many users had the same password for LinkedIn, Facebook, Gmail, and work accounts.
- Hackers tested LinkedIn credentials on other platforms, leading to thousands of compromised accounts.
- Business accounts were targeted in phishing & BEC attacks, costing companies millions in damages.

● **Lesson**: One breach can compromise multiple accounts when users reuse passwords.

5. Preventing Password Reuse & Strengthening Security

5.1 Enforcing Unique Passwords

- Use a password manager like Bitwarden, 1Password, or LastPass.
- Generate random, strong passwords for each service.

5.2 Enabling Multi-Factor Authentication (MFA)

◆ Even if a password is leaked, MFA blocks unauthorized logins.
◆ Use authenticator apps (Google Authenticator, Authy) instead of SMS-based 2FA.

5.3 Regularly Checking for Breaches

◆ Set up HIBP email alerts for real-time breach notifications.
◆ Conduct internal security audits to identify employees reusing passwords.

5.4 Implementing Password Policies for Organizations

◆ Require unique passwords for work accounts.
◆ Use SSO (Single Sign-On) solutions to manage credentials securely.
◆ Restrict the use of weak or common passwords.

● **Example:**

✓ Require 12+ character passwords with letters, numbers, and symbols.

✓ Prevent employees from using "Password123" or "CompanyName2024".

✓ Force password changes after a breach.

Password reuse is one of the biggest security risks in cybersecurity. By identifying reused credentials, investigators can prevent attacks, protect users, and strengthen digital security. Organizations must enforce strong password policies, monitor for breaches, and educate users to minimize the risks of credential reuse.

3.5 Tracing Email Use Across Dark Web Leak Sites

When an email address is leaked in a data breach, it often finds its way to dark web marketplaces, hacking forums, and credential dumps. Cybercriminals buy, sell, and share these emails for phishing attacks, credential stuffing, identity theft, and financial fraud. For OSINT analysts and cybersecurity professionals, tracing an email across dark web leak sites can:

✓ Identify compromised credentials before they are misused

✓ Reveal cybercriminal activity tied to an email address

✓ Uncover linked accounts, usernames, and leaked personal data

✓ Assist in tracking cyber threats targeting individuals and organizations

In this chapter, we'll explore:

- Where leaked emails appear on the dark web
- How to search for an email in dark web databases
- OSINT tools for tracking email use in breaches
- Dark web monitoring techniques
- Mitigation steps for compromised email accounts

1. Where Leaked Emails Appear on the Dark Web

1.1 Data Dump Marketplaces

◆ Criminal marketplaces sell bulk email-password databases from breaches.
◆ Users can purchase leaked credentials for hacking, fraud, and spam campaigns.

● **Example:**

- The Genesis Market specialized in selling stolen email credentials & digital fingerprints.

1.2 Hacking Forums & Paste Sites

◆ Public and private forums contain shared email lists and credential dumps.
◆ Pastebin, Ghostbin, and Doxbin have been used to distribute stolen emails.

● **Example:**

- The "Cit0day Breach Market" exposed 23,000 hacked databases before it was shut down.

1.3 Dark Web Search Engines & Leak Aggregators

- ◈ Some Tor-based search engines index breach dumps and leaked databases.
- ◈ These allow cybercriminals to search for exposed emails & passwords.

◆ Common Dark Web Search Engines:

✓ Onion Search Engine

✓ **Ahmia** – Indexes Tor-based sites
✓ **Dark.fail** – Directory of dark web marketplaces

1.4 Telegram & Discord Leak Channels

- ◈ Cybercriminals use encrypted messaging apps to share leaked credentials.
- ◈ These groups provide live breach updates and credential sales.

● Example:

- The "Combolist Telegram Group" shares thousands of stolen email-password pairs daily.

2. Searching for a Leaked Email in Breach Databases

2.1 Public OSINT Breach Databases

✓ **Have I Been Pwned (HIBP)** – Checks if an email appears in breaches.
✓ **DeHashed** – Searches email, username, or IP in data leaks.
✓ **LeakCheck** – Looks up email-password leaks.

● Example:

A company finds an executive's corporate email in multiple breaches using HIBP. This means their credentials could be at risk of compromise.

2.2 Dark Web Monitoring & Paid Services

Some tools provide real-time alerts when an email appears in dark web leaks.

◆ Dark Web Monitoring Tools:

✅ **DarkOwl** – Dark web intelligence for businesses.
✅ **SpyCloud** – Tracks stolen credentials on hacker sites.
✅ **Constella Intelligence** – Monitors leaked personal data.

⬤ **Example:**

A cybersecurity firm sets up SpyCloud alerts for their executives' emails. They receive a notification when an email appears in a new credential dump.

2.3 Searching Paste Sites & Leaked Database Repositories

◆ Some open-source OSINT tools help search paste sites and leaked data dumps.

◆ **Common Tools for Pastebin & Breach Search:**

✅ **Pastebin Scrapers** – Track leaked emails on paste sites.
✅ **H8mail** – Searches breaches for email addresses.
✅ **Scylla.sh** – OSINT search engine for leaked data.

⬤ **Example:**

An investigator uses H8mail to search for an employee's email and finds it linked to a leaked Dropbox password from a past breach.

3. Tracing Stolen Emails on the Dark Web

3.1 Analyzing Credential Dumps

◆ If an email appears in a breach dump, investigators check:

✓☐ Associated passwords (to detect reuse risks)
✓☐ Linked accounts & usernames
✓☐ IP addresses & locations tied to leaks

⬤ **Example:**

A company finds employee emails in a ransomware gang's leak site, confirming a data breach attack.

3.2 Tracking Email Mentions in Hacking Forums

◆ Investigators monitor Tor-based hacker forums for discussions about specific emails or companies.

◆ Dark Web Forum OSINT Techniques:

✓ Use Onion search engines to find mentions of an email.

✓ Set up Google Dorking alerts (e.g., "johndoe@gmail.com site:pastebin.com").

✓ Analyze forum threads discussing targeted breaches.

● Example:

A cybersecurity analyst finds an attacker discussing a phishing attack targeting a CEO's leaked email on a dark web forum.

3.3 Investigating Stolen Cookies & Session Tokens

◆ Some breaches include session cookies that allow attackers to log in without a password.
◆ These cookies are sold on dark web markets and used for session hijacking.

◆ Tools to Detect Compromised Sessions:

✓ **CyberChef** – Analyzes cookies from leaked breaches.
✓ **Chkrootkit** – Detects session hijacks.
✓ **Burp Suite** – Examines cookie security.

● Example:

An attacker buys a stolen Gmail cookie from a dark web forum and logs into a victim's account without needing a password.

4. Case Study: Dark Web Investigation of a Corporate Email Leak

Incident:

A financial company discovered that several employee emails were listed in a dark web credential dump.

Investigation Steps:

1☐ The cybersecurity team used Have I Been Pwned to confirm the emails were leaked in the LinkedIn and Dropbox breaches.

2☐ They ran the emails through DeHashed and found that some passwords were reused for corporate logins.

3☐ Monitoring tools like SpyCloud flagged that stolen credentials were being sold on dark web forums.

4☐ Analysts accessed Tor-based marketplaces and found the company's executive emails for sale.

5☐ The company forced password resets, enabled multi-factor authentication (MFA), and monitored for further breaches.

● **Outcome:**

✓ Prevented potential business email compromise (BEC) attacks.

✓ Blocked attackers from using stolen credentials for fraud.

✓ Strengthened corporate security policies against leaked emails.

5. Mitigation & Protection Strategies

5.1 Enabling Multi-Factor Authentication (MFA)

◆ Even if an email-password pair is leaked, MFA prevents unauthorized logins.

5.2 Regular Dark Web Monitoring

- Companies should use SpyCloud, DarkOwl, or Constella Intelligence to monitor leaked credentials.

5.3 Immediate Action on Leaked Credentials

- Reset passwords for any leaked accounts.
- Warn affected users about phishing risks.
- Monitor accounts for unusual login attempts.

5.4 Educating Employees & Users on Dark Web Risks

- Train employees to:

✓ Avoid password reuse

✓ Recognize phishing emails

✓ Report suspicious login activity

Tracing email use across dark web leak sites is essential for identifying compromised credentials, preventing fraud, and mitigating cyber threats. By monitoring breach databases, searching dark web forums, and analyzing credential dumps, OSINT investigators and security teams can proactively protect individuals and organizations.

3.6 Case Study: Tracking a Hacked Corporate Email Account

Corporate email accounts are prime targets for cybercriminals. A compromised corporate email can lead to data breaches, financial fraud, business email compromise (BEC), and ransomware attacks. In this case study, we analyze how an OSINT investigation helped track a hacked corporate email, exposing cybercriminal activity and preventing further damage.

Case Background

Incident:

A multinational finance company, GlobalTrust Financial, detected suspicious login attempts on an executive's corporate email account:

Email: cfo@globaltrust.com
Unusual Login Location: Russia & Brazil
Access Attempts: Multiple failed logins from Tor exit nodes
Suspicious Activity: Phishing emails sent from the CFO's email to internal employees

Initial Investigation Questions:

1☐ How was the CFO's email compromised?

2☐ Was the email part of a data breach or dark web sale?

3☐ Who is behind the attack?

4☐ What steps can be taken to contain the breach?

Phase 1: Identifying the Source of the Compromise

Step 1: Checking Data Breach Exposure

The cybersecurity team used Have I Been Pwned (HIBP) and DeHashed to check if the CFO's email was leaked in a past data breach.

◆ **Findings:**

✓ The CFO's email was found in the 2019 LinkedIn breach

✓ The leaked credentials contained an old, reused password: "Finance2020!"

✓ The same password was used for multiple corporate accounts

● **Conclusion:**

The attacker likely obtained the CFO's email and password from the LinkedIn breach and attempted to use it for credential stuffing attacks.

Step 2: Analyzing Dark Web Mentions

Investigators searched the dark web using:

✓ **DarkOwl** – To check for the email in hacker forums
✓ **Onion search engines** – To find leaks in dark web marketplaces

✅ **Telegram & Discord leak groups** – To look for credential sales

◆ **Findings:**

✅ The CFO's email appeared on a hacker forum post offering corporate logins

✅ The credentials were bundled in a "Finance Sector Email Leak"

✅ The post was active on a Tor-based dark web market

● **Conclusion:**

The CFO's email was actively sold on hacking forums, which increased the likelihood of multiple cybercriminals attempting to access the account.

Phase 2: Tracing the Attacker's Activity

Step 3: Investigating Suspicious Logins & IP Tracing

The company's security logs revealed:

- First unauthorized login attempt: Moscow, Russia
- Subsequent login attempts: Brazil, Germany, and U.S. (via VPN)
- Some logins originated from Tor exit nodes

◆ **Investigative Actions:**

✅ Used ipinfo.io to analyze attacker IPs

✅ Checked WHOIS records to identify VPN services used

✅ Monitored internal email activity for suspicious messages

◆ **Findings:**

✅ One IP belonged to a well-known bulletproof hosting provider used for cybercrime.

✅ Another IP was traced back to a compromised AWS server.

● **Conclusion:**

The attacker used VPNs, Tor, and hacked cloud servers to mask their identity.

Step 4: Analyzing Phishing Emails Sent from the Hacked Account

After gaining access to the CFO's email, the attacker sent phishing emails to internal employees.

◆ Phishing Email Details:

Subject: "Urgent Payment Request – CFO Approval Required"
Spoofed Signature: Mimicked the CFO's real email signature
Malicious Link: Redirected users to a fake Microsoft login page
Sender IP: Matched one of the attacker's VPN servers

◆ Investigative Actions:

✓ Extracted email headers to analyze sender information

✓ Used URL analysis tools (VirusTotal, Any.Run) to check the phishing link

✓ Investigated whether employees clicked the link or entered credentials

◆ Findings:

✓ At least 3 employees clicked the malicious link

✓ One employee entered their corporate login credentials, exposing their account

✓ The phishing domain was hosted on a fast-flux hosting network, making it difficult to trace

● Conclusion:

The attack was an attempt at Business Email Compromise (BEC), aimed at gaining deeper access to corporate financial systems.

Phase 3: Mitigating the Threat & Strengthening Security

Immediate Incident Response Actions:

✓ Forced a password reset for the CFO's and affected employees' accounts

✓ Enabled Multi-Factor Authentication (MFA) on all executive accounts

✓ Blocked known attacker IPs and VPNs from corporate networks

✓ Warned all employees to ignore phishing emails

✓ Reported phishing domains to hosting providers and law enforcement

Post-Incident OSINT Actions:

✓ Continued dark web monitoring for any new leaks involving corporate emails

✓ Set up automated breach alerts for corporate emails on SpyCloud & DarkOwl

✓ Investigated dark web vendors selling corporate logins to identify possible leads

◆ **Further Findings:**

- Investigators found a dark web vendor selling a "GlobalTrust Finance Access Package", including other corporate logins.
- This suggested the company's network was already being targeted for further attacks.

● **Conclusion:**

The breach was part of a larger cybercriminal operation targeting financial firms.

Final Outcome & Lessons Learned

Outcome of the Investigation:

✓☐ The hacked email was traced back to dark web forums
✓☐ The phishing attack was contained before financial loss occurred
✓☐ The company strengthened security policies and breach detection
✓☐ Law enforcement was notified to investigate dark web sellers offering corporate credentials

Key Lessons Learned:

◆ **Password Reuse is Dangerous** – The CFO's LinkedIn breach led to a corporate compromise.

◆ **MFA is Critical** – Without it, attackers easily gained access.

◆ **Dark Web Monitoring is Essential** – Threat actors actively sell corporate logins.

◆ **Phishing Awareness Saves Companies** – Employee training can prevent further compromise.

This case study highlights how a single compromised corporate email can escalate into a full-scale cyber threat. Through OSINT techniques, breach database searches, dark web monitoring, and phishing analysis, investigators were able to track the attacker's methods, contain the threat, and prevent further damage.

4. Investigating Phishing Attacks & Scam Emails

In this chapter, we will dive into the critical task of investigating phishing attacks and scam emails, which are among the most common forms of cybercrime. These deceptive emails are designed to trick individuals into revealing sensitive information, such as login credentials, financial details, or personal data. We'll explore the techniques used by attackers to craft convincing phishing emails, including the manipulation of email headers, sender addresses, and content. By understanding the red flags and patterns of phishing attempts, investigators can effectively identify, trace, and disrupt these attacks. We'll also cover tools and methods for analyzing scam emails, verifying their authenticity, and tracing them back to their origins. This knowledge is vital for protecting users and organizations from falling victim to one of the most pervasive and damaging cyber threats.

4.1 How Phishing Campaigns Work & How to Spot Them

Phishing is one of the most common and effective cyber threats used by attackers to steal credentials, deploy malware, and gain unauthorized access to systems. These attacks rely on social engineering, deception, and technical manipulation to trick users into revealing sensitive information.

For OSINT analysts, cybersecurity professionals, and investigators, understanding how phishing campaigns operate is essential to detecting, preventing, and mitigating these attacks. This chapter explores:

✓ The different types of phishing attacks

✓ How phishing campaigns are launched

✓ How to spot phishing attempts using OSINT techniques

✓ Real-world phishing case studies

1. Understanding Phishing Campaigns

1.1 What is Phishing?

Phishing is a cyberattack where an attacker impersonates a trusted entity to deceive victims into:

- Providing login credentials
- Downloading malware
- Giving away financial or personal information

Phishing is often carried out via email, SMS (smishing), social media, and phone calls (vishing).

● **Example:**

A hacker impersonates a company's IT department, sending an email urging employees to reset their passwords on a fake login page. Once employees enter their credentials, the attacker gains access to their accounts.

1.2 Common Types of Phishing Attacks

Phishing Type	Description	Example
Email Phishing	Mass emails sent to trick users into revealing information.	A fake PayPal email asking users to verify their accounts.
Spear Phishing	Targeted emails aimed at specific individuals or organizations.	A fake email to a CFO pretending to be from the CEO, asking for a wire transfer.
Whaling	Spear phishing attack targeting high-profile executives.	A phishing email impersonating a legal department sending an "urgent document" to a CEO.
Smishing	Phishing attempts via SMS messages.	A text message claiming to be from a bank, asking to confirm account details.
Vishing	Phishing over voice calls.	A scammer pretending to be from tech support, asking for remote access to fix a "virus."
Angler Phishing	Phishing through social media messages or fake customer support.	A fake Twitter support account responding to users with malicious links.

● **Real-World Example:**

In 2020, Twitter was compromised through a spear-phishing attack targeting employees with access to internal tools. Attackers convinced employees to provide login credentials, allowing them to hijack high-profile accounts like Elon Musk and Barack Obama.

2. How Phishing Campaigns Work

A phishing campaign typically follows a structured process:

Step 1: Reconnaissance & Target Research

Attackers gather OSINT on targets using:

- **Data breaches & leaks** (e.g., Have I Been Pwned, DeHashed)
- **Social media footprints** (LinkedIn, Twitter, Facebook)
- **Corporate websites** (employee names, contact details)

● **Example:**

An attacker finds an executive's email address in a LinkedIn breach and uses it for a targeted phishing attack.

Step 2: Crafting the Phishing Message

A phishing email is designed to appear legitimate, using:

- ✓ **Spoofed sender addresses** (e.g., "support@micros0ft.com")
- ✓ **Urgent language** ("Your account will be locked in 24 hours!")
- ✓ **Fake login pages** (clone of Office 365 or PayPal)
- ✓ **Malicious attachments** (infected PDFs, Word documents)

● **Example:**

A fake Amazon email asks users to update their billing information through a spoofed website.

Step 3: Delivery of the Attack

Attackers distribute phishing emails through:

- ✓ **Compromised business accounts** (previously hacked emails)
- ✓ **Mass email spam campaigns** (using botnets)
- ✓ **Social engineering tactics** (posing as IT staff)

● Example:

Attackers send phishing emails from a real but compromised CFO email account, making it more convincing to employees.

Step 4: Exploitation & Data Theft

Once a victim clicks a phishing link or downloads a malicious file:

- **Credentials are stolen** (stored in attacker databases)
- **Malware is installed** (keyloggers, ransomware)
- Victim's accounts are used to spread more phishing emails

● Example:

A user clicks on a fake Microsoft login page, unknowingly giving their credentials to an attacker who then logs into the real account.

3. How to Spot Phishing Emails

3.1 Key Indicators of Phishing Emails

◆ Suspicious Sender Address

- Attackers use lookalike domains (e.g., paypal@secure-paypa1.com)
- Check sender domain with MXToolbox or Whois Lookup

◆ Generic Greetings & Urgency

- Attackers use "Dear User" instead of your real name
- Fake urgency: "Act now or your account will be closed!"

◆ Suspicious Links

- Hover over links (without clicking) to check real URLs
- Use URLVoid or VirusTotal to scan for malicious sites

◆ Attachments & Embedded Malware

- Attackers send infected PDFs, ZIP files, Word macros
- Use Any.Run or Hybrid Analysis to test suspicious files

◆ **Unusual Requests for Sensitive Data**

- No legitimate company asks for passwords or banking info via email

● **Example:**

A phishing email from "Apple Support" claims "Your Apple ID is locked. Click here to verify." The link leads to a fake login page designed to steal credentials.

4. OSINT Tools for Phishing Investigation

Tool	Purpose	Link
Have I Been Pwned	Check if an email was leaked in a breach	https://haveibeenpwned.com/
MXToolbox	Analyze email headers & sender IPs	https://mxtoolbox.com/
URLVoid	Scan links for phishing & malware	https://www.urlvoid.com/
VirusTotal	Check attachments & links for malicious content	https://www.virustotal.com/
Any.Run	Analyze suspicious files in a sandbox	https://any.run/

5. Preventing Phishing Attacks

5.1 Implementing Security Measures

✓ Enable Multi-Factor Authentication (MFA) on all accounts

✓ Use email filtering solutions (e.g., Proofpoint, Mimecast)

✓ Train employees to recognize phishing emails

✓ Block known phishing domains & malicious IPs

5.2 Reporting & Responding to Phishing Attacks

✓ **If you receive a phishing email:**

- Do not click any links or open attachments

- Report it to your IT/security team
- Block the sender and phishing domain

✅ **If you fall for a phishing scam:**

- Change your passwords immediately
- Enable MFA if not already active
- Monitor for suspicious logins

Phishing campaigns remain one of the biggest cyber threats to individuals and organizations. Attackers use OSINT techniques to craft realistic phishing emails that deceive even tech-savvy users. By understanding how phishing attacks work and recognizing red flags, security professionals can prevent attacks before they cause harm.

4.2 Investigating Suspicious Links & Attachments

Cybercriminals frequently use malicious links and attachments in phishing emails, scam messages, and malware distribution campaigns. These payloads can lead to credential theft, financial fraud, or malware infections.

For OSINT analysts, cybersecurity investigators, and threat hunters, understanding how to analyze suspicious links and attachments is critical in tracking phishing operations and identifying cybercriminal infrastructure.

This chapter will cover:

✅ How to analyze suspicious links and identify phishing domains

✅ How to investigate malicious attachments without executing them

✅ OSINT tools and techniques for URL and file analysis

✅ Real-world examples of link and attachment investigations

1. Investigating Suspicious Links

1.1 Common Malicious Link Techniques

Attackers use various URL manipulation techniques to disguise their phishing and malware delivery links:

Technique	Example	Description
Lookalike Domains	`paypa1.com` (instead of `paypal.com`)	Attackers use slight variations of legitimate domains to trick users.
Subdomain Tricks	`paypal.com.secure-login.com`	The real domain is `secure-login.com`, not `paypal.com`.
Shortened URLs	`bit.ly/2Xyz123`	Attackers use link shorteners to hide malicious URLs.
Hex/Unicode Encoding	`https://%77%77%77.%70%68%69%73%68.com`	URLs are encoded to bypass filters.
Data URI Attacks	`data:text/html;base64,PHNjcmlwdD5hbGVydC`	Malicious code is embedded directly in the URL.

● **Example:**

A user receives an email claiming to be from Microsoft Support with a link:

☞ https://microsoft-support-login.com

Hovering over the link reveals the real URL:

🔒 https://securelogin.phishing.com

1.2 How to Analyze Suspicious Links

🔎 **Step 1: Hover Over the Link**

Before clicking, hover over the link to reveal the actual destination URL.

🔎 **Step 2: Check URL Reputation with OSINT Tools**

Tool	Purpose	Link
VirusTotal	Scans URLs for malware and phishing indicators	https://www.virustotal.com
URLVoid	Checks a website's reputation against security databases	https://www.urlvoid.com
CheckPhish	Identifies phishing pages using AI detection	https://checkphish.ai
Unshorten.It	Expands shortened URLs to reveal the real destination	https://unshorten.it

🔎 Step 3: Analyze WHOIS & DNS Records

- Use WHOIS lookups to check domain registration details.
- Use MXToolbox to check mail servers and DNS records.

Tool	Purpose	Link
Whois Lookup	Finds domain owner & registration details	https://whois.domaintools.com
MXToolbox	Checks domain mail servers & SPF records	https://mxtoolbox.com

🔎 Step 4: Open URL in a Secure Environment

- If further investigation is needed, use a sandboxed browser or a virtual machine to visit the URL safely.
- Use Any.Run or Hybrid Analysis to check for hidden malware.

2. Investigating Suspicious Attachments

2.1 Common Malicious File Types

Cybercriminals often disguise malware inside legitimate-looking files:

File Type	Example	Threat
Executable Files	`invoice.exe`	Ransomware, trojans, keyloggers
Microsoft Office Files	`report.docm`	Macro-based malware
PDF Files	`receipt.pdf`	Embedded malicious links
ZIP/RAR Archives	`documents.zip`	Packed malware
ISO/IMG Disk Images	`setup.iso`	Used to bypass email filters

● **Example:**

An email attachment named "Urgent_Payment_Invoice.pdf" actually contains an embedded JavaScript file that downloads malware when opened.

2.2 How to Analyze Suspicious Attachments

🔎 Step 1: Do Not Open the File

- Never open an unknown file on your main device.
- Use a virtual machine (VM) or a sandbox environment.

🔎 Step 2: Check File Hashes Against Malware Databases

Compute the file's SHA-256 or MD5 hash and check against known malware databases.

Tool	Purpose	Link
VirusTotal	Scans files for malware signatures	https://www.virustotal.com
Hybrid Analysis	Runs the file in a sandbox to detect hidden threats	https://www.hybrid-analysis.com
MetaDefender	Analyzes files for threats using multiple engines	https://metadefender.opswat.com

🔎 Step 3: Extract & Analyze Metadata

Metadata can reveal the true source of a file.
Use ExifTool to check file creation date, author, and hidden data.

Tool	Purpose	Link
ExifTool	Extracts metadata from images, PDFs, and Office files	https://exiftool.org

🔎 Step 4: Open File in a Secure Sandbox

Use Any.Run or Cuckoo Sandbox to safely execute and observe file behavior.

3. Real-World Case Study: Investigating a Malicious PDF

Incident:

A financial company received an email from "CEO@FinanceGlobal.com" with an attached "Investment_Report.pdf".

◆ Red Flags:

✓ The CEO's email address was slightly altered (financeglobal.com vs. financeglobal.com).

✓ The email contained urgent language asking the recipient to open the PDF.

✓ The attachment was flagged as suspicious by email filters.

Investigation Steps:

1▢ Checked the Sender's Email

- MXToolbox WHOIS Lookup showed that the domain was registered 2 days ago—a common sign of phishing.

2▢ Analyzed the PDF File

- VirusTotal scan flagged the PDF as containing an embedded JavaScript payload.
- ExifTool analysis showed the PDF was created using a suspicious tool.

3▢ Opened the File in a Sandbox

Hybrid Analysis revealed that opening the PDF triggered a remote PowerShell script to download malware.

● The PDF was a trojan downloader designed to infect the recipient's computer. The phishing attempt was part of a business email compromise (BEC) attack targeting financial institutions.

4. Preventing Link & Attachment-Based Attacks

✓ Enable email filtering to block known phishing links.

✓ Educate employees on spotting malicious links & attachments.

✓ Use endpoint protection with real-time malware scanning.

✓ Block executable attachments in emails.

✓ Always verify unexpected attachments before opening them.

Suspicious links and attachments remain a major cyber threat. OSINT techniques and cybersecurity tools can help investigators analyze phishing domains, detect malicious files, and track cybercriminal activity.

4.3 Reverse Engineering Phishing Domains & Infrastructure

Cybercriminals behind phishing attacks rely on domains, hosting providers, and various backend infrastructure to operate their campaigns. While phishing emails may be easy to identify, tracking down the attackers and dismantling their operations requires reverse engineering phishing domains and mapping out their infrastructure.

For OSINT analysts and cybersecurity investigators, understanding how phishing domains are registered, where they are hosted, and how they connect to other malicious assets can provide valuable intelligence on threat actors.

This chapter will cover:

✓ How to investigate phishing domains

✓ Techniques for tracking hosting providers and infrastructure

✓ OSINT tools for mapping connected domains and IP addresses

✓ Real-world case study of a phishing infrastructure takedown

1. Understanding Phishing Domains & Their Lifecycle

1.1 How Phishing Domains Are Created

Attackers use different techniques to create deceptive phishing websites:

Method	Description	Example
Lookalike Domains (Typosquatting)	Attackers register domains that resemble legitimate ones.	`paypa1.com` instead of `paypal.com`
Subdomain Spoofing	Using deceptive subdomains under a legitimate-looking domain.	`paypal.com.secure-login.com`
Homograph Attacks (Unicode Spoofing)	Attackers use **visually similar characters** to trick users.	`apple.com` (Cyrillic 'a' instead of Latin 'a')
Compromised Websites	Attackers hijack legitimate sites to host phishing pages.	`example.com/login.php` (hacked to serve phishing content)
Bulletproof Hosting	Attackers use **offshore hosting providers** that ignore takedown requests.	Hosted on **anonymous VPS services**

1.2 Investigating Phishing Domains

🔍 Step 1: Identify the Domain from the Phishing Email

- Extract the URL from the phishing email.
- Expand shortened links using Unshorten.It.

🔍 Step 2: Perform a WHOIS Lookup

WHOIS records can reveal:

✅ Domain owner details (if not protected)

✅ Registration date (new domains = red flag ⚑)

✅ Registrar and hosting provider

Tool	Purpose	Link
Whois Lookup	Retrieves domain registration details	https://whois.domaintools.com
ICANN Lookup	Checks domain ownership information	https://lookup.icann.org
ViewDNS.info	Provides WHOIS history and DNS records	http://viewdns.info

🔍 Step 3: Check Hosting & Server Details

Find where the phishing website is hosted using:

✅ IP address lookups

✅ Reverse DNS lookups

✅ Hosting provider identification

Tool	Purpose	Link
MXToolbox	Finds hosting provider & mail servers	https://mxtoolbox.com
Shodan	Scans for open ports & services	https://www.shodan.io
Censys	Maps internet-facing infrastructure	https://censys.io

🔎 Step 4: Analyze SSL Certificates & Subdomains

- Many phishing sites reuse SSL certificates, which can help track related sites.
- Use Crt.sh to find all domains using the same SSL certificate.

Tool	Purpose	Link
Crt.sh	Searches for SSL certificates linked to a domain	https://crt.sh
Sublist3r	Finds subdomains of phishing sites	https://github.com/aboul3la/Sublist3r

2. Mapping Phishing Infrastructure

2.1 Tracking Connected Domains & IPs

Attackers often reuse the same infrastructure across multiple phishing campaigns. By analyzing IP addresses, name servers, and hosting providers, we can map out their full network.

🔎 **Step 1: Reverse Lookup the IP Address**

- Many phishing domains share the same IP address as other malicious sites.
- Use Reverse IP Lookup to find related domains.

Tool	Purpose	Link
SecurityTrails	Reverse IP & DNS lookup	https://securitytrails.com
Spyse	Identifies shared IP addresses	https://spyse.com

🔎 Step 2: Find Related Domains Using Passive DNS

- Passive DNS databases store historical DNS records.
- This helps track other phishing sites operated by the same attacker.

Tool	Purpose	Link
RiskIQ PassiveTotal	Tracks domain history & connected IPs	https://community.riskiq.com
Farsight Security	Provides passive DNS data	https://www.farsightsecurity.com

🔎 Step 3: Identify Bulletproof Hosting Providers

- Some hosting providers specialize in hosting cybercriminal operations.
- If a phishing site is hosted on a known bulletproof provider, it's likely part of a larger operation.

Tool	Purpose	Link
AbuseIPDB	Checks if an IP is linked to cybercrime	https://www.abuseipdb.com
IPinfo.io	Identifies hosting provider & ASN info	https://ipinfo.io

3. Real-World Case Study: Dismantling a Phishing Network

Incident:

A financial institution reported a phishing campaign targeting its customers with a fake login page.

🔎 Investigation Steps:

1️⃣ Extracted the Phishing URL

Found in a phishing email: secure-banking-login.com

2️⃣ Performed WHOIS & Hosting Analysis

WHOIS lookup revealed:

✅ The domain was registered two weeks ago

✅ The registrar was located in Russia

✅ The hosting provider was a known bulletproof host

3️⃣ Mapped Connected Domains

Reverse IP lookup found six additional phishing domains hosted on the same server:

✅ bank-login-secure.com

✅ account-verification-banking.com

4️⃣ Analyzed SSL Certificates

Crt.sh showed that all domains shared the same SSL certificate, confirming they were related.

5️⃣ Takedown Action

- The financial institution reported the domains to their registrar.
- The phishing sites were blacklisted by security vendors.
- Abuse reports were sent to the hosting provider.

Outcome:

🏦 The phishing network was shut down within 72 hours, preventing further customer credential theft.

4. Preventing & Mitigating Phishing Infrastructure

✅ Monitor domains similar to your organization's name using WHOIS alerts.

☑ Blacklist known phishing domains using security appliances.

☑ Report phishing sites to Google Safe Browsing & Microsoft Defender.

☑ Use AI-driven threat intelligence platforms for domain monitoring.

☑ Educate users on checking URLs before entering credentials.

Reverse engineering phishing domains and their infrastructure is crucial for tracking cybercriminals and disrupting their operations. By using OSINT tools, passive DNS lookups, and SSL certificate analysis, investigators can uncover hidden phishing networks and take action before they cause harm.

4.4 Tracking Down Phishing Kit Sellers on the Dark Web

The Dark Web has become a marketplace for cybercriminals selling phishing kits, which are pre-built packages that allow attackers to deploy phishing campaigns with minimal technical knowledge. These kits often include ready-made phishing pages, automated scripts, and credential-stealing mechanisms that mimic legitimate websites like banks, social media platforms, and email providers.

For OSINT analysts and cybersecurity investigators, identifying and tracking phishing kit sellers is crucial in understanding emerging threats, mapping cybercriminal networks, and taking down operations before they cause damage.

This chapter will cover:

☑ How phishing kits work and what they contain

☑ Where phishing kits are sold on the Dark Web

☑ OSINT techniques to track phishing kit sellers

☑ Case study: Investigating a major phishing kit operation

1. Understanding Phishing Kits & Their Components

1.1 What is a Phishing Kit?

A phishing kit is a pre-configured set of files designed to replicate a legitimate website and steal user credentials. These kits are often sold on Dark Web marketplaces or shared in underground forums.

Component	Description
Cloned Website	A fake version of a login page (e.g., PayPal, Microsoft, Facebook).
PHP Scripts	Captures and stores credentials entered by victims.
Email Sender Module	Sends phishing emails automatically to potential targets.
Redirection Script	Sends victims to the real website after stealing credentials.
Admin Panel	Allows attackers to monitor stolen credentials in real time.

● **Example**: A cybercriminal purchases a PayPal phishing kit on the Dark Web for $50. They upload the files to a compromised server and launch a phishing campaign. When victims enter their PayPal login details, the credentials are sent directly to the attacker's email or database.

2. Where Are Phishing Kits Sold on the Dark Web?

Phishing kits are available on various Dark Web platforms, including:

2.1 Dark Web Marketplaces

🔎 **Common marketplaces selling phishing kits:**

Marketplace Name	Type of Products Sold
AlphaBay (re-emerged)	Stolen credentials, phishing kits, and hacking tools.
Genesis Market	Digital fingerprints and phishing kits.
DarkFox Market	Malware, exploit kits, and phishing scripts.

💡 **OSINT Tip**: Most Dark Web marketplaces require invitation codes or PGP verification before access. Investigators often use forum monitoring and network infiltration techniques to gather intelligence.

2.2 Cybercriminal Forums & Telegram Groups

🔎 Popular phishing kit distribution channels:

Platform	Type of Activity
Exploit.in	Discussions on phishing techniques and kit sales.
Breached Forums	Leaked databases, phishing kits, and carding discussions.
Telegram Channels	Direct sales and automated bots selling phishing tools.

💡 **OSINT Tip**: Use Telegram OSINT tools like Telegra.ph and Tgstat to track phishing kit sellers on Telegram.

2.3 Private Dark Web Shops

- Some sellers host private storefronts with Monero (XMR) or Bitcoin (BTC) payments.
- These sites use hidden services (.onion domains) and require referrals or purchases via escrow.

💡 **OSINT Tip**: Use Ahmia.fi or Dark.fail to discover hidden phishing kit stores.

3. OSINT Techniques to Track Phishing Kit Sellers

Tracking phishing kit sellers requires a combination of Dark Web monitoring, cryptocurrency analysis, and infrastructure mapping.

3.1 Identifying Sellers & Their Profiles

Sellers often use pseudonyms across different forums and marketplaces. Investigators can:

✅ Cross-reference usernames and contact details on multiple forums.

✅ Use Google Dorking and BreachData leaks to check if sellers reused credentials.

✅ Search Bitcoin addresses linked to sales on blockchain explorers.

💡 **Example**: A seller using the username "PhishMasterX" on a Dark Web forum was found using the same alias on Telegram.

3.2 Tracking Cryptocurrency Transactions

Phishing kit sellers typically accept Bitcoin (BTC), Monero (XMR), or Litecoin (LTC) for payments. Investigators can track transactions using:

Tool	Purpose	Link
Blockchain Explorer	Tracks Bitcoin transactions	https://www.blockchain.com/explorer
Chainalysis Reactor	Analyzes illicit cryptocurrency transactions	(Paid tool)
Elliptic	Identifies crypto addresses linked to cybercrime	(Paid tool)

💡 **OSINT Tip**: If a seller reuses a Bitcoin address, their transactions can be traced back to an exchange, leading to KYC (Know Your Customer) data exposure.

3.3 Mapping Hosting & Infrastructure

Phishing kit sellers often host their sites on bulletproof hosting services. Investigators can:

✔ Scan for related phishing domains using Passive DNS tools.

✔ Use Shodan and Censys to find servers hosting phishing kit stores.

✔ Check SSL certificate reuse to link multiple sites together.

Tool	Purpose	Link
Crt.sh	Finds SSL certificates linked to phishing domains	https://crt.sh
SecurityTrails	Tracks IPs, domains, and DNS history	https://securitytrails.com
Shodan	Scans for open ports and vulnerabilities	https://www.shodan.io

💡 **Example**: An OSINT investigator found three phishing kit websites hosted on the same IP address, exposing a cybercriminal network.

4. Case Study: Investigating a Phishing Kit Operation

Incident:

A cybersecurity team discovered a phishing campaign targeting a major bank. The phishing emails linked to a fake login page hosted on a recently registered domain.

Investigation Steps:

1⬜ Extracted Phishing Kit Files

The phishing page contained hidden metadata revealing the original developer's username.

2⬜ Tracked the Seller on Dark Web Forums

The username was found selling similar kits on Exploit.in and DarkFox Market.

3⬜ Followed Cryptocurrency Transactions

The seller's Bitcoin wallet was traced to a crypto exchange with KYC verification.

4⬜ Identified Additional Phishing Domains

Using Passive DNS lookups, investigators found more phishing sites linked to the same attacker.

Outcome:

🏛 The seller's Bitcoin wallet was flagged, leading to their funds being seized by law enforcement.
🏛 Phishing domains were taken down, stopping further attacks.

5. Preventing & Disrupting Phishing Kit Operations

✅ Monitor Dark Web forums for emerging phishing kit trends.

✅ Track cryptocurrency transactions linked to phishing-related payments.

✅ Use web crawlers to detect new phishing kit deployments.

✅ Report phishing sites & domains to takedown services.

✅ Educate businesses & individuals on phishing threats.

Tracking phishing kit sellers on the Dark Web is a critical part of cyber threat intelligence and OSINT investigations. By leveraging Dark Web monitoring, cryptocurrency tracing, and infrastructure analysis, investigators can map out cybercriminal networks and disrupt phishing operations before they escalate.

4.5 Analyzing Phishing Tactics Targeting Individuals vs. Companies

Phishing attacks come in many forms, but they generally target two main groups: individuals and companies. While both are susceptible to phishing, the tactics used against them differ significantly in complexity, delivery methods, and objectives.

Cybercriminals tailor their strategies based on their targets:

◆ Individuals are often targeted for personal data, financial credentials, or identity theft.
◆ Companies face more sophisticated phishing attempts aimed at stealing corporate secrets, financial fraud, or breaching entire networks.

For OSINT analysts and cybersecurity professionals, understanding the differences in these phishing tactics is essential for effective investigation and mitigation.

This chapter explores:

✅ Common phishing tactics targeting individuals vs. companies

✅ How attackers customize their strategies

✅ OSINT techniques for detecting and preventing these threats

1. Phishing Attacks on Individuals

1.1 Common Tactics Targeting Individuals

Phishing attacks against individuals rely on emotional manipulation, urgency, and deception. The most common tactics include:

Tactic	Description	Example
Credential Theft (Email Phishing)	Fake emails trick users into providing login details.	A fake email from "Netflix" asks users to update their password.
Spear Phishing	A highly targeted phishing attack customized for the victim.	An email impersonating a bank requests identity verification.
Smishing (SMS Phishing)	Phishing attempts via text messages.	A text from "FedEx" asks the victim to click a link to track a package.
Vishing (Voice Phishing)	Attackers use phone calls to impersonate legitimate entities.	A scammer calls, pretending to be from "Apple Support," and asks for an Apple ID login.
Social Media Phishing	Fake accounts or messages attempt to steal credentials.	A Facebook message from a "friend" asks the victim to check a suspicious link.

💡 Real-World Example:

Facebook phishing scams: Attackers send fake messages pretending to be from Facebook, warning users of an account issue and directing them to a malicious login page.

1.2 How Attackers Customize Phishing for Individuals

Phishing attacks against individuals exploit personal interests, habits, and online behavior.

♦ **Data from breaches**: Cybercriminals use leaked credentials from breaches (e.g., from Have I Been Pwned) to personalize phishing emails.
♦ **Psychological triggers**: Messages use fear (account lockout), excitement (you won a prize), or urgency (immediate action needed) to trick victims.
♦ **Spoofed brands**: Attackers impersonate well-known companies like PayPal, Amazon, or Google to appear legitimate.

💡 OSINT Tip:

- Use email header analysis to identify spoofed senders.
- Search email addresses in breach databases to see if they've been compromised.

2. Phishing Attacks on Companies

2.1 Common Tactics Targeting Companies

Attacks on businesses are usually more sophisticated and aim for higher rewards.

Tactic	Description	Example
Business Email Compromise (BEC)	Attackers impersonate executives or vendors to trick employees into transferring funds.	A fake email from the "CFO" asks for an urgent wire transfer.
Whaling	A type of spear phishing targeting high-level executives.	A CEO receives an email from a "law firm" requesting sensitive data.
Supply Chain Attacks	Attackers compromise a vendor to infiltrate a company.	A breached IT provider is used to deliver malware to clients.
Malware-Injected Emails	Phishing emails contain **malicious attachments** or links.	An employee receives a fake invoice containing a **Trojan or ransomware.**
Credential Harvesting Attacks	Fake login portals trick employees into revealing corporate credentials.	A fake Office365 login page captures employee credentials.

💡 Real-World Example:

Google & Facebook Phishing Scam: Attackers impersonated a supplier, sending fake invoices and stealing over $100 million.

2.2 How Attackers Customize Phishing for Companies

Phishing attacks against businesses require extensive reconnaissance and social engineering.

◆ **Targeted Approach**: Attackers research company employees via LinkedIn, job postings, and press releases to craft convincing emails.
◆ **Executive Impersonation**: Emails appear to be from high-ranking officials or trusted vendors to increase credibility.
◆ **Use of Legitimate Services**: Cybercriminals send phishing emails from compromised company accounts to bypass security filters.

💡 OSINT Tip:

- Investigate suspicious emails by analyzing DKIM, SPF, and DMARC records to detect spoofing.
- Search Dark Web marketplaces for leaked corporate credentials that may fuel phishing attacks.

3. Key Differences: Individuals vs. Companies

Aspect	Individuals	Companies
Target	General public, consumers	Employees, executives, suppliers
Objective	Financial fraud, personal data theft	Corporate espionage, financial fraud, network access
Attack Sophistication	Basic (mass emails, SMS)	Advanced (spear phishing, BEC, malware)
Tactics Used	Emotional manipulation, urgency	Social engineering, impersonation, technical exploits
Attack Methods	Email, SMS, social media	BEC, supply chain compromise, executive impersonation
Prevention	Email filtering, user education	Advanced threat detection, employee training, DMARC enforcement

💡 Example:

- A phishing email targeting an individual may claim they won an iPhone and need to "verify their identity."
- A phishing email targeting a company may impersonate the CEO, requesting a confidential wire transfer.

4. OSINT Techniques to Detect & Prevent Phishing

4.1 Detecting Phishing Against Individuals

🔍 Use these OSINT tools to analyze phishing threats targeting individuals:

Tool	Purpose	Link
Have I Been Pwned	Checks if an email is in a data breach	https://haveibeenpwned.com
EmailRep.io	Checks email reputation & phishing risk	https://emailrep.io
PhishTank	Identifies known phishing sites	https://www.phishtank.com

4.2 Detecting Phishing Against Companies

🔍 Investigate corporate phishing attacks with these tools:

Tool	Purpose	Link
MXToolbox	Analyzes email headers & SPF/DKIM/DMARC records	https://mxtoolbox.com
RiskIQ PassiveTotal	Maps phishing domains & infrastructure	https://community.riskiq.com
AbuseIPDB	Checks if an IP is linked to cybercrime	https://www.abuseipdb.com

5. Preventing Phishing Attacks

For Individuals:

✅ Use multi-factor authentication (MFA) on all accounts.

✅ Avoid clicking links in unexpected emails or texts.

✅ Check email headers for suspicious senders.

✅ Use a password manager to avoid reused credentials.

For Companies:

✅ Enforce email authentication standards (SPF, DKIM, DMARC).

✅ Train employees to recognize phishing attacks.

✅ Monitor Dark Web for leaked corporate credentials.

✅ Implement endpoint security & anti-phishing solutions.

Phishing tactics vary significantly depending on whether they target individuals or businesses. By understanding these differences and leveraging OSINT tools, investigators can detect, analyze, and prevent phishing campaigns before they cause harm.

4.6 Case Study: Investigating a Global Phishing Operation

Global phishing operations are increasingly sophisticated, well-organized, and financially motivated, often involving cybercriminal syndicates operating across multiple countries.

These operations exploit email phishing, fake websites, malware, and social engineering to steal credentials, financial data, and sensitive corporate information.

In this case study, we will examine the investigation of a global phishing operation that targeted thousands of individuals and businesses worldwide. This investigation involved:

✔ Identifying phishing emails & fake websites

✔ Tracking cybercriminals through OSINT techniques

✔ Tracing cryptocurrency payments linked to stolen credentials

✔ Collaborating with law enforcement to dismantle the operation

1. The Discovery of a Large-Scale Phishing Campaign

1.1 Initial Incident: A Surge in Phishing Emails

In early 2023, cybersecurity analysts detected a spike in phishing emails impersonating well-known financial institutions. These emails contained:

✦ Fake login pages mimicking banks and payment services.
✦ Malicious attachments disguised as invoices or security alerts.
✦ Phishing links designed to steal email and banking credentials.

1.2 Early Clues from OSINT Investigation

Researchers analyzed hundreds of reported phishing emails and found:

🔎 Email headers revealing the use of compromised email servers.
🔎 Fake domains registered to mimic legitimate financial services.
🔎 Common sender IP addresses, linking multiple phishing campaigns together.

💡 **Key Finding**: The phishing emails originated from multiple countries, indicating a coordinated global operation rather than isolated attacks.

2. Identifying the Infrastructure Behind the Operation

2.1 Tracking Phishing Domains

Using Passive DNS analysis and WHOIS records, investigators discovered that over 500 domains were registered within a short period, mimicking:

🏦 Major banks (Chase, HSBC, Wells Fargo)
✉@ Email providers (Outlook, Gmail, Yahoo)
💳 Payment platforms (PayPal, Venmo, Apple Pay)

◆ Many of these domains were hosted on the same IP ranges in bulletproof hosting services, commonly used by cybercriminals.
◆ Some domains used previously seen phishing kit templates, indicating they were likely sold as Phishing-as-a-Service (PhaaS).

💡 **Key Finding**: The phishing infrastructure was not just one actor—multiple cybercriminals were using a shared platform to deploy phishing campaigns.

2.2 Analyzing Email Headers & Sender Metadata

Researchers extracted email headers from multiple phishing emails and used MXToolbox and EmailRep.io to analyze them.

📌 Identified common SMTP servers used to send phishing emails.
📌 Linked the sender's IP addresses to known phishing campaigns.
📌 Cross-referenced email addresses in data breach databases.

💡 **Key Finding**: Many phishing emails were sent from compromised business email accounts, a tactic known as Business Email Compromise (BEC).

3. Following the Money: Cryptocurrency & Payment Trails

3.1 Tracking Stolen Credentials & Financial Transactions

After victims entered their credentials into phishing sites, cybercriminals:

💰 Sold stolen logins on Dark Web marketplaces.
💰 Used compromised accounts for wire fraud.
💰 Converted funds into cryptocurrency (Bitcoin, Monero, Litecoin).

🔍 Using Blockchain forensics tools (Chainalysis, Elliptic, Bitcoin Explorer), investigators tracked stolen funds flowing through:

📌 Multiple Bitcoin wallets associated with illicit transactions.

📌 Mixers/Tumblers to obscure the money trail.

📌 Cryptocurrency exchanges where stolen funds were cashed out.

💡 **Key Finding**: The cryptocurrency payments led to wallet addresses associated with a known cybercrime group operating in Eastern Europe.

4. Infiltrating the Cybercriminal Networks

4.1 Dark Web & Telegram Monitoring

Investigators monitored Dark Web forums and Telegram groups where phishing kits and stolen credentials were being sold.

🔍 **Key Findings from Underground Marketplaces:**

📌 Phishing kits and fake login pages were sold for as little as $50–$300.

📌 Cybercriminals were offering "guaranteed bypass" techniques for email security.

📌 Telegram bots were being used for automated credential checking.

💡 **Breakthrough**: A seller using the alias "PhishKing99" was promoting a new phishing kit that matched the templates used in this global campaign.

4.2 Undercover OSINT Operation

To gather intelligence, investigators:

✅ Created sock puppet (fake) accounts on Dark Web forums.

✅ Engaged in conversations with sellers to track their operations.

✅ Collected Bitcoin addresses linked to sales of phishing kits.

💡 **Key Finding**: One phishing kit reseller was previously involved in a similar operation taken down in 2021—suggesting repeat offenders were active.

5. Law Enforcement Action & Operation Takedown

5.1 Coordinating with Authorities

☐ Investigators shared their findings with international law enforcement agencies (FBI, Europol, Interpol).
☐ Domain registrars and hosting providers were alerted to take down phishing websites.
☐ Crypto exchanges were notified to freeze illicit accounts.

5.2 The Bust: Phishing Network Dismantled

✅ 20+ cybercriminals arrested across multiple countries (Russia, Ukraine, Nigeria, Brazil).

✅ Over 200 phishing websites shut down.

✅ $5 million in cryptocurrency seized from cybercriminal wallets.

✅ Multiple phishing-as-a-service (PhaaS) platforms shut down.

💡 **Key Takeaway**: The coordinated use of OSINT, blockchain analysis, and Dark Web monitoring was critical in dismantling the phishing operation.

6. Lessons Learned & Prevention Strategies

◆ Individuals & Businesses Must Stay Vigilant

✅ Enable multi-factor authentication (MFA) to prevent credential theft.

✅ Educate employees on how to identify phishing emails.

✅ Use email security tools (DMARC, SPF, DKIM) to detect spoofing.

◆ Cybercrime is Increasingly Sophisticated

✅ Attackers use compromised business email accounts to bypass security.

✅ Phishing-as-a-Service (PhaaS) allows even low-skilled attackers to launch campaigns.

✅ Cryptocurrency and Dark Web marketplaces make tracking harder but not impossible.

◆ OSINT & Blockchain Forensics Are Key

✅ Tracking phishing domains, email metadata, and cryptocurrency transactions can uncover cybercriminal networks.

✅ Dark Web monitoring provides early warning signs of emerging threats.

This global phishing investigation highlights the power of OSINT in tracking cybercriminals, from email headers to cryptocurrency transactions. By leveraging OSINT techniques, blockchain analysis, and Dark Web infiltration, cybersecurity professionals were able to expose and dismantle a major phishing operation.

5. Using Data Breach Databases & Leak Sites

In this chapter, we will explore how to leverage data breach databases and leak sites to enhance email investigations. As cybercriminals increasingly share or sell stolen data on the dark web and other platforms, these leak sites and databases have become invaluable resources for OSINT analysts. We will examine the most prominent breach databases, such as Have I Been Pwned and other specialized leak sites, and demonstrate how to search for compromised email addresses or domain names. By cross-referencing email addresses and other identifiers against these databases, investigators can quickly determine if an email account has been part of a known breach, assess the scope of the leak, and track the potential consequences for the affected individuals or organizations. Understanding how to navigate these resources and extract actionable intelligence is essential for any investigator working in the realm of email security and data breach response.

5.1 The Role of Data Leak Marketplaces & Paste Sites

Data leak marketplaces and paste sites play a crucial role in the underground economy of cybercrime. These platforms serve as repositories for stolen data, where cybercriminals trade, sell, and distribute leaked credentials, personally identifiable information (PII), and sensitive corporate data.

For OSINT investigators, cybersecurity professionals, and law enforcement, these sites provide valuable intelligence on breaches, compromised accounts, and emerging threats. This chapter explores:

✅ What data leak marketplaces & paste sites are

✅ How cybercriminals use them

✅ OSINT techniques to track and analyze leaked data

✅ How law enforcement and security teams mitigate risks

1. What Are Data Leak Marketplaces & Paste Sites?

1.1 Data Leak Marketplaces

◈ Dark Web marketplaces where stolen data is sold.

◈ Commonly found on Tor, I2P, and underground Telegram channels.

◈ Sell corporate databases, stolen login credentials, credit card data, SSNs, and more.

💡 **Example**: Breached data from LinkedIn, Facebook, and financial institutions often appears on these marketplaces before public disclosure.

1.2 Paste Sites (Public & Private)

◈ Websites where users can anonymously share and store text-based data.

◈ Originally designed for code sharing, but now widely used for dumping leaked credentials.

◈ Some pastes contain email-password combos, API keys, or internal company data.

💡 **Popular Paste Sites:**

✅ **Pastebin** – One of the most well-known pasting services.

✅ **Ghostbin** – Often used for illegal data dumps.

✅ **Hastebin** – A more ephemeral pasting service.

✅ **Dark Web paste sites** – Private sites hosting high-value leaks.

2. How Cybercriminals Use These Platforms

2.1 Selling & Trading Stolen Data

◆ **Cybercriminals sell leaked credentials in bulk, often organized by:**

✅ **Email accounts** (e.g., Gmail, Outlook, corporate emails).

✅ **Financial data** (credit card numbers, banking details).

✅ **Company databases** (usernames, hashed passwords, internal documents).

💡 **Example:**

- A hacker breaches an e-commerce platform and leaks customer data on BreachForums before selling it to the highest bidder.

2.2 Credential Stuffing & Account Takeover (ATO)

◆ Attackers use leaked email-password combos to test logins across multiple platforms.

◆ If users reuse passwords, cybercriminals can take over social media, banking, or work accounts.

💡 Example:

Credentials from a Dropbox breach might work on LinkedIn, Netflix, or corporate accounts if passwords are reused.

2.3 Blackmail & Extortion

◆ Leaked private messages, explicit photos, or confidential corporate documents can be used for:

✔ **Ransom demands** – "Pay or we release your data."

✔ **Corporate espionage** – Leaking competitors' trade secrets.

✔ **Doxxing** – Exposing personal details to harm reputations.

💡 Example:

A ransomware group leaks internal emails from a Fortune 500 company to pressure them into paying millions in Bitcoin.

3. OSINT Techniques for Investigating Data Leaks

3.1 Searching Paste Sites for Leaked Credentials

Investigators can use the following tools to monitor and analyze paste sites:

Tool	Purpose	Website
Have I Been Pwned (HIBP)	Checks if an email has been leaked	https://haveibeenpwned.com
DeHashed	Advanced search for leaked data	https://www.dehashed.com
Intelligence X	Searches leaked databases & paste sites	https://intelx.io
Pastebin Scrapers	Automates searches for leaked credentials	Custom tools required

🔍 How to Investigate:

✅ Search for specific email addresses, usernames, or domains in paste sites.

✅ Monitor recent pastes containing sensitive data.

✅ Extract hashes or encrypted passwords and attempt to decrypt them.

3.2 Investigating Dark Web Marketplaces

Since many data leaks occur on Dark Web markets, OSINT analysts use:

✅ **Tor Search Engines (Ahmia, OnionLand, Recon)** – To find leaked data.
✅ **Dark Web forums & marketplaces** – To track emerging leaks.
✅ **Blockchain forensics** – To analyze cryptocurrency payments linked to stolen data sales.

💡 **Example:**

A company finds leaked employee credentials on a Dark Web forum and resets all affected passwords before hackers can exploit them.

3.3 Tracking Data Brokers & Sellers

🔍 OSINT analysts investigate who is selling stolen data by:

✅ Examining username patterns across forums.

✅ Tracking Bitcoin transactions linked to stolen data sales.

✅ Searching Telegram groups & Discord servers for breach discussions.

💡 **Example:**

A hacker using the alias "DataLord" sells stolen bank logins. Investigators trace their crypto transactions to an exchange and identify them.

4. Law Enforcement & Corporate Response

4.1 Law Enforcement Actions Against Data Marketplaces

☐ **Major takedowns of leak sites & markets:**

✓ **RaidForums (2022)** – A top data marketplace seized by authorities.
✓ **BreachForums (2023)** – Taken down after being linked to massive leaks.
✓ **Genesis Market (2023)** – A marketplace for stolen credentials dismantled.

💡 **Impact**: Cybercriminals migrate to Telegram, Discord, and private forums, requiring new OSINT monitoring strategies.

4.2 How Companies Mitigate Risks

◆ **Dark Web monitoring** – Scanning for leaked corporate credentials.
◆ Forcing password resets when breaches occur.
◆ Employee security training to prevent credential reuse.
◆ Implementing multi-factor authentication (MFA) to reduce risk of stolen credentials being exploited.

💡 **Example:**

After a GitHub data leak, a company forces all developers to reset their SSH keys and API tokens.

Data leak marketplaces and paste sites fuel the cybercrime ecosystem, but they also serve as valuable sources of intelligence for investigators. By monitoring these platforms, OSINT analysts can:

🔍 Detect breaches before they are exploited.
🔍 Track cybercriminal activity and emerging threats.
🔍 Assist law enforcement in identifying and taking down data brokers.

5.2 Searching for Compromised Credentials & PII

Every year, billions of email addresses, passwords, and personally identifiable information (PII) are leaked online through data breaches, phishing campaigns, and credential-stuffing attacks. Cybercriminals exploit this data for identity theft, financial fraud, and corporate espionage.

For OSINT analysts and cybersecurity professionals, searching for compromised credentials is essential to:

✅ Identify exposed email addresses, passwords, and sensitive data.

✅ Assess risks for individuals and organizations.

✅ Track cybercriminal activity linked to stolen credentials.

✅ Protect victims by mitigating potential damage.

This chapter explores how to search for compromised credentials and PII, using both open-source intelligence (OSINT) tools and Dark Web investigations.

1. Understanding Compromised Credentials & PII

1.1 What Are Compromised Credentials?

Compromised credentials refer to leaked usernames, passwords, and account details that have been exposed due to a data breach or cyberattack. They often include:

📌 Email-password combinations (plain text or hashed).
📌 Social media or corporate login details.
📌 API keys, SSH credentials, and security tokens.

💡 **Example:**

- The Yahoo data breach (2013–2014) leaked over 3 billion user accounts, exposing email addresses, passwords, security questions, and personal data.

1.2 What is Personally Identifiable Information (PII)?

PII refers to sensitive data that can identify an individual. This includes:

📌 Full name, date of birth, and address.
📌 Social Security Number (SSN), passport number, or driver's license.
📌 Bank account details, credit card numbers, or medical records.
📌 Phone numbers, IP addresses, or biometric data.

💡 **Example:**

The Equifax breach (2017) exposed the SSNs, birth dates, and credit data of 147 million Americans, leading to widespread identity fraud.

2. Searching for Compromised Credentials

2.1 Using Public Leak Databases

Several online services provide free or paid access to data breach records. These tools help users check whether their email or password has been exposed.

Tool	Description	Website
Have I Been Pwned (HIBP)	Checks if an email or password has been leaked in known breaches.	https://haveibeenpwned.com
DeHashed	Searches breached data for emails, usernames, phone numbers, and IPs.	https://www.dehashed.com
IntelX	Advanced search for leaked data, Dark Web pastes, and financial records.	https://intelx.io
SnusBase	Paid access to leaked credentials, hashed passwords, and PII.	https://snusbase.com

2.2 How to Search for Leaked Credentials

✅ Enter an email, username, or domain in tools like HIBP or DeHashed.

✅ Review leak details (which breach, what data was exposed).

✅ If passwords were leaked, immediately reset credentials and enable multi-factor authentication (MFA).

💡 **Example:**

A journalist finds their email was exposed in a LinkedIn breach. They change all reused passwords and enable MFA on sensitive accounts.

3. Investigating Stolen Credentials on the Dark Web

3.1 Searching Dark Web Marketplaces & Forums

Many high-value credential dumps (bank logins, corporate accounts, financial records) never appear on public leak databases. Instead, they are sold in Dark Web marketplaces and Telegram groups.

🔎 **Where stolen credentials are sold:**

✅ **Dark Web forums** (e.g., Exploit, RAMP, BreachForums)

✅ **Telegram & Discord** (automated credential-checking bots)

✅ **Marketplaces** (Genesis Market, Russian Market)

3.2 OSINT Techniques to Find Stolen Credentials

◆ Use Dark Web search engines (Ahmia, OnionLand) to locate hidden marketplaces.
◆ Monitor Telegram/Discord channels where credential dumps are shared.
◆ Check Bitcoin transactions linked to stolen data sales.
◆ Use OSINT tools like Lampyre or DarkTracer to analyze Dark Web leaks.

💡 **Example:**

An OSINT investigator finds a corporate credential dump on a Dark Web forum and alerts the affected company before hackers exploit the accounts.

4. Tracking Leaked PII & Identity Theft Risks

4.1 Finding Leaked PII in Data Breaches

PII exposure can lead to identity fraud, doxxing, and financial theft. OSINT analysts use specialized tools to track leaked PII.

Tool	Purpose	Website
People Data Labs (PDL)	Finds leaked PII from breaches	https://www.peopledatalabs.com
SpyCloud	Monitors corporate identity theft risks	https://spycloud.com
Social Links	Finds compromised social media & financial data	https://sociallinks.io

💡 **Example:**

A security analyst uses SpyCloud to monitor leaked employee credentials and forces password resets before attackers can exploit them.

5. How Companies & Individuals Protect Themselves

5.1 How Companies Respond to Leaked Credentials

✅ **Dark Web monitoring** – Scanning for corporate credential leaks.
✅ **Forced password resets** – If employee credentials appear in breaches.
✅ **Multi-factor authentication (MFA)** – To prevent account takeovers.
✅ **Employee security training** – To prevent phishing-based credential theft.

💡 **Example:**

A financial institution detects leaked customer account credentials and immediately locks the accounts and notifies affected users.

5.2 How Individuals Can Protect Their Data

✅ Use unique passwords for every account (use a password manager).

✅ Enable MFA on all critical accounts.

✅ Monitor emails for breach alerts using HIBP or DeHashed.

✅ Freeze credit if SSN or financial data is leaked.

✅ Be cautious of phishing emails requesting login details.

💡 **Example:**

A user finds their email leaked in a breach but had MFA enabled, preventing attackers from taking over their account.

Searching for compromised credentials and PII is critical for preventing cybercrime. By monitoring public databases, investigating the Dark Web, and using OSINT tools, investigators can:

🔍 Identify leaked credentials before they are exploited.
🔍 Mitigate identity theft and account takeover risks.

🔍 Track cybercriminal activities linked to stolen data.

5.3 How Criminals Monetize Stolen Email Data

Stolen email data is one of the most valuable assets in the cybercrime economy. Cybercriminals don't just leak or sell credentials; they monetize stolen email data in multiple ways, ranging from financial fraud to corporate espionage. The exploitation of compromised email accounts enables identity theft, business email compromise (BEC), phishing scams, ransomware attacks, and more.

For OSINT investigators and cybersecurity professionals, understanding how attackers profit from stolen emails is essential to tracking, mitigating, and preventing these threats. This chapter explores:

✅ How cybercriminals use stolen email data

✅ The underground economy of credential trading

✅ Financial fraud techniques leveraging compromised emails

✅ How threat actors exploit corporate emails for BEC attacks

✅ Dark Web marketplaces where email credentials are sold

1. The Value of Stolen Email Accounts in Cybercrime

1.1 Why Stolen Email Data is Valuable

A compromised email address is often the key to multiple accounts because:

- Many users reuse passwords across platforms.
- Emails serve as the primary method for account recovery.
- Emails contain sensitive information, invoices, and financial data.
- Compromised corporate emails provide access to internal company systems.

💡 **Example:**

A hacker steals a user's Gmail credentials and gains access to their PayPal, Amazon, and banking accounts due to password reuse.

1.2 Where Stolen Emails Are Sold

Stolen emails are traded in Dark Web markets, Telegram groups, and hacker forums. Prices vary depending on the type of account:

Type of Stolen Email Account	Estimated Price (USD)
Personal Gmail/Yahoo accounts	$1 – $10 per account
Corporate email accounts	$20 – $100 per account
Financial email accounts (linked to PayPal, banking, crypto)	$50 – $500 per account
Bulk email dumps (thousands of emails & passwords)	$100 – $5,000

💡 Example:

A hacker sells a database of 50,000 leaked corporate emails on a Dark Web forum for $2,500, which buyers use for phishing and fraud.

2. How Criminals Monetize Stolen Email Data

2.1 Credential Stuffing & Account Takeovers (ATO)

◆ Attackers use credential stuffing tools to check stolen emails against popular services (Netflix, Amazon, banking sites).
◆ If users reuse passwords, criminals gain access to multiple accounts.
◆ Automated bots speed up the process, checking thousands of logins per minute.

💡 Example:

A hacker finds a user's email & password from a LinkedIn breach, then uses the same credentials to hack their PayPal account.

Common Tools Used:

✅ **Sentry MBA** – Credential stuffing automation.
✅ **OpenBullet** – Custom scripts for account brute-forcing.
✅ **SNIPR** – Cracks email-password combos across multiple sites.

2.2 Business Email Compromise (BEC) Scams

- ◆ Criminals hijack corporate emails and impersonate executives.
- ◆ They send fake invoices or request urgent wire transfers.
- ◆ These scams cost businesses billions annually.

💡 Example:

A cybercriminal hacks a CFO's email, sends an urgent payment request to an employee, and steals $150,000 before detection.

OSINT Investigation Tips:

✓ Check for suspicious login attempts on corporate email logs.

✓ Analyze email headers for unusual forwarding rules.

✓ Search Dark Web forums for hacked corporate emails on sale.

2.3 Phishing & Malware Distribution

- ◆ Stolen email accounts are used to send phishing emails to contacts.
- ◆ Attackers distribute malicious attachments (keyloggers, RATs, ransomware).
- ◆ Some phishing emails spoof legitimate brands (banks, Microsoft, Google).

💡 Example:

A hacked CEO's email sends fake job offers with an infected PDF to employees, spreading malware across the company network.

OSINT Investigation Tips:

✓ Use VirusTotal to scan suspicious email attachments.

✓ Check if phishing links are flagged on URLVoid.

✓ Investigate shortened URLs for redirection traps.

2.4 Selling Access to Compromised Accounts

◆ Instead of using the emails themselves, cybercriminals sell account logins to other hackers.

◆ High-value targets include Netflix, Hulu, PayPal, eBay, and online banking accounts.

◆ Stolen credentials are bundled into "combo lists" and sold in Dark Web markets.

💡 Example:

A hacker sells a PayPal email-password combo on a Telegram channel for $300 to another fraudster, who then withdraws funds.

Common Dark Web Markets Selling Stolen Emails:

✅ Genesis Market (seized in 2023 but similar markets exist).

✅ Russian Market (specializes in banking logins).

✅ BreachForums (before being shut down, it hosted credential leaks).

2.5 Ransomware & Blackmail Using Leaked Emails

◆ Attackers use compromised emails to threaten victims.

◆ Blackmail tactics include:

✅ Claiming to have hacked a webcam or recorded explicit content.

✅ Threatening to expose sensitive information unless a ransom is paid.

✅ Sending fake "sextortion" emails demanding Bitcoin payments.

💡 Example:

A cybercriminal sends an extortion email claiming to have "hacked a webcam", demanding $800 in Bitcoin—even though the claim is false.

OSINT Investigation Tips:

✅ Analyze Bitcoin wallet addresses linked to extortion demands.

✅ Trace email origins using SPF/DKIM/DMARC analysis.

☑ Check if similar scams are reported on abuse databases (e.g., ScamWarners).

3. How OSINT Investigators & Cybersecurity Teams Track Stolen Emails

3.1 Monitoring Dark Web & Leak Sites

OSINT analysts use Dark Web tools and breach monitoring services to track compromised emails.

☑ **DarkTracer** – Monitors Dark Web credential leaks.
☑ **IntelX** – Searches hidden breaches and PII leaks.
☑ **BreachAlarm** – Alerts companies to newly leaked emails.

💡 **Example:**

A company finds its employees' email credentials on a Dark Web forum, forcing immediate password resets.

3.2 Tracing Cryptocurrency Transactions from Fraud

Since many email-related frauds involve Bitcoin and Monero payments, OSINT investigators:

☑ Use Bitcoin forensics tools like Chainalysis & Crystal Blockchain.

☑ Track ransomware payments made from hacked emails.

☑ Identify crypto wallets linked to fraud campaigns.

💡 **Example:**

Investigators track a BEC scammer's Bitcoin wallet and find connections to previous ransomware payments.

Stolen email credentials are highly valuable in cybercrime, fueling financial fraud, phishing, ransomware, and corporate espionage. OSINT investigators play a crucial role in:

🔍 Tracking stolen credentials on Dark Web forums.

🔍 Analyzing phishing & BEC scams.

🔍 Tracing cryptocurrency payments linked to fraud.

🔍 Helping organizations secure compromised email accounts.

5.4 Investigating "Combolists" & Corporate Breaches

When email data is stolen in breaches, cybercriminals don't just use it for direct attacks—they compile massive databases called "combolists". These lists contain email-password pairs from multiple leaks and are used for credential stuffing, phishing, and fraud.

For OSINT investigators, analyzing combolists and corporate breaches is critical for tracking cybercriminals, mitigating threats, and preventing future attacks. In this chapter, we will explore:

✅ What combolists are and how they are created

✅ How attackers use them for large-scale cybercrime

✅ Where combolists are traded on the Dark Web

✅ Techniques for investigating corporate breaches linked to combolists

✅ OSINT methods for tracking exposed credentials and mitigating risks

1. Understanding Combolists & Their Role in Cybercrime

1.1 What Are Combolists?

A combolist (short for combination list) is a massive database of email-password pairs collected from multiple breaches. These lists contain:

📌 Usernames & passwords from past breaches.

📌 Email addresses linked to leaked passwords.

📌 Sometimes additional metadata (IP addresses, phone numbers, locations).

Unlike raw data breaches, which expose credentials from a single hacked platform, combolists merge data from multiple breaches, making them more powerful for attackers.

💡 **Example:**

A hacker compiles LinkedIn, Dropbox, and Adobe breach data into a single combolist and sells it for credential stuffing attacks.

1.2 How Are Combolists Created?

Cybercriminals aggregate, clean, and filter leaked credentials to make them more usable. They:

1☐ Extract raw data from public breaches, Dark Web leaks, and private hacks.

2☐ Remove duplicates and merge valid login pairs.

3☐ Check password validity using automated credential stuffing tools.

4☐ Sort email-password pairs by category, such as banking, corporate, or streaming accounts.

5☐ Sell or distribute the final combolist via Telegram, Dark Web forums, or private hacking groups.

1.3 How Attackers Use Combolists

Once created, combolists are used for:

✅ **Credential Stuffing Attacks** – Automated bots try leaked passwords on popular sites (Netflix, PayPal, Amazon).

✅ **Phishing & Social Engineering** – Attackers use email-password pairs to craft personalized phishing attacks.

✅ **Business Email Compromise (BEC)** – Hacked corporate emails from combolists are used for financial fraud.

✅ **Ransomware Deployment** – Attackers use stolen corporate logins to deploy malware inside organizations.

💡 **Example:**

A hacker uses a Netflix combolist to hijack thousands of user accounts, selling them for $1 each on the Dark Web.

2. Investigating Combolists on the Dark Web

2.1 Where Are Combolists Traded?

🔎 Dark Web Forums & Marketplaces

☑ **BreachForums (before shutdown)** – One of the largest forums for credential dumps.
☑ **Russian Market** – Specializes in stolen logins for financial services.
☑ **Genesis Market (seized in 2023, but similar markets exist)** – Sold verified corporate credentials.

🔎 Telegram & Discord Channels

☑ Private groups where hacked data is sold in bulk.

☑ Some groups offer subscription-based access to daily credential leaks.

🔎 Pastebin & Leak Sites

☑ Hackers sometimes leak partial combolists as teasers for full lists.

☑ OSINT analysts monitor Pastebin clones for newly posted credentials.

💡 Example:

A Telegram channel posts a sample of 100,000 emails from a "fresh" combolist, offering the full database for $500 in Bitcoin.

2.2 How OSINT Investigators Find & Analyze Combolists

☑ Monitor Data Breach Aggregators

- **Have I Been Pwned (HIBP):** Check if corporate emails appear in past breaches.
- **DeHashed**: Search for leaked credentials by email, username, or domain.
- **IntelX**: Deep search across leaked datasets, including Dark Web sources.

☑ Track Dark Web Marketplaces & Forums

- Use Ahmia, OnionLand, and DarkSearch to find credential dumps.
- Monitor Telegram groups that advertise fresh combolists.

✅ Analyze Leaked Password Patterns

- Check if users reused passwords across multiple platforms.
- Identify common password structures used in combolists.

💡 Example:

An OSINT analyst discovers employee credentials from a hacked law firm on BreachForums, helping the firm reset compromised accounts before attackers use them.

3. Investigating Corporate Breaches Linked to Combolists

3.1 How Corporate Email Credentials End Up in Combolists

Corporate accounts appear in combolists due to:

📌 **Third-Party Breaches** – If employees use work emails for external services (e.g., Dropbox, LinkedIn) and those services are hacked.

📌 **Phishing Attacks** – Employees unknowingly enter credentials into fake login pages.

📌 **Credential Reuse** – If an employee reuses the same password for multiple accounts, hackers gain access to corporate systems.

📌 **Dark Web Leaks** – Insiders or attackers sell corporate login credentials on forums.

💡 Example:

A hacker steals an HR manager's credentials from a Dropbox breach, then uses them to access internal payroll systems.

3.2 Steps to Investigate Corporate Breaches

🔍 Step 1: Identify Affected Emails

✅ Check if corporate domains appear in breach databases (HIBP, DeHashed).

✅ Monitor Dark Web marketplaces for leaked corporate email lists.

🔍 Step 2: Trace Source of the Breach

✅ Determine if the breach was internal (company hacked) or external (third-party service breach).

✅ Use email headers and security logs to identify unusual login attempts.

🔎 Step 3: Check for Active Exploitation

✅ Investigate if stolen credentials are being used in BEC scams or phishing attacks.

✅ Look for password reset requests or unauthorized logins in corporate logs.

🔎 Step 4: Take Immediate Action

✅ Force password resets for exposed accounts.

✅ Enable Multi-Factor Authentication (MFA) to prevent future takeovers.

✅ Warn employees about phishing threats targeting leaked emails.

💡 Example:

A tech company finds 200 employee emails in a leaked combolist, so they reset passwords and enforce MFA before hackers can exploit them.

4. How Companies Can Defend Against Combolist Threats

✅ Implement Dark Web Monitoring

Use services like SpyCloud, DarkTracer, or IntelX to detect leaked credentials.

✅ Force Regular Password Updates

Require unique, strong passwords that are changed every 90 days.

✅ Enable Multi-Factor Authentication (MFA)

Even if credentials are leaked, MFA prevents attackers from logging in.

✅ **Monitor for Unusual Login Activity**

Use SIEM tools (Splunk, Graylog) to detect suspicious logins from new locations.

✅ **Educate Employees on Credential Security**

Teach staff to avoid using work emails for personal accounts.

💡 **Example:**

A financial institution detects leaked customer logins in a Telegram group, so they freeze affected accounts and notify users to change passwords.

5. Conclusion

Investigating combolists and corporate breaches is essential for OSINT analysts and cybersecurity teams. Understanding how criminals use stolen credentials, where combolists are traded, and how to mitigate corporate breaches helps prevent cybercrime.

🔍 **Key Takeaways:**

✅ Combolists aggregate leaked credentials from multiple breaches.

✅ Attackers use them for credential stuffing, phishing, and corporate fraud.

✅ OSINT tools help track stolen emails in Dark Web markets.

✅ Companies must monitor for leaked credentials and enforce MFA.

5.5 Using Open-Source Tools to Monitor for Leaks

Cybercriminals constantly leak, sell, and trade stolen email credentials, making it crucial for OSINT analysts, cybersecurity professionals, and businesses to actively monitor leaks. Open-source tools provide powerful, cost-effective ways to track breaches, detect exposed credentials, and mitigate risks before attackers can exploit them.

This chapter will cover:

✅ Why monitoring for leaks is important

✅ How to use open-source tools for email breach detection

✅ Tracking Dark Web leaks with OSINT techniques

✅ Automating alerts for leaked credentials

✅ Best practices for responding to exposed data

By the end, you'll have a clear workflow for proactively detecting email leaks using publicly available tools.

1. Why Monitoring for Email Leaks is Critical

Cybercriminals use stolen email credentials for:

📌 **Account Takeovers (ATO)** – Logging into banking, social media, or corporate accounts.
📌 **Business Email Compromise (BEC)** – Sending fraudulent invoices and impersonating executives.
📌 **Phishing & Malware Attacks** – Using leaked emails to spread malware and scams.
📌 **Dark Web Resale** – Selling credentials to other hackers for profit.

💡 **Example:**

- A corporate email from a Dropbox breach appears in a combolist, allowing hackers to access internal company data.
- By using open-source tools, organizations and investigators can detect leaked emails before they are exploited.

2. Open-Source Tools for Monitoring Email Leaks

Several free and open-source tools allow OSINT investigators to track email breaches. Here are some of the most effective ones:

2.1 Have I Been Pwned (HIBP) & Its API

🔎 **What It Does:**

✅ Checks if an email has been leaked in a past breach.

✅ Provides breach details (date, source, exposed data types).

✅ Offers a free API for automated monitoring.

How to Use It:

- Visit haveibeenpwned.com.
- Enter an email address to check for leaks.
- Use the HIBP API to automate email monitoring.

💻 **Example API Query:**

*curl -H "hibp-api-key: YOUR_API_KEY" *
"https://haveibeenpwned.com/api/v3/breachedaccount/example@email.com"

💡 **Use Case:**

A company monitors employee emails via the HIBP API and forces password resets for exposed accounts.

2.2 DeHashed: Searching for Exposed Credentials

🔎 **What It Does:**

✅ Searches leaked email, username, password, and phone number databases.

✅ Provides breach sources and exposed data details.

✅ Has an API for automated monitoring.

How to Use It:

- Visit dehashed.com.
- Enter an email, username, or domain.
- Check if leaked credentials are linked to your target.

💡 **Use Case:**

An OSINT analyst searches a phishing victim's email on DeHashed and finds past password leaks, helping them identify account compromises.

2.3 Intelligence X: Deep Searching Leaked Data

🔎 What It Does:

✅ Searches for leaked emails, passwords, and documents across breach data.

✅ Includes Dark Web and open-source intelligence (OSINT) archives.

✅ Provides Tor network search capabilities.

How to Use It:

- Visit intelx.io.
- Enter a target email, domain, or leaked dataset name.
- Analyze exposed records and take action.

💡 Use Case:

An investigator searches for a leaked email address and discovers it is tied to a ransomware leak site.

2.4 Holehe: Checking Where an Email is Registered

🔎 What It Does:

✅ Finds all online accounts linked to an email (Google, PayPal, LinkedIn, etc.).

✅ Helps track compromised accounts and credential reuse risks.

✅ Works as a Python command-line tool.

How to Use It:

Install Holehe:

pip install holehe

Run a search for an email:

holehe example@email.com

💡 Use Case:

An OSINT analyst discovers that a leaked email is linked to multiple social media accounts, helping trace an attacker's identity.

2.5 LeakCheck: Automating Dark Web Leak Detection

🔎 What It Does:

✅ Monitors Dark Web leak databases for compromised emails.

✅ Provides JSON-formatted data for automation.

✅ Uses a paid API with free trial access.

How to Use It:

Register at leakcheck.net.

Use the API to query leaked emails:

curl "https://leakcheck.net/api?key=YOUR_API_KEY&check=email@example.com"

💡 Use Case:

A security team integrates LeakCheck API into their SIEM system for real-time breach alerts.

3. Tracking Dark Web Leaks with OSINT

3.1 Searching Dark Web Paste Sites

🔎 Dark Web tools like:

✅ **Ahmia.fi** – Searches Tor websites for leaked data.
✅ **OnionLand Search** – Finds hidden Dark Web forums.
✅ **Hunchly** – Captures OSINT investigations for documentation.

💡 Example:

An OSINT investigator searches for leaked corporate emails on Pastebin clones and finds a recent dump.

3.2 Using SpiderFoot for Automated Leak Detection

🔍 What It Does:

✅ Automates OSINT collection on email leaks.

✅ Scans Dark Web, data breaches, and OSINT sources.

✅ Has integration with Shodan, HIBP, and other services.

How to Use It:

Install SpiderFoot:

```
git clone https://github.com/smicallef/spiderfoot.git
cd spiderfoot
python3 sf.py
```

Run an email leak scan:

```
python3 sf.py -m email_leak_check -t example@email.com
```

💡 Use Case:

A cybersecurity team runs SpiderFoot weekly to detect newly leaked employee credentials.

4. Automating Alerts for Leaked Credentials

To stay ahead of leaks, organizations should set up automated alerts.

4.1 Monitoring Leaks with a Python Script

Use Python with HIBP API to check for leaks:

```
import requests
```

```
API_KEY = "YOUR_HIBP_API_KEY"
EMAIL = "example@email.com"

url = f"https://haveibeenpwned.com/api/v3/breachedaccount/{EMAIL}"
headers = {"hibp-api-key": API_KEY}

response = requests.get(url, headers=headers)
if response.status_code == 200:
    print(f"WARNING: {EMAIL} has been breached in the following incidents:
{response.json()}")
else:
    print("No breaches found.")
```

💡 Use Case:

A company runs this script daily to check for employee emails in new breaches.

5. Best Practices for Responding to Leaked Emails

✅ **Force Password Resets** – Immediately reset exposed accounts.

✅ **Enable Multi-Factor Authentication (MFA)** – Adds extra security against breaches.

✅ **Notify Affected Users** – Inform them of compromised credentials.

✅ **Investigate Source of the Leak** – Determine whether the breach came from a third-party service or an internal system.

✅ **Monitor for Further Exploitation** – Watch for BEC scams, phishing, or Dark Web resales.

🔎 Key Takeaways:

✅ Open-source tools help track email leaks in real-time.

✅ Dark Web searches reveal where credentials are sold.

✅ Automated alerts detect new leaks before cybercriminals act.

✅ MFA and strong passwords protect against credential-based attacks.

5.6 Case Study: How a Data Breach Exposed Millions of Users

Data breaches occur daily, but some stand out due to their scale, impact, and consequences. In this case study, we analyze a real-world data breach that exposed millions of users, examine how investigators uncovered it, and explore how criminals exploited the leaked information.

This chapter will cover:

✅ How the breach happened and who was affected

✅ The role of OSINT in tracking the leaked data

✅ How cybercriminals monetized the stolen credentials

✅ Steps investigators took to mitigate the damage

✅ Key lessons for cybersecurity professionals and OSINT analysts

1. The Breach: What Happened?

In 2019, a massive database containing over 770 million email addresses and passwords appeared on a Dark Web forum. This breach, known as Collection #1, was one of the largest credential dumps in history.

🔎 Key Details:

📌 **Size of the breach**: 773 million unique email addresses, 21 million unique passwords.
📌 **Source**: A mix of previously leaked breaches and newly stolen data.
📌 **First discovered by**: Troy Hunt, creator of Have I Been Pwned (HIBP).
📌 **Where it appeared**: A popular hacker forum and Dark Web marketplaces.
📌 **Data type exposed**: Emails, plaintext passwords, hashed credentials.

💡 Why This Breach Mattered:

- Unlike single-company breaches, Collection #1 was an aggregated dataset compiled from multiple leaks.
- It included both new and previously exposed credentials, increasing its value to hackers.

- The scale of this leak made credential stuffing attacks easier.

2. How OSINT Investigators Discovered the Breach

The breach was first identified when cybersecurity researchers spotted a Dark Web post advertising a massive data dump.

2.1 Monitoring Dark Web Forums & Leak Sites

OSINT analysts used several techniques to track the leaked data:

✅ Dark Web Marketplaces & Telegram Groups

- Researchers scanned hacker forums like RaidForums (now shut down) for leaked databases.
- Criminal groups on Telegram advertised the dataset for sale.

✅ Pastebin & Leak Monitoring

- Parts of the Collection #1 dataset appeared on public leak sites before being removed.
- OSINT analysts monitored paste sites and indexed leaks for early detection.

✅ Data Breach Search Engines

- Tools like DeHashed and IntelX helped confirm the data's authenticity.

💡 Example:

A cybersecurity analyst found a Collection #1 sample on a hacker forum, allowing companies to warn users before full exploitation.

3. How Cybercriminals Used the Stolen Data

Once leaked, the credentials were used in multiple cybercrimes:

3.1 Credential Stuffing Attacks

📌 Hackers used automated bots to test leaked email-password pairs across Netflix, PayPal, Amazon, and banking sites.
📌 Users who reused passwords were most at risk.
📌 Attackers sold access to hacked accounts on the Dark Web.

💡 **Example:**

100,000 Spotify accounts were hijacked because users reused leaked passwords.

3.2 Business Email Compromise (BEC) Scams

📌 Corporate emails from the breach were exploited in fraudulent invoice scams.
📌 Attackers used spoofing techniques to impersonate executives.
📌 Victims transferred millions of dollars to hacker-controlled accounts.

💡 **Example:**

A phishing attack targeted a law firm using stolen credentials from Collection #1.

3.3 Phishing & Social Engineering

📌 Hackers sent fake security alerts tricking users into revealing updated credentials.
📌 Stolen emails helped attackers create highly convincing phishing campaigns.

💡 **Example:**

Victims received fake "reset your password" emails, leading them to phishing sites.

4. How Investigators Responded

After the breach was discovered, OSINT analysts, cybersecurity professionals, and companies took action.

4.1 Identifying Affected Users

🔍 Investigators used Have I Been Pwned (HIBP) to check if their accounts were in the dataset.
🔍 Companies ran internal scans to find affected employee emails.

🔎 Security teams cross-referenced passwords with internal databases.

💡 **Example:**

Google & Microsoft forced password resets for users exposed in Collection #1.

4.2 Notifying Victims & Forcing Password Changes

🔎 Companies sent security alerts to users affected by the breach.
🔎 Organizations forced mandatory password resets and enabled MFA.
🔎 Individuals used password managers to create unique, strong passwords.

💡 **Example:**

Dropbox notified users whose credentials were found in the dataset, preventing unauthorized access.

4.3 Law Enforcement Actions

🔎 Cybercrime units traced the origins of the dataset.
🔎 Some Dark Web forums hosting the data were taken down.
🔎 Authorities arrested criminals selling credentials from Collection #1.

💡 **Example:**

The FBI launched investigations into sellers of stolen credentials, leading to several arrests.

5. Key Lessons for OSINT Analysts & Cybersecurity Professionals

This breach highlighted critical takeaways for security experts and investigators:

✅ Monitor Dark Web forums & leak sites for early breach detection.

✅ Use OSINT tools like HIBP, DeHashed, and IntelX to track leaked credentials.

✅ Automate alerts for breached emails to take immediate action.

✅ Implement Multi-Factor Authentication (MFA) to prevent unauthorized logins.

✅ Educate users about password hygiene to reduce credential reuse risks.

6. Conclusion: Why Continuous Monitoring is Essential

The Collection #1 breach was one of the largest email leaks ever. It exposed millions of users to cyber threats and demonstrated how hackers aggregate and exploit stolen credentials.

🔍 **Key Takeaways:**

✅ Massive breaches fuel Dark Web markets and cybercrime.

✅ OSINT tools help track leaked credentials before attackers act.

✅ Cybercriminals use credential stuffing, phishing, and BEC fraud to exploit stolen data.

✅ Organizations must proactively monitor leaks and enforce security measures.

6. Dark Web Basics: Accessing & Investigating

In this chapter, we will introduce the dark web, a hidden layer of the internet that hosts illicit activities and underground marketplaces where stolen data, including email addresses and other sensitive information, is frequently traded. We will guide you through the process of accessing the dark web securely using tools like Tor and explain the safety protocols necessary to navigate these spaces without compromising your privacy or security. As we explore the dark web's structure, we'll focus on how to investigate relevant forums, marketplaces, and sites where data leaks, breaches, and cybercrime activities are often discussed or sold. Understanding how to operate in this shadowy part of the web is a critical skill for any investigator aiming to uncover the truth behind data breaches and protect against emerging cyber threats.

6.1 What is the Dark Web? Myths vs. Reality

The term "Dark Web" often conjures images of cybercriminals, illicit markets, and hackers operating in complete anonymity. While some of that is true, much of what is said about the Dark Web is exaggerated, misunderstood, or entirely fictional.

In this chapter, we'll break down:

✅ What the Dark Web actually is

✅ How it differs from the Deep Web and Surface Web

✅ Common myths vs. reality about the Dark Web

✅ Legitimate vs. criminal uses of Dark Web networks

✅ Why OSINT analysts, journalists, and investigators monitor it

By the end of this section, you'll have a clear understanding of what the Dark Web is—and what it isn't.

1. Understanding the Layers of the Internet

The internet is often categorized into three layers:

1.1 The Surface Web (4-5% of the Internet)

★ This is the part of the web that is indexed by search engines like Google, Bing, and Yahoo.

★ Includes websites like Wikipedia, news sites, social media, and company homepages.

★ Easily accessible to anyone with a standard web browser.

🔎 **Example**: If you can find it through a Google search, it's on the Surface Web.

1.2 The Deep Web (~90% of the Internet)

★ The Deep Web consists of web pages that aren't indexed by search engines.

★ This includes password-protected content such as:

- Online banking portals
- Corporate intranets
- Private emails
- Subscription-based content (e.g., academic databases, Netflix)

★ Not illegal—just private.

🔎 **Example**: Your Gmail inbox is part of the Deep Web because it's not publicly searchable.

1.3 The Dark Web (~5-6% of the Internet)

★ The Dark Web is a small portion of the Deep Web that requires special tools like Tor or I2P to access.

★ Dark Web sites are not indexed by normal search engines and often use .onion or .i2p domains.

★ Used for both legitimate and illegal activities.

🔎 **Example**: A whistleblower using SecureDrop (a Dark Web service) to leak government corruption to journalists.

2. Common Myths vs. Reality About the Dark Web

There's a lot of misinformation surrounding the Dark Web. Let's separate myth from fact.

Myth #1: The Dark Web is Only for Criminals

⊘ False

✓ **Reality**: While the Dark Web hosts illegal activities, it also serves journalists, activists, researchers, and privacy-conscious users.

🔍 **Example:**

Journalists use the Dark Web to safely communicate with sources in authoritarian regimes.
Whistleblowers use Dark Web platforms like SecureDrop to expose corruption.

Myth #2: You Can Find Anything on the Dark Web Instantly

⊘ False
✓ **Reality**: Unlike Google, there's no centralized search engine for the Dark Web.

🔍 **Example**:

Finding a reliable marketplace for stolen data requires networking and trust—it's not as simple as typing "buy credit card info" in a search bar.

Myth #3: The Dark Web is 100% Anonymous

⊘ False

✓ **Reality**: Law enforcement agencies actively monitor the Dark Web, and many criminals have been arrested.

🔍 **Example:**

- Silk Road (a major Dark Web drug market) was taken down by the FBI in 2013, and its founder, Ross Ulbricht, was arrested.
- Many Tor users make OPSEC mistakes that expose their real identity.

Myth #4: The Dark Web is Impossible to Shut Down

⊘ False
✓ **Reality**: Governments regularly take down illegal marketplaces and forums.

🔍 **Example:**

- AlphaBay, one of the largest Dark Web markets, was shut down in 2017 by the FBI and Europol.
- RaidForums, a popular leak site, was taken down in 2022.

Myth #5: The Dark Web is Huge Compared to the Surface Web

🚫 False
✓ **Reality**: The Deep Web is massive, but the Dark Web is relatively small—only a few thousand active sites exist at any given time.

🔍 **Example**:

In 2021, Tor had only ~100,000 active .onion sites—a fraction of the Surface Web.

3. Legitimate vs. Criminal Uses of the Dark Web

Not everything on the Dark Web is illegal. Here's a breakdown of legitimate vs. criminal use cases:

3.1 Legitimate Uses of the Dark Web

✓ **Journalists & Whistleblowers** – Platforms like SecureDrop allow safe communication.
✓ **Privacy Advocates** – People in oppressive regimes use the Dark Web to bypass censorship.
✓ **Researchers & OSINT Investigators** – Security analysts monitor the Dark Web for threats.
✓ **Political Activists** – Citizens in countries with internet censorship use the Dark Web to access information.

🔍 **Example:**

Edward Snowden leaked classified NSA documents via Dark Web platforms.

3.2 Criminal Uses of the Dark Web

⊘ **Stolen Data Marketplaces** – Selling hacked emails, passwords, and credit card details.

⊘ **Illegal Drug & Weapon Sales** – Similar to Silk Road and AlphaBay.

⊘ **Hitman-for-Hire Scams** – Often fake services designed to scam people.

⊘ **Ransomware Groups** – Threat actors use Dark Web leak sites to publish stolen data.

🔎 **Example:**

The Conti ransomware group hosted a Dark Web leak site to extort companies.

4. Why OSINT Analysts & Cybersecurity Experts Monitor the Dark Web

Cybercrime investigators and security teams actively track Dark Web activity to:

🔎 Detect leaked corporate credentials before hackers exploit them.

🔎 Monitor ransomware groups and their extortion tactics.

🔎 Track cybercriminal forums to identify emerging threats.

🔎 Collect intelligence on illicit marketplaces and cyber threat actors.

💡 **Example:**

A cybersecurity firm finds stolen employee login details on a Dark Web marketplace before hackers use them.

5. Key Takeaways: Dark Web Myths vs. Reality

✍ The Dark Web is not just for criminals—it has legitimate uses.

✍ It is not as big or as anonymous as people think.

✍ Law enforcement agencies actively monitor and take down illegal marketplaces.

✍ OSINT analysts track cyber threats by monitoring Dark Web forums and leak sites.

Conclusion: Understanding the Dark Web for OSINT Investigations

The Dark Web is a critical intelligence source for OSINT professionals. By separating myths from reality, investigators can:

🔎 Identify cyber threats before they escalate

🔎 Understand criminal tactics and tools

🔎 Use Dark Web monitoring to protect individuals and organizations

6.2 How Tor, I2P & Other Anonymous Networks Work

The Dark Web operates on specialized anonymous networks that make it difficult to track users or websites. These networks are designed to protect privacy, security, and censorship resistance, but they are also used by criminals to conceal illicit activities.

This chapter covers:

✅ How Tor, I2P, and other anonymity networks work

✅ Key differences between these technologies

✅ How cybercriminals use them to hide their identities

✅ How OSINT investigators can track activity within these networks

By understanding these technologies, investigators can better analyze threats, trace cybercriminals, and navigate the hidden corners of the internet.

1. The Role of Anonymity Networks

Anonymous networks serve three main purposes:

1️⃣ **Privacy Protection** – Hides users' IP addresses and encrypts communication.

2️⃣ **Censorship Resistance** – Allows access to restricted content in oppressive regimes.

3️⃣ **Anonymity for Criminals** – Enables black markets, fraud, and illegal activities.

🔎 **Example:**

- A journalist in China uses Tor to bypass censorship.
- A ransomware group hosts a leak site on the Dark Web using Tor.

The two most widely used anonymous networks are Tor (The Onion Router) and I2P (Invisible Internet Project).

2. How Tor Works: The Onion Routing System

2.1 What is Tor?

Tor (The Onion Router) is a network that routes internet traffic through multiple encrypted relays, making it difficult to trace users' activities. Websites using Tor have ".onion" addresses, which are only accessible through the Tor Browser.

2.2 How Tor Hides Identities

When a user accesses a .onion site:

1☐ Their request is encrypted multiple times (like layers of an onion).

2☐ The request is routed through at least three random nodes:

- **Entry Node (Guard Node)** – Knows the user's IP but not the destination.
- **Middle Node** – Passes encrypted traffic without knowing the source or destination.
- **Exit Node** – Knows the destination but not the original sender.

3☐ The website sees only the last node (exit node), not the user's real IP.

🔍 **Example:**

If a hacker accesses a Dark Web forum via Tor, law enforcement can only see the exit node's IP, not the hacker's real location.

2.3 How Tor is Used

✅ **Legitimate Uses:**
-
- Privacy-focused browsing to prevent tracking.
- Journalists and whistleblowers using SecureDrop.
- Bypassing government censorship in restrictive countries.

🚫 **Criminal Uses:**

- Hosting Dark Web marketplaces (e.g., Silk Road, AlphaBay).
- Selling stolen data, drugs, and weapons on illicit forums.
- Hosting ransomware leak sites to extort victims.

Investigators use Tor analysis tools like OnionScan to detect vulnerabilities in Dark Web sites.

3. How I2P Works: The Invisible Internet Project

3.1 What is I2P?

I2P (Invisible Internet Project) is another anonymity network similar to Tor but designed for hidden services and peer-to-peer communication rather than accessing the regular web.

3.2 How I2P Differs from Tor

Feature	Tor	I2P
Routing Type	Onion Routing	Garlic Routing
Purpose	Access both **Dark Web & Surface Web**	Internal anonymous network
Website Domains	.onion	.i2p
Entry/Exit Nodes	**Has exit nodes** (can access regular internet)	**No exit nodes** (fully internal)
Speed	Slower due to **longer relay paths**	Faster than Tor

💡 **Key Difference:**

- Tor can access the regular internet (e.g., visiting Facebook via Tor).
- I2P is a closed system—all activity stays within the I2P network.

3.3 How I2P is Used

✅ **Legitimate Uses:**

- Privacy-focused file sharing (e.g., researchers and journalists).
- Decentralized communication for activists.

🚫 **Criminal Uses:**

- Ransomware gangs use I2P to communicate securely.
- Darknet forums selling stolen credentials.

💡 OSINT Tip:

Tracking criminals on I2P is harder than Tor because there are no exit nodes.

4. Other Anonymous Networks

4.1 Freenet

📌 A decentralized peer-to-peer network for anonymous file sharing.
📌 Focuses on data persistence—once a file is uploaded, it's stored across many nodes.
📌 Used for censorship-resistant content hosting.

🔎 Example:

Freenet has been used to store banned books and whistleblower documents.

4.2 ZeroNet

📌 A peer-to-peer web hosting system with Bitcoin cryptography.
📌 No central servers—websites stay online as long as users share them.
📌 Can be accessed without Tor, making it faster than traditional Dark Web sites.

🔎 Example:

Cybercriminals host decentralized forums that are harder to shut down.

5. How OSINT Investigators Track Activity in Anonymous Networks

Despite the anonymity, OSINT analysts and law enforcement use various techniques to track cybercriminals operating on these networks.

5.1 Traffic Analysis & Exit Node Monitoring

📌 Law enforcement monitors Tor exit nodes for suspicious activity.
📌 Some malicious exit nodes perform SSL stripping attacks to steal credentials.

💡 **Example:**

The FBI ran fake Tor exit nodes to monitor Dark Web traffic and trace criminals.

5.2 Metadata & OPSEC Mistakes

📌 Many criminals make mistakes that reveal their identity.
📌 Investigators look for:

- Reused usernames from Surface Web accounts.
- Mistyped URLs that leak real IP addresses.
- Accidentally revealing personal details in forum posts.

💡 **Example:**

The creator of Silk Road was arrested because he used his real email address in a forum post.

5.3 Monitoring Dark Web Marketplaces & Forums

📌 OSINT tools track cybercriminal discussions on forums.
📌 Investigators infiltrate criminal groups to gather intelligence.

💡 **Example:**

The FBI infiltrated AlphaBay, leading to its takedown in 2017.

6. Key Takeaways: Understanding Anonymity Networks

🔎 Tor and I2P are the primary anonymous networks used on the Dark Web.
🔎 Tor uses Onion Routing and has exit nodes, while I2P is fully internal.
🔎 Both networks have legitimate and criminal uses.
🔎 OSINT analysts track activity by monitoring exit nodes, analyzing metadata, and infiltrating forums.

Conclusion: Why OSINT Analysts Need to Understand Tor & I2P

Understanding how anonymity networks work is critical for cyber investigations. Whether tracking a ransomware group, monitoring a Dark Web market, or investigating a cyber threat, knowing the tools criminals use can help uncover valuable intelligence.

6.3 Using OSINT to Monitor the Dark Web Legally & Ethically

The Dark Web is a crucial source of intelligence for cybersecurity professionals, law enforcement, threat intelligence analysts, and OSINT investigators. However, monitoring it requires a deep understanding of ethical boundaries, legal considerations, and investigative best practices.

This chapter covers:

✓ How OSINT professionals monitor the Dark Web

✓ Legal challenges and ethical concerns

✓ Best practices for staying compliant while gathering intelligence

✓ Real-world examples of Dark Web OSINT investigations

By the end of this section, you'll know how to conduct Dark Web investigations responsibly—without violating laws or ethical standards.

1. Why Monitor the Dark Web?

The Dark Web is a hub for cybercrime, but it also contains critical intelligence that can help:

🔎 Cybersecurity teams detect stolen credentials and data leaks before they're exploited.

🔎 Law enforcement track criminal activities like fraud, drug trafficking, and hacking.

🔎 Companies protect their employees and customers from cyber threats.

🔎 Researchers analyze emerging cyber threats such as ransomware groups.

💡 **Example:**

A security team finds stolen corporate credentials on a Dark Web forum before they are used in a cyberattack.

However, monitoring the Dark Web comes with risks. Investigators must be aware of legal and ethical boundaries to avoid unintentionally breaking the law.

2. Legal Considerations for Dark Web Investigations

Dark Web investigations can cross legal lines if not conducted properly. Investigators must consider:

2.1 Laws Vary by Country

📌 Different countries have different laws on accessing Dark Web content, downloading data, and interacting with criminals.

📌 Some actions that may be legal in one country could be illegal in another.

🔍 **Example:**

- Germany prohibits accessing certain types of illegal content, even for research.
- The U.S. allows monitoring forums but prohibits direct engagement with cybercriminals.

💡 **OSINT Tip:**

Always check local and international laws before conducting Dark Web investigations.

2.2 Passive vs. Active Investigation

📌 **Passive Monitoring = Legal in most cases**

✓ Browsing forums and marketplaces

✓ Collecting publicly available data

✓ Using automated tools to monitor Dark Web leaks

📌 **Active Engagement = Risky & Possibly Illegal**

🚫 Creating fake identities to interact with criminals

🚫 Buying stolen data to investigate its source

🚫 Participating in illegal forums (even for research)

🔎 Example:

- Browsing a ransomware group's leak site is legal.
- Pretending to buy stolen credit cards to infiltrate a forum could be illegal.

💡 OSINT Tip:

Stick to passive intelligence gathering to avoid legal issues.

2.3 Handling Stolen Data

📌 Many Dark Web forums sell or share leaked personal data (PII, emails, passwords, financial records).
📌 Downloading, storing, or sharing this data could be illegal.

🔎 Example:

"Have I Been Pwned" (HIBP) monitors breaches without storing or distributing stolen credentials.

💡 Best Practice:

Never download stolen data—instead, report findings to affected parties.

2.4 Dark Web Marketplace Laws

📌 Many Dark Web forums sell illegal goods, including:

🚫 Stolen credit cards & personal data
🚫 Hacking tools & malware
🚫 Drugs, weapons, counterfeit documents

💡 Important:

Even browsing illegal marketplaces could trigger legal scrutiny in some jurisdictions.

🔎 Example:

In 2019, U.S. federal agents arrested a researcher who accessed a Dark Web drug marketplace as part of his study.

💡 OSINT Tip:

Never make purchases or create accounts on criminal marketplaces.

3. Ethical Challenges in Dark Web OSINT

Beyond legal concerns, ethical dilemmas arise when investigating the Dark Web.

3.1 Ethical Dilemma: Should You Infiltrate Criminal Groups?

📌 Some investigators use fake identities to blend into cybercriminal forums.
📌 This raises ethical and legal concerns, especially if deception is involved.

💡 Best Practice:

- Avoid direct interaction with criminals.
- Instead, monitor discussions and analyze open-source data.

3.2 Ethical Dilemma: What to Do If You Find a Major Threat?

📌 OSINT analysts sometimes discover planned cyberattacks, leaked government documents, or threats against individuals.

💡 Best Practice:

- Report critical threats to appropriate authorities.
- If working for a company, alert security teams about leaked credentials.

🔎 Example:

A researcher finds an upcoming ransomware attack on a hospital. The ethical choice is to alert law enforcement immediately.

4. Best Practices for Legal & Ethical Dark Web OSINT

To legally and ethically monitor the Dark Web, follow these guidelines:

✅ **Use Read-Only Access** – Avoid engaging in criminal discussions.

✅ **Use a Secure, Isolated Environment** – A dedicated virtual machine (VM) and VPN prevent accidental exposure.

✅ **Follow Corporate & Legal Policies** – Always get legal approval before starting an investigation.

✅ **Don't Download or Store Illegal Data** – Collect metadata, not stolen files.

✅ **Report Major Threats** – Share findings with affected organizations or law enforcement.

💡 **OSINT Tip:**

Create a clear documentation process to record findings without breaking laws.

5. Real-World Examples of Legal Dark Web OSINT

5.1 Identifying Stolen Corporate Credentials

📌 Many cybersecurity teams use automated tools to scan for corporate emails and passwords appearing in Dark Web leaks.

🔎 **Example:**

- A bank's security team finds leaked employee credentials on a hacker forum.
- They force password resets before hackers exploit the data.

💡 **OSINT Tool:**

SpyCloud monitors stolen credentials in Dark Web databases.

5.2 Tracking Ransomware Groups

📌 Threat intelligence teams monitor ransomware groups' leak sites for new victims.

🔎 **Example:**

- The Conti ransomware group had a Dark Web site where they published stolen data.

- Security firms tracked Conti's operations and helped companies defend against attacks.

💡 Best Practice:

Monitoring is legal, but engaging with hackers is risky.

5.3 Investigating Dark Web Marketplaces

📌 Law enforcement agencies track transactions on illegal marketplaces using cryptocurrency tracing tools.

🔎 Example:

In 2021, Europol shut down DarkMarket, one of the largest illegal Dark Web markets, by tracing Bitcoin transactions.

💡 OSINT Tip:

Use tools like CipherTrace and Chainalysis for crypto tracking.

6. Key Takeaways: Legal & Ethical Dark Web OSINT

🚀 Passive OSINT (monitoring forums, scanning leaks) is usually legal.
🚀 Active engagement (creating accounts, pretending to buy illegal goods) can be illegal.
🚀 Downloading stolen data is risky—stick to metadata analysis.
🚀 Report serious threats to law enforcement or affected organizations.
🚀 Always operate within legal and ethical boundaries.

Conclusion: Why Ethical Dark Web OSINT Matters

Dark Web intelligence is a powerful tool for cybersecurity and law enforcement, but it must be used responsibly. Legal and ethical violations can lead to criminal charges—even for well-intentioned researchers.

By following legal guidelines, ethical standards, and best practices, OSINT professionals can gather intelligence effectively while staying compliant.

6.4 Dark Web Search Engines & Intelligence Gathering

The Dark Web contains vast amounts of hidden data, but unlike the Surface Web, it does not have centralized search engines like Google or Bing. Instead, investigators must rely on specialized Dark Web search engines, OSINT techniques, and manual intelligence gathering to find relevant information.

This chapter covers:

✅ How Dark Web search engines work

✅ The limitations of searching the Dark Web

✅ Best practices for gathering intelligence safely

✅ Tools and techniques used by OSINT analysts

By the end of this section, you'll know how to navigate the Dark Web efficiently while maintaining security, anonymity, and ethical standards.

1. Why Search the Dark Web?

The Dark Web is a hub for cybercriminal activities, but it is also a valuable source of intelligence for cybersecurity professionals, law enforcement, and OSINT investigators.

Common Intelligence Use Cases

🔎 **Cyber Threat Intelligence**: Monitoring ransomware groups, hacking forums, and data leak sites.

🔎 **Tracking Stolen Credentials**: Identifying breached company accounts or personal data.

🔎 **Investigating Dark Web Marketplaces**: Analyzing trends in illicit trade, such as stolen credit cards or malware.

🔎 **Monitoring Threat Actors**: Gathering intelligence on cybercriminal groups and their operations.

🔎 **Preventing Fraud**: Detecting fraudulent schemes, phishing kits, and identity theft operations.

💡 **Example:**

- A cybersecurity team discovers a new ransomware leak site containing stolen data from a financial institution.
- They warn the affected company before the data is exploited.

However, finding relevant Dark Web content is not as easy as using Google. This is where specialized search engines and OSINT techniques come in.

2. How Dark Web Search Engines Work

Unlike Google, which indexes trillions of Surface Web pages, Dark Web search engines operate in a fragmented and unreliable way due to:

📌 **Limited indexing**: Most .onion sites do not allow search engines to crawl them.
📌 **Frequent site shutdowns**: Dark Web sites often disappear or change addresses.
📌 **Access restrictions**: Many marketplaces and forums require registration or invite-only access.
📌 **Encryption & anonymity**: Data is intentionally hidden to prevent tracking.

💡 **OSINT Tip:**

Dark Web search engines can be useful, but they should be combined with manual research and OSINT tools for deeper intelligence gathering.

3. Popular Dark Web Search Engines

Several search engines are designed specifically for .onion sites on the Tor network. Below are some of the most commonly used ones:

3.1 Ahmia

📌 URL: https://ahmia.fi
📌 Ahmia indexes Dark Web sites but only lists legal content.
📌 It allows users to search for specific keywords in .onion pages.

💡 **Best for:**

- Finding general Dark Web sites and forums.

3.2 Torch (Tor Search Engine)

- 📌 One of the largest Dark Web search engines.
- 📌 Indexes millions of .onion pages.

📷 Limitations:

- Many search results contain malicious or fraudulent links.
- Low reliability—frequent downtime and spam.

💡 Best for:

Locating hidden services and marketplaces (requires verification).

3.3 DarkSearch.io

- 📌 A Surface Web-accessible search engine for .onion sites.
- 📌 Provides direct links to Dark Web marketplaces, forums, and leak sites.

💡 Best for:

Quick searches without using the Tor browser.

3.4 Haystak

- 📌 Claims to index 1.5 billion+ pages on the Dark Web.
- 📌 Provides better filtering than most Dark Web search engines.

💡 Best for:

Searching Dark Web forums and leaks.

📷 Limitations:

Paid features limit full access.

4. Limitations of Dark Web Search Engines

While these search engines help locate Dark Web content, they have major limitations:

⊘ Most Dark Web content is unindexed.
⊘ Marketplaces and criminal forums require manual access.
⊘ Search results often include scams and inactive sites.
⊘ Search engines can be manipulated with fake listings.

💡 Best Practice:

Combine search engines with OSINT tools and manual intelligence gathering.

5. OSINT Techniques for Dark Web Intelligence Gathering

Since search engines have limitations, OSINT analysts use additional methods to find valuable information on the Dark Web.

5.1 Monitoring Dark Web Forums & Marketplaces

📌 Many cybercriminals operate private forums where they sell or discuss stolen data.
📌 These forums often require manual registration or insider access.

💡 OSINT Tip:

Use leak monitoring services like SpyCloud, Recorded Future, and DarkOwl to track stolen credentials.

5.2 Searching Paste Sites & Data Dumps

📌 Dark Web paste sites (similar to Pastebin) are commonly used to dump stolen credentials, email lists, and financial data.

🔎 Popular Paste Sites:

- **Dread Paste** – Used by cybercriminals to share leaked data.
- **DeepPaste** – Hosts leaked credentials and database dumps.

💡 OSINT Tip:

Use "Have I Been Pwned" to check if an email or password has appeared in a data breach.

5.3 Cryptocurrency Tracking for Dark Web Transactions

📌 Many Dark Web transactions use Bitcoin, Monero, or other cryptocurrencies.

📌 OSINT investigators use crypto tracing tools to follow illicit transactions.

💡 **Tools for Crypto OSINT:**

- **CipherTrace** – Tracks cryptocurrency transactions.
- **Chainalysis** – Used by law enforcement for blockchain investigations.

🔎 **Example:**

FBI used Bitcoin tracking to arrest administrators of Silk Road and AlphaBay.

5.4 Tracking Ransomware Leak Sites

📌 Many ransomware groups publish stolen data on Dark Web leak sites to pressure victims into paying ransoms.

💡 **Best Practice:**

Security teams monitor these sites to detect leaked corporate data before it's misused.

🔎 **Example:**

The REvil ransomware group published stolen files from major corporations before demanding ransom payments.

6. Best Practices for Safe & Ethical Dark Web OSINT

✅ **Use an Isolated & Secure Environment**

Always access the Dark Web via a virtual machine (VM) and VPN to prevent leaks.

✅ **Avoid Interacting with Criminals**

Do not create accounts, post in forums, or attempt to buy illegal goods.

✅ Use Passive Collection Methods

Rely on search engines, OSINT tools, and monitoring services rather than direct engagement.

✅ Verify Findings from Multiple Sources

Dark Web information is often manipulated or false—cross-check data before acting on it.

✅ Report Serious Threats

If investigating ransomware, fraud, or cyberattacks, report findings to law enforcement or affected organizations.

7. Key Takeaways: Dark Web Intelligence Gathering

🚀 Dark Web search engines exist, but they have major limitations.
🚀 Most valuable intelligence comes from manual research and OSINT tools.
🚀 Threat actors use the Dark Web to sell stolen data, malware, and credentials.
🚀 Investigators must follow legal and ethical guidelines when gathering intelligence.

Conclusion: Why OSINT Professionals Need Dark Web Monitoring

The Dark Web remains a critical source of cyber threat intelligence. While search engines provide a starting point, deeper investigations require specialized OSINT techniques and tools.

By combining Dark Web search engines, OSINT methodologies, and strong cybersecurity practices, analysts can uncover threats, breaches, and cybercriminal activity while staying safe and compliant.

6.5 Understanding the Hidden Economy of the Dark Web

The Dark Web operates as a shadow economy, where stolen data, illicit goods, hacking tools, and cybercrime services are bought and sold in underground marketplaces. Unlike traditional markets, this economy is fueled by cryptocurrency transactions, anonymity, and decentralized trust systems.

This chapter explores:

✅ How the Dark Web economy functions

✅ The main types of illicit goods and services sold

✅ How cybercriminals establish trust and reputation

✅ The role of cryptocurrencies in Dark Web transactions

✅ How OSINT analysts track financial activity in these markets

By understanding the economic structures of the Dark Web, investigators can gain valuable insights into cybercriminal operations, emerging threats, and potential intelligence sources.

1. How the Dark Web Economy Works

The Dark Web's economy mimics the legitimate global market, but with no central regulation or oversight. Instead, it operates on:

📌 **Anonymity** – Transactions and communications are hidden via Tor and encrypted messaging.

📌 **Cryptocurrency payments** – Bitcoin, Monero, and other cryptocurrencies are used to ensure untraceable transactions.

📌 **Marketplace structures** – Just like Amazon or eBay, Dark Web marketplaces have product listings, seller reviews, and escrow systems.

📌 **Decentralization** – When a marketplace is shut down, new ones quickly take its place.

💡 **OSINT Tip:**

Understanding the flow of money and data in these markets can help track criminal operations and identify emerging threats.

2. What is Sold on Dark Web Marketplaces?

Dark Web marketplaces facilitate the sale of both digital and physical illicit goods. Below are the most common categories:

2.1 Stolen Data & Hacked Credentials

📌 Compromised personal and corporate accounts (email, banking, social media).
📌 Database dumps containing usernames, passwords, and credit card details.
📌 Government and medical records (passport scans, SSNs, medical histories).

💡 **Example:**

The Genesis Market sold stolen browser fingerprints and login sessions, allowing cybercriminals to bypass two-factor authentication (2FA).

📷 **Security Risk:**

Attackers buy and use stolen credentials for account takeovers, fraud, and espionage.

2.2 Cybercrime-as-a-Service (CaaS)

📌 **Ransomware-as-a-Service (RaaS)** – Hackers sell ready-made ransomware kits.
📌 **Botnets for hire** – Attackers rent infected computers to launch DDoS attacks.
📌 **Phishing kits** – Complete packages for running email and website scams.
📌 **Malware & exploit sales** – Zero-day vulnerabilities and keyloggers.

💡 **Example:**

The "Emotet" botnet was rented out to hackers for distributing malware campaigns.

📷 **Security Risk:**

Even low-skilled criminals can launch major cyberattacks using rented services.

2.3 Fake Documents & Fraudulent Services

📌 Counterfeit passports, driver's licenses, and identity documents.
📌 Fake credit cards and cloned ATM cards.
📌 Fraudulent tax returns, fake pay stubs, and loan documents.

💡 **Example:**

Some fraudsters offer identity packages ("fullz") that include SSNs, credit reports, and utility bills for impersonation.

🔒 Security Risk:

Identity theft leads to financial fraud, loan scams, and fake job applications.

2.4 Drugs, Weapons, & Illegal Goods

📌 **Narcotics** – Dark Web drug markets operate like illegal versions of Amazon.
📌 **Weapons sales** – Firearms, explosives, and military-grade equipment.
📌 **Human trafficking** – Some sites offer illegal migration services and forged documents.

💡 Example:

The infamous Silk Road marketplace was a major hub for illegal drug sales before it was shut down by the FBI in 2013.

🔒 Security Risk:

Law enforcement agencies monitor these markets to track organized crime.

3. How Cybercriminals Establish Trust on the Dark Web

Since the Dark Web is anonymous and unregulated, fraud is common—even among criminals. To establish trust, cybercriminals use:

3.1 Reputation Systems & Escrow Services

📌 **Buyer reviews and ratings** – Like eBay, sellers have ratings and customer feedback.
📌 **Escrow payments** – Marketplaces hold cryptocurrency payments in escrow until buyers confirm delivery.
📌 **Trusted vendor status** – Some marketplaces require a deposit to become a verified seller.

💡 OSINT Tip:

Investigators can analyze vendor reputations and past sales history to track cybercriminal activity.

3.2 Invite-Only Forums & Vetting Processes

📌 Some high-level cybercrime forums require:

✅ Proof of experience (successful hacks, stolen data).

✅ Payment of membership fees (in cryptocurrency).

✅ Invitations from trusted members.

💡 **OSINT Tip:**

These invite-only groups are harder to infiltrate, but leaks and insider reports sometimes expose key details.

3.3 Encrypted Communication Channels

📌 **Jabber (XMPP) & PGP encryption** – Used for secure messaging.
📌 **Telegram & Discord channels** – Some criminals operate private groups.
📌 End-to-end encrypted email services (e.g., ProtonMail, Tutanota).

💡 **OSINT Tip:**

Monitoring Telegram channels has become a crucial method for tracking cybercriminal discussions.

4. The Role of Cryptocurrencies in the Dark Web Economy

4.1 Why Criminals Use Cryptocurrencies

📌 **Anonymity**: Transactions do not require identity verification.
📌 **Decentralization**: No central authority can freeze funds.
📌 **Cross-border payments**: Cryptocurrencies allow international trade without regulation.

💡 **Example:**

Bitcoin was the primary currency on Silk Road, but newer marketplaces prefer Monero (XMR) for better privacy.

4.2 Tracking Cryptocurrency Transactions

Despite its anonymity, cryptocurrency is traceable using blockchain analysis.

💡 **Tools for Crypto OSINT:**

- **Chainalysis** – Used by law enforcement to track illicit Bitcoin flows.
- **CipherTrace** – Identifies Dark Web financial transactions.
- **Elliptic** – Analyzes money laundering patterns in cryptocurrency.

🔎 **Example:**

In 2021, law enforcement tracked Bitcoin transactions to dismantle the DarkSide ransomware group.

5. OSINT Strategies for Investigating the Dark Web Economy

✓ **Monitor Marketplaces & Forums** – Use search engines like Ahmia, DarkSearch.io, and OSINT tools.

✓ **Track Cryptocurrency Transactions** – Use blockchain analysis tools to trace payments.

✓ **Analyze Leaked Vendor Data** – Cybercriminal forums sometimes get hacked, exposing usernames and transactions.

✓ **Use Passive Collection Methods** – Avoid direct engagement with threat actors.

🚨 **Legal & Ethical Caution:**

Accessing illegal marketplaces is risky—investigators should use legal monitoring tools instead of direct participation.

6. Key Takeaways: The Dark Web's Hidden Economy

🚀 The Dark Web operates as a decentralized cybercrime economy.

🚀 Stolen data, hacking services, and fraud tools are traded daily.

🚀 Cybercriminals establish trust using reviews, escrow, and encrypted communication.

🚀 Cryptocurrency fuels most transactions, but blockchain analysis can trace illicit funds.

🚀 OSINT tools help investigators track criminal activities without breaking the law.

Conclusion: Why OSINT Professionals Must Understand the Dark Web Economy

The Dark Web's underground economy is constantly evolving, with new marketplaces, scams, and cybercriminal services emerging daily. By understanding how these markets operate, OSINT analysts can better predict, track, and disrupt cyber threats.

6.6 Case Study: A Law Enforcement Dark Web Takedown

Dark Web marketplaces and cybercriminal networks operate under the assumption of anonymity, but law enforcement agencies worldwide have developed sophisticated methods to infiltrate, track, and dismantle these illicit operations.

This case study explores a real-world Dark Web takedown, detailing:

✅ The criminal marketplace that was targeted

✅ How law enforcement gathered intelligence

✅ The technical and OSINT techniques used

✅ How cryptocurrency tracking played a role

✅ The arrests and aftermath of the operation

By analyzing this case, we gain insights into how investigators successfully disrupt Dark Web activities and the challenges they face in doing so.

1. Background: The Targeted Dark Web Marketplace

One of the most famous law enforcement takedowns was Operation Bayonet, which led to the seizure of AlphaBay, the largest Dark Web marketplace at the time.

What Was AlphaBay?

📌 Launched in 2014 as a successor to Silk Road.

📌 Hosted over 400,000 users and 250,000 listings.

✦ Sold illicit goods, including stolen data, drugs, malware, and hacking services.
✦ Operated with Bitcoin and Monero for transactions.

🎗 At its peak, AlphaBay facilitated transactions worth an estimated $600 million annually.

🚨 **Security Risk:**

Criminals used AlphaBay to buy and sell stolen credentials, run phishing campaigns, and distribute ransomware.

2. Law Enforcement's Intelligence Gathering

The FBI, DEA, Europol, and multiple national agencies worked together to bring down AlphaBay. Their investigation involved:

🔎 **OSINT and Dark Web Monitoring** – Agents monitored forums and vendor listings to identify key sellers and their digital footprints.
🔎 **Blockchain Analysis** – Investigators tracked cryptocurrency transactions linked to AlphaBay accounts.
🔎 **Traffic Analysis** – They analyzed Tor network traffic to locate potential weaknesses in the marketplace's security.
🔎 **Undercover Operations** – Agents posed as buyers to infiltrate vendor networks and collect intelligence.

3. The Breakthrough: How Investigators Unmasked AlphaBay's Admin

The key to cracking the case came from a simple mistake made by Alexandre Cazes, AlphaBay's creator.

3.1 The Email Slip-Up

✦ Cazes used his personal email address (pimp.alex@yahoo.com) in an early AlphaBay promotional email.
✦ OSINT analysts cross-referenced this email with other online accounts, linking it to his real identity.

🎗 **OSINT Lesson:**

Even small pieces of leaked information can unravel an entire operation.

3.2 Cryptocurrency Forensics

✦ Cazes failed to properly launder AlphaBay's Bitcoin earnings.
✦ Investigators traced wallet transactions leading to his financial accounts and luxury assets.

🔏 Crypto Mistake:

Despite using Monero for transactions, Bitcoin's blockchain allowed investigators to track payments.

4. The Takedown: Operation Bayonet

4.1 Coordinated Law Enforcement Raid

✦ On July 5, 2017, police arrested Alexandre Cazes in Thailand, where he was living.
✦ His house, cars, and computers were seized, containing incriminating evidence.
✦ Law enforcement took control of AlphaBay's servers, shutting down the marketplace.

4.2 The Aftermath

✦ Cazes died in custody a week later, reportedly by suicide.
✦ Authorities seized over $23 million in cryptocurrency and assets.
✦ Many AlphaBay users moved to other Dark Web marketplaces, but trust in these platforms was shaken.

💡 Impact on the Dark Web:

After AlphaBay's shutdown, many vendors switched to decentralized markets, making law enforcement investigations harder.

5. Key Takeaways: How OSINT & Crypto Forensics Helped

🚀 Small OSINT mistakes (like an exposed email) can take down massive criminal networks.
🚀 Cryptocurrency tracking is a powerful tool against cybercrime.
🚀 International cooperation is crucial in Dark Web takedowns.

🚀 Marketplace shutdowns disrupt cybercrime but lead to new challenges.

Conclusion: The Future of Dark Web Investigations

While AlphaBay was dismantled, new marketplaces continue to emerge. Law enforcement agencies are constantly adapting, using advanced OSINT, blockchain forensics, and cyber intelligence to track criminals operating in the Dark Web economy.

7. Marketplaces & Criminal Forums on the Dark Web

In this chapter, we will delve into the dark web's underground marketplaces and criminal forums, which are hotspots for cybercriminal activity, including the buying and selling of stolen data, hacked credentials, and other illicit services. We will explore how these forums operate, the types of transactions they host, and the tools available to investigators for tracking and infiltrating these spaces. By examining the interactions and transactions on these platforms, investigators can gather crucial intelligence on the perpetrators behind breaches and leaks. Additionally, we will discuss the methods used by cybercriminals to hide their tracks, as well as strategies to identify key players and uncover hidden networks. Understanding the dark web's marketplaces and forums is essential for anyone looking to investigate data leaks and cybercrime in depth, providing insight into how stolen email

7.1 The Evolution of Dark Web Marketplaces

Dark Web marketplaces have evolved significantly over the past two decades, adapting to law enforcement crackdowns, technological advancements, and shifting cybercriminal strategies. From early darknet drug markets like Silk Road to modern decentralized markets, these platforms continue to facilitate illicit trade, cybercrime services, and stolen data sales.

This chapter explores:

✅ The history of Dark Web marketplaces

✅ Major marketplace takedowns and their impact

✅ How criminals adapt to law enforcement actions

✅ The rise of decentralized and encrypted trading networks

Understanding the evolution of these markets helps OSINT analysts and investigators anticipate future trends and emerging cyber threats.

1. The Early Days: Silk Road & the Rise of Dark Web Commerce (2011-2013)

1.1 What Was Silk Road?

Silk Road was the first major Dark Web marketplace, launched in 2011 by Ross Ulbricht ("Dread Pirate Roberts"). It was built on Tor for anonymity and Bitcoin for payments, allowing users to trade drugs, fake documents, and hacking tools with relative safety.

📌 **Key Features of Silk Road:**

- Escrow system to prevent scams.
- Vendor and buyer reputation system (like eBay).
- Strong libertarian ideology – banned certain activities like child exploitation.

1.2 The Fall of Silk Road

🏛 **Takedown Date**: October 2013
🏛 **Reason**: FBI traced Bitcoin transactions and found Ulbricht's unencrypted laptop during his arrest.
🏛 **Impact**: Showed that even Tor and Bitcoin aren't foolproof against OSINT and blockchain analysis.

💡 **OSINT Lesson:**

Ulbricht's mistake? Using personal email and forum usernames that linked back to him.

2. The Rise of Successor Marketplaces (2013-2017)

After Silk Road's fall, multiple marketplaces filled the void, each improving security but making similar mistakes.

2.1 Silk Road 2.0 (2013-2014)

📌 Created by former Silk Road moderators.
📌 Used improved encryption but reused old usernames, exposing key players.
🏛 Shutdown by FBI in 2014.

2.2 Evolution Market (2013-2015)

📌 Gained popularity after Silk Road 2.0 fell.

💰 Exit scam in 2015: Admins disappeared with $12 million in Bitcoin, proving fraud risk in anonymous markets.

2.3 AlphaBay (2014-2017)

📌 Became the largest Dark Web market, offering drugs, malware, and cybercrime tools.
📌 Introduced Monero payments for privacy.
💰 Shutdown in Operation Bayonet (2017) – AlphaBay's admin used a personal email, exposing his identity.

💡 Takeaway:

Every marketplace improved on the last but also made OSINT mistakes, leading to law enforcement takedowns.

3. The Shift to Decentralization (2017-Present)

With repeated takedowns, criminals shifted to decentralized models:

3.1 OpenBazaar (2016-2021) – A Failed Experiment

📌 A peer-to-peer (P2P) marketplace without central servers.
📌 Harder to shut down but lacked escrow and trust systems, leading to low adoption.

3.2 Monero & Privacy Coins Dominate

📌 Bitcoin is traceable, leading cybercriminals to adopt Monero (XMR), Zcash, and Dash.
📌 Law enforcement developed Monero-tracking tools, reducing its effectiveness.

3.3 Telegram & Encrypted Chat-Based Markets

📌 Many sellers moved to Telegram, Discord, and WhatsApp for direct sales.
📌 Reduces law enforcement visibility but increases scam risks for buyers.

💡 Current Trend:

No single marketplace dominates; instead, many smaller, private invite-only forums exist.

4. How Law Enforcement Adapts

Despite decentralization, authorities still find ways to track and disrupt criminal markets.

4.1 OSINT & Dark Web Monitoring

📌 Law enforcement monitors forums, marketplaces, and encrypted chats.
📌 AI-powered tools track vendor reputations and marketplace discussions.

4.2 Cryptocurrency Forensics

📌 Agencies use Chainalysis, CipherTrace, and Elliptic to track illicit crypto transactions.
📌 Even Monero transactions can sometimes be correlated through exchange deposits.

4.3 Undercover Operations

📌 FBI, Europol, and Interpol infiltrate Dark Web markets, posing as buyers or vendors.
📌 Seized servers reveal transaction data, leading to mass arrests.

🔍 **Example:**

Wall Street Market (2019) – Shut down after German authorities seized servers and deanonymized users.

5. The Future of Dark Web Marketplaces

✓ **Decentralized Finance (DeFi) & Crypto Tumblers** – Criminals are moving towards privacy-focused crypto mixing services.
✓ **Artificial Intelligence (AI) in OSINT** – AI-driven tools improve law enforcement's ability to monitor and track illicit activity.
✓ **More Secure Private Markets** – Future markets may use decentralized networks (IPFS, blockchain-based marketplaces) to evade detection.

💡 **Final Takeaway:**

The battle between cybercriminals and law enforcement is ongoing, with each side constantly evolving.

Conclusion: Why OSINT Analysts Must Track Dark Web Evolution

The history of Dark Web marketplaces reveals that:

🚀 Every takedown leads to smarter, more resilient replacements.

🚀 Decentralization and privacy coins are key trends.

🚀 OSINT and cryptocurrency forensics remain the best investigative tools.

🚀 Law enforcement still wins by exploiting human errors (email leaks, poor OPSEC).

By understanding how these markets evolve, OSINT professionals and cybersecurity experts can stay ahead of emerging threats.

7.2 How Stolen Data is Bought & Sold

Stolen data is the lifeblood of the Dark Web economy, fueling cybercrime activities ranging from identity theft and financial fraud to corporate espionage and nation-state attacks. Criminal marketplaces provide a platform for buying, selling, and trading compromised credentials, personal data, and sensitive business information.

This chapter explores:

✓ The types of stolen data sold on Dark Web marketplaces

✓ How cybercriminals acquire, price, and distribute stolen information

✓ The role of "combolists," data dumps, and underground auctions

✓ How OSINT investigators track stolen data and monitor Dark Web transactions

By understanding these underground markets, investigators can detect breaches early, prevent fraud, and disrupt cybercriminal operations.

1. What Kind of Data is Sold on the Dark Web?

Cybercriminals trade various types of stolen information, often categorized based on monetization potential.

1.1 Personal Identifiable Information (PII)

📌 Includes: Names, addresses, phone numbers, Social Security numbers (SSNs), passport details.

📌 Use Cases: Identity theft, fake document creation, social engineering attacks.

📌 Price: $1 - $10 per record, depending on completeness.

💡 **Example**: In 2022, a major leak exposed over 1 billion Chinese citizens' PII, reportedly stolen from a government database and sold for 10 Bitcoin (~$200,000 at the time).

1.2 Stolen Login Credentials

📌 **Includes**: Email-password combinations, corporate accounts, streaming service logins (Netflix, Spotify, etc.).

📌 **Use Cases**: Credential stuffing attacks, account takeovers, ransomware infections.

📌 **Price**: $2 - $50 per account, depending on service (e.g., banking logins are more valuable).

💡 **Example**: Cybercriminals use "combolists" (massive collections of stolen credentials) for automated brute-force attacks on various platforms.

1.3 Financial & Payment Data

📌 **Includes**: Credit card numbers, PayPal logins, bank account details, cryptocurrency wallets.

📌 **Use Cases**: Fraudulent transactions, cash-out schemes, money laundering.

📌 **Price**: $5 - $120 per card, depending on balance and region.

💡 **Example**: Dark Web vendors often bundle "fullz" (full identity + financial details), allowing criminals to impersonate victims for fraud or wire transfers.

1.4 Corporate & Government Data Breaches

📌 **Includes**: Internal emails, intellectual property, customer databases, software exploits.

📌 **Use Cases**: Ransomware extortion, insider trading, espionage, targeted attacks.

📌 **Price**: $500 - $100,000+, depending on data sensitivity.

💡 **Example**: In 2023, Ransomware group ALPHV leaked hundreds of GBs of stolen corporate data after a company refused to pay a ransom.

2. How Cybercriminals Acquire Stolen Data

Dark Web vendors obtain stolen data through various cyberattack methods:

2.1 Data Breaches & Hacking

📌 Cybercriminals target poorly secured databases, cloud storage, or employee credentials.
📌 Stolen databases are either sold outright or held for ransom.

🔎 **Example**: In 2021, the LinkedIn data leak exposed 700 million user records, including emails and job histories, scraped and sold on Dark Web forums.

2.2 Phishing & Social Engineering

📌 Hackers use fake emails, SMS, or websites to trick users into revealing credentials.
📌 Stolen logins are compiled into "credential stuffing" databases.

🔎 **Example**: In 2022, a fake Coinbase login page tricked users into revealing passwords, which were then sold for $150 per account.

2.3 Malware & Keyloggers

📌 Trojans, spyware, and keyloggers steal login credentials and sensitive files.
📌 Sold in bulk on malware-as-a-service platforms.

🔎 **Example**: Infostealer malware like RedLine Stealer sells stolen crypto wallet credentials and saved passwords on the Dark Web.

2.4 Insider Threats & Leaked Credentials

📌 Employees leak company data for financial gain or revenge.
📌 Access credentials are sold in private cybercrime Telegram groups.

🔎 **Example**: A Tesla employee allegedly leaked internal software source code to a Dark Web buyer in 2021.

3. How Stolen Data is Sold & Distributed

Cybercriminals have various methods for selling stolen data, including marketplaces, private forums, and encrypted messaging platforms.

3.1 Dark Web Marketplaces

✦ Operate like Amazon or eBay for cybercrime.
✦ Vendors list stolen credit cards, credentials, and hacking services.
✦ Payments made in Bitcoin, Monero, or privacy-focused cryptocurrencies.

🔎 **Example**: Joker's Stash was a major marketplace specializing in stolen credit card data, shut down in 2021 after law enforcement action.

3.2 Cybercrime Forums & Private Channels

✦ Russian-language and invite-only forums are used for high-profile transactions.
✦ Telegram, Discord, and Signal allow encrypted data sales.

🔎 **Example**: Genesis Market sold "browser fingerprints" stolen from malware-infected devices, enabling session hijacking and bypassing 2FA security.

3.3 Ransomware Extortion & Data Auctions

✦ Ransomware gangs steal sensitive corporate data and threaten to leak it unless paid.
✦ Some groups auction off stolen data to the highest bidder.

🔎 **Example**: The REvil ransomware group auctioned data from hacked law firms and celebrities, demanding millions in cryptocurrency ransom.

4. How OSINT Analysts & Cybersecurity Teams Track Stolen Data

Despite criminals' efforts to remain anonymous, OSINT professionals and law enforcement use various methods to track stolen data and disrupt illicit trade.

4.1 Monitoring Data Leak Sites & Pastebins

✦ Websites like RaidForums (shut down in 2022), BreachForums, and Pastebin host stolen data dumps.
✦ OSINT analysts use automated scrapers to detect leaked credentials linked to their organizations.

🔎 **Tool Example**: Have I Been Pwned (HIBP) helps users check if their emails appear in known breaches.

4.2 Cryptocurrency Transaction Tracking

📌 Law enforcement uses Chainalysis, CipherTrace, and Elliptic to trace Bitcoin and Monero transactions linked to cybercriminal wallets.
📌 Some criminals use crypto mixers (Tumblers), but investigators have techniques to deanonymize them.

🔎 **Example**: The FBI tracked Bitcoin payments from the Colonial Pipeline ransomware attack, recovering $2.3 million.

4.3 Undercover Operations & Marketplace Takedowns

📌 Law enforcement agencies infiltrate Dark Web forums by posing as buyers.
📌 Once enough evidence is gathered, marketplaces are seized, and servers provide IP logs and transaction histories.

🔎 **Example**: Operation Bayonet (2017) took down AlphaBay, exposing thousands of cybercriminals.

Conclusion: The Arms Race Between Cybercriminals & Investigators

The trade of stolen data is a multi-billion-dollar underground economy, but law enforcement, OSINT analysts, and cybersecurity professionals continue to develop new techniques to track, disrupt, and prevent these illegal activities.

💡 **Key Takeaways:**

✅ Stolen data is monetized in various ways, from identity fraud to corporate extortion.

✅ Marketplaces evolve after every major takedown, but new OSINT tools help track cybercriminals.

✅ Blockchain forensics, data leak monitoring, and OSINT investigations are crucial for disrupting Dark Web trade.

7.3 Investigating Cybercrime Forums & Vendor Trust Ratings

Cybercrime forums and marketplaces serve as hubs for buying and selling stolen data, hacking tools, and illicit services. Unlike mainstream e-commerce sites, these underground markets operate on trust and reputation systems, allowing buyers to assess vendor reliability before making purchases.

This chapter explores:

✅ How cybercrime forums function

✅ The structure of trust ratings & vendor reputations

✅ Techniques for investigating forum users and transactions

✅ How OSINT analysts can track and infiltrate cybercrime networks

Understanding the dynamics of these forums is essential for identifying cybercriminals, tracking illicit activity, and disrupting underground economies.

1. The Role of Cybercrime Forums in the Dark Web Economy

Cybercrime forums act as online black markets and networking spaces, where criminals share techniques, trade illegal goods, and recruit new members.

1.1 Types of Cybercrime Forums

Cybercrime forums vary based on their focus and audience:

Forum Type	Primary Activities	Access Level
Hacking Forums	Malware development, exploits, botnets	Public or private
Fraud Forums	Credit card fraud, phishing, fake documents	Invite-only
Ransomware Affiliate Programs	Ransomware-as-a-Service (RaaS), data extortion	Highly restricted
Data Leak & Dump Sites	Selling breached databases, personal information	Open or semi-private
Carding Forums	Stolen credit card trade, payment fraud	Invite-only

📖 **Example**: RaidForums (shut down in 2022) was a popular data breach forum where users bought and sold stolen credentials.

1.2 Public vs. Private Forums

📌 **Public Forums**: Easily accessible, often used for recruiting or low-level discussions.

📌 **Private/Invite-Only Forums**: Require vetting, reputation, or membership fees to prevent law enforcement infiltration.

💡 **OSINT Strategy**: Researchers often track public forums for emerging threats and attempt to gain access to private groups through sock puppet accounts.

2. How Vendor Trust Ratings Work

Since cybercriminals operate anonymously, they rely on trust ratings and reputation scores to determine vendor credibility.

2.1 Reputation Systems on Dark Web Marketplaces

Most cybercrime marketplaces use a rating system similar to eBay or Amazon, where buyers leave feedback based on:

- ◆ **Successful transactions** – Did the vendor deliver as promised?
- ◆ **Product/service quality** – Was the stolen data valid?
- ◆ **Communication & support** – Did the vendor provide after-sale support?
- ◆ **Escrow compliance** – Did they use the site's escrow system or attempt a scam?

📌 **Trust Level Categories:**

✓ **Trusted Vendors**: Long transaction history, high positive feedback.

⚠️ **Unverified Vendors**: New sellers with little to no reputation.

✗ **Scammers/Exit Scammers**: Vendors who take money but fail to deliver goods.

🔎 **Example**: AlphaBay (before its shutdown in 2017) had a tiered vendor system, where top vendors earned "gold" or "platinum" badges based on transaction volume and reviews.

2.2 How Vendors Establish Credibility

To build trust, vendors often:

✅ Offer free samples of stolen data to prove authenticity.

✅ Participate in "escrow" transactions—funds are held by the forum until the buyer confirms delivery.

✅ Maintain consistent usernames across forums to build long-term reputations.

💡 **OSINT Tip**: Tracking vendor usernames across multiple platforms can reveal linked identities or past activities.

3. Investigating Cybercrime Forums & Vendors

Cybercrime forum investigations involve analyzing user activity, tracking financial transactions, and identifying key players.

3.1 Analyzing User Profiles & Activity

Most forums have detailed user profiles with:

📌 Join date, post count, and activity history.
📌 Trust score or reputation ranking.
📌 Past transactions and feedback from buyers.

🔍 **Example**: A vendor with 10+ successful sales and positive feedback is likely more active than a newly registered account.

💡 **OSINT Strategy:**

- Look for recurring usernames, email addresses, or wallet addresses used in multiple forums.
- Monitor post patterns—some vendors use identical phrasing or signatures across different platforms.

3.2 Tracking Cryptocurrency Transactions

Since Dark Web markets rely on Bitcoin, Monero, and other cryptocurrencies, OSINT analysts use blockchain forensics tools to:

✅ Identify wallet addresses linked to transactions.

✅ Track Bitcoin tumbler/mixing services used to launder funds.

✅ Map connections between vendors and known cybercriminal groups.

🔎 **Example**: The FBI tracked Bitcoin payments linked to AlphaBay vendors, leading to multiple arrests after the site's takedown.

💡 **OSINT Tools for Crypto Tracking:**

- **Chainalysis** – Blockchain forensics platform.
- **CipherTrace** – Tracks illicit crypto transactions.
- **Elliptic** – Identifies Dark Web-linked wallets.

3.3 Infiltrating Forums & Gaining Access

Some investigators create sock puppet accounts (fake identities) to access private forums and gain insider intelligence.

📌 **Methods of Access:**

- **Social engineering** – Gaining trust by participating in discussions.
- **Paid memberships** – Some forums require an entry fee in Bitcoin.
- **Sponsorship by an existing member** – Some sites require referrals from trusted users.

🔏 **Risk**: If cybercriminals suspect an investigator, they may expose or dox them. Good OPSEC (Operational Security) is critical.

💡 **OSINT Tip**: Never reuse real-world credentials or personal information when creating sock puppet accounts.

4. Law Enforcement & OSINT Success Stories

Despite criminals' efforts to remain anonymous, law enforcement has successfully infiltrated and taken down multiple cybercrime forums.

4.1 Operation Bayonet (2017) – AlphaBay Takedown

📌 **What Happened?**

- FBI & Europol infiltrated AlphaBay, the biggest Dark Web marketplace.
- Admin "DeSnake" used a personal email address in early transactions, exposing his identity.
- Law enforcement seized servers, gaining user data and transaction histories.

🔍 **Key Takeaway**: Even skilled cybercriminals make OSINT mistakes—tracking early online activity is crucial.

4.2 RaidForums & BreachForums Seizures

📌 **What Happened?**

- These forums specialized in data breaches and stolen credentials.
- Law enforcement posed as buyers, gathering intelligence.
- Forum admin "Omnipotent" was arrested in 2022, leading to site shutdowns.

🔍 **Key Takeaway**: Undercover operations remain one of the most effective ways to infiltrate and dismantle cybercrime networks.

5. How OSINT Analysts Can Monitor Cybercrime Forums

To track and investigate cybercrime forums effectively:

✅ Monitor public data leak sites for breached credentials.

✅ Use blockchain analytics to trace cryptocurrency payments.

✅ Analyze vendor reputation scores to identify major players.

✅ Deploy sock puppet accounts for passive intelligence gathering.

✅ Work with law enforcement to share findings on major cybercrime networks.

Conclusion: The Importance of Investigating Cybercrime Forums

Cybercrime forums play a critical role in the underground economy, enabling fraud, hacking, and stolen data trade. However, trust ratings, financial transactions, and user activity leave digital footprints that OSINT analysts and law enforcement can track.

💡 **Key Takeaways:**

✅ Cybercrime forums rely on trust and reputation systems—analyzing them reveals key players.

✅ Cryptocurrency transactions can be traced using OSINT and blockchain forensics tools.

✅ Law enforcement and OSINT professionals successfully infiltrate and take down cybercrime forums by leveraging poor OPSEC practices of criminals.

7.4 Identifying Connections Between Different Marketplaces

The underground cybercrime economy is not confined to a single marketplace or forum. Instead, it is a network of interconnected platforms, where vendors, buyers, and illicit service providers operate across multiple sites. Criminals often spread their operations across different marketplaces to maximize profits, avoid law enforcement detection, and rebuild after a takedown.

This chapter explores:

✅ How different Dark Web marketplaces and forums are interconnected

✅ Techniques for tracking vendors, buyers, and transactions across multiple sites

✅ How cybercriminals migrate after law enforcement crackdowns

✅ OSINT tools and strategies for mapping connections between marketplaces

By analyzing vendor activity, cryptocurrency transactions, and forum communications, investigators can uncover links between various illicit platforms and gain insights into how cybercriminal networks operate.

1. The Interconnected Nature of Dark Web Marketplaces

Dark Web markets operate as a decentralized network rather than isolated entities. Vendors and buyers frequently migrate between different marketplaces due to:

◆ **Market shutdowns & law enforcement takedowns** (e.g., AlphaBay → Empire Market → DarkFox)

◆ **Changes in market rules or escrow policies** (e.g., some sites ban ransomware sales)

◆ **Desire to reach a larger customer base** (e.g., vendors listing on multiple forums)

◆ **Exit scams** (market admins steal user funds, forcing migration)

★ **Example**: After AlphaBay was shut down in 2017, many of its vendors moved to Dream Market, while others transitioned to Empire Market, Wall Street Market, and DarkMarket.

1.1 Types of Marketplaces & Forums

Category	Primary Focus	Examples
General Dark Web Markets	Stolen data, malware, drugs, weapons	AlphaBay, Empire Market, DarkFox
Data Breach Forums	Leaked databases, credentials, corporate breaches	RaidForums, BreachForums, Cracked.io
Hacking & Exploit Markets	Malware, zero-day exploits, RaaS	Exploit.in, RAMP, XSS
Fraud & Carding Forums	Stolen credit cards, PayPal accounts, fake IDs	Joker's Stash, Carding Mafia, Verified
Ransomware & Extortion Groups	Ransomware-as-a-Service (RaaS), corporate extortion	LockBit, ALPHV, REvil

2. How Vendors & Buyers Connect Across Multiple Marketplaces

Many cybercriminals reuse usernames, wallets, and contact methods across different platforms, making it possible to track their movements.

2.1 Username & Alias Reuse

Even on anonymous platforms, many vendors and buyers use the same or similar usernames across multiple sites.

🔍 **Example**: The vendor "MasterCarder" sold stolen credit card data on AlphaBay, Empire Market, and DarkMarket before being arrested in 2021.

💡 OSINT Strategy:

- Search for identical or slightly modified usernames on multiple marketplaces.
- Look for pattern similarities in vendor descriptions, products, and pricing.
- Use tools like Dehashed, IntelX, or manual scraping to find reused identities.

2.2 Cryptocurrency Wallet Reuse

Many criminals reuse Bitcoin or Monero addresses across multiple sites, which can expose their transactions.

🔍 **Example**: The FBI tracked Bitcoin transactions linked to AlphaBay vendors, leading to the seizure of millions of dollars in illicit funds.

💡 OSINT Strategy:

- Use blockchain forensics tools like Chainalysis, CipherTrace, or Elliptic to track reused wallets across multiple sites.
- Cross-check wallet addresses from transaction logs, escrow payments, and forum posts.

2.3 PGP Key & Contact Information Reuse

Some vendors use the same PGP encryption key across different markets, allowing investigators to link accounts.

🔍 **Example**: A vendor selling hacking tools on Exploit.in was linked to a fraud marketplace account due to reusing the same PGP key.

💡 OSINT Strategy:

- Extract PGP keys from vendor profiles and search for matches on other platforms.
- Use OSINT tools like Keybase, MIT PGP Directory, or public key servers to track reused keys.

3. Tracking Market Migrations After a Takedown

When law enforcement seizes a major marketplace, vendors and buyers quickly relocate to new platforms.

📌 **Common Migration Patterns:**

Marketplace Shutdown	Where Vendors Moved
AlphaBay (2017)	Dream Market, Empire Market
Hansa Market (2017)	Wall Street Market, Valhalla Market
Joker's Stash (2021)	Brian's Club, UniCC
RaidForums (2022)	BreachForums, Cracked.io

3.1 Identifying Migration Trends

🔍 **Example**: After RaidForums was taken down in 2022, many users moved to BreachForums, which was then seized by the FBI in 2023.

💡 **OSINT Strategy:**

- Monitor forum discussions and Telegram groups for migration plans.
- Use web crawling tools to track where vendors resurface.
- Analyze onion site redirects—some marketplaces set up temporary landing pages guiding users to the new site.

3.2 Tracking Admins & Moderators

When marketplaces shut down, admins and moderators often reappear on new platforms.

🔍 **Example**: The Empire Market admin resurfaced as an admin on DarkFox Market, using similar language and policies.

💡 **OSINT Strategy:**

- Compare forum moderation styles, language, and security policies.
- Look for wallet addresses used for escrow fees.
- Monitor admin announcements and darknet mirrors.

4. OSINT Tools & Techniques for Mapping Marketplace Connections

Investigators can use a combination of automated tools and manual techniques to map connections between different Dark Web markets.

4.1 Web Scraping & Dark Web Monitoring

- **OnionLink, Ahmia, and DarkSearch** – Search Dark Web marketplaces for vendor aliases.
- **HTTrack, Scrapy** – Automated scraping of vendor profiles.
- **Wayback Machine** – Archive marketplace pages before takedowns.

4.2 Blockchain Analysis & Cryptocurrency Tracking

- **Chainalysis, CipherTrace, Elliptic** – Track Bitcoin, Monero, and other crypto transactions.
- **BitcoinAbuse.com** – Check reported scam wallets.

4.3 Forum & Marketplace Profiling

- **Dehashed, HavelBeenPwned, IntelX** – Find reused usernames, emails, or passwords.
- **Keybase, MIT PGP Lookup** – Track reused PGP keys.
- **Maltego, SpiderFoot** – Map connections between vendors, buyers, and marketplaces.

Conclusion: Why Mapping Marketplace Connections is Crucial

Cybercriminals rely on an interconnected network of Dark Web forums and markets, allowing them to evade law enforcement and continue operations even after major takedowns. By identifying links between different platforms, OSINT analysts and cybersecurity professionals can:

✅ Track vendor migrations after law enforcement operations.

✅ Identify recurring usernames, cryptocurrency wallets, and PGP keys.

✅ Disrupt cybercriminal activity by mapping connections and exposing vulnerabilities.

7.5 How Marketplaces Handle Disputes & Escrow Services

Dark Web marketplaces rely on trust and reputation systems to facilitate illicit transactions, but trust is fragile in an anonymous, lawless environment. Buyers and sellers need mechanisms to resolve disputes, ensure payment security, and prevent scams. This is where escrow services and dispute resolution processes play a critical role.

This chapter explores:

✅ How escrow services work in Dark Web marketplaces

✅ Common dispute resolution mechanisms between buyers and vendors

✅ How cybercriminals exploit escrow systems

✅ OSINT techniques to investigate escrow transactions and dispute patterns

Understanding these processes helps law enforcement, cybersecurity professionals, and OSINT analysts track financial transactions, identify marketplace vulnerabilities, and uncover cybercriminal networks.

1. How Escrow Services Work in Dark Web Marketplaces

Escrow services are used to hold funds securely until a transaction is completed. They prevent fraud by ensuring that:

- The buyer doesn't lose money to an untrustworthy vendor.
- The vendor gets paid once the buyer confirms delivery.
- The marketplace admin acts as a neutral party in case of disputes.

1.1 The Typical Escrow Process

1️⃣ **Buyer places an order** – Sends funds (usually Bitcoin or Monero) to the marketplace's escrow system.

2️⃣ **Vendor ships/delivers goods** – This could be digital (stolen data, malware) or physical (drugs, weapons).

3️⃣ **Buyer confirms receipt** – If satisfied, the escrow releases payment to the vendor.

4️⃣ **Automatic release if no dispute** – If the buyer doesn't confirm, funds are released after a set time.

📌 **Example**: On Empire Market, the escrow automatically released payments after 7 days unless a dispute was filed.

💡 **OSINT Tip**: Tracking escrow release times can provide insights into marketplace policies and user behavior.

2. Types of Escrow Systems on Dark Web Marketplaces

Not all marketplaces use the same escrow system. Some have automated processes, while others involve manual admin intervention.

Escrow Type	How It Works	Pros & Cons	Examples
Traditional Escrow	Marketplace holds funds until buyer confirms	☑ Secure, reduces fraud ⚠ Slow	AlphaBay, DarkMarket
Multi-Signature Escrow	Requires approval from buyer, seller & admin	☑ More security ⚠ Requires technical knowledge	White House Market
FE (Finalizing Early)	Vendor receives payment immediately	☑ Faster ⚠ High risk of scams	High-trust vendors on Empire Market
Wallet-less Escrow	Uses an external wallet instead of marketplace funds	☑ Reduces risk of exit scams ⚠ Requires off-market transactions	AlphaBay 2.0 (revived in 2021)

📌 **Example**: White House Market (before shutting down in 2021) used multi-signature escrow to increase transaction security.

💡 **OSINT Tip**: Some vendors exploit escrow policies by demanding FE (Finalizing Early), tricking buyers into direct payments.

3. Common Disputes in Dark Web Marketplaces

Even among criminals, scams and disputes happen frequently. Some marketplaces have moderators or dispute resolution panels to handle conflicts.

3.1 Common Reasons for Disputes

Dispute Type	Description	Who Usually Wins?
Non-Delivery Scam	Vendor takes money but never delivers goods	Buyer (if evidence is provided)
Defective Goods	Malware doesn't work, stolen data is fake	Mixed, depends on marketplace rules
Law Enforcement Sting	Buyer claims they were scammed by undercover LE	Vendor (LE doesn't get refunds)
Fake Dispute Scam	Vendor files a dispute against a legitimate buyer	Vendor (if they have strong rep)
Exit Scam by Marketplace	Marketplace shuts down and steals all escrow funds	Nobody wins

📌 **Example**: In 2019, Wall Street Market exit scammed its users, stealing over $14 million from escrow accounts.

💡 **OSINT Tip:** Monitoring escrow disputes can reveal marketplace vulnerabilities and scam patterns.

4. How Marketplaces Handle Disputes

4.1 Admin Mediation

Marketplace administrators act as judges in disputes, reviewing evidence from buyers and sellers.

🚩 **Problems with Admin Mediation:**

- Corrupt admins side with high-volume vendors.
- Some admins sell dispute information to competitors.
- If the marketplace is an undercover law enforcement operation, all dispute records become evidence.

📌 **Example**: In 2017, Hansa Market was secretly controlled by Dutch police before its takedown.

💡 **OSINT Tip**: Tracking dispute resolutions can help determine if a marketplace is under law enforcement control.

4.2 Marketplace Arbitration Panels

Some larger markets (like AlphaBay) had arbitration panels where senior users helped resolve disputes.

☐ **Problems with Arbitration Panels:**

- Can be biased towards high-reputation vendors.
- Some members sell inside information.
- Law enforcement infiltrators can gain moderator positions.

📌 **Example**: Dream Market's arbitration system was notorious for favoring veteran vendors over new buyers.

5. OSINT & Law Enforcement Investigations into Escrow Systems

Escrow transactions create a trail of cryptocurrency payments, usernames, and dispute logs, which OSINT analysts can track.

5.1 Tracking Cryptocurrency Transactions in Escrow

Bitcoin and Monero transactions in escrow can be analyzed using blockchain forensics.

🔍 **Example**: The FBI tracked Bitcoin escrow transactions on AlphaBay, leading to the arrest of its admin.

💡 **OSINT Tools for Crypto Tracking:**

- **Chainalysis** – Blockchain forensic platform.
- **CipherTrace** – Tracks illicit crypto transactions.
- **Elliptic** – Identifies wallets linked to Dark Web escrow.

5.2 Identifying Suspicious Dispute Patterns

Investigators can track vendors with frequent disputes to detect potential scams.

💡 **OSINT Strategy:**

- Scrape dispute resolution logs (some forums leak case details).
- Analyze refund rates—high refund rates may indicate a scam vendor.

- Compare vendor disputes across multiple marketplaces (some criminals use the same scam tactics on different sites).

6. How Criminals Exploit Escrow & Dispute Systems

Cybercriminals manipulate escrow and disputes to commit fraud, extortion, and deception.

6.1 Fake Buyer Scams

◆ Vendor creates fake buyer accounts to generate positive dispute outcomes.
◆ Gains high trust ratings, then runs an exit scam.

6.2 Forced Finalization (FE Scams)

◆ Vendor demands upfront payment to bypass escrow.
◆ Buyer pays directly, then vendor disappears.

6.3 Marketplace Exit Scams

◆ Marketplaces pretend to have a "technical issue", locking all escrow funds.
◆ Admins disappear with millions in cryptocurrency.

📌 **Example**: Empire Market exit scammed its users in 2020, stealing $30 million in Bitcoin.

💡 **OSINT Tip**: Sudden changes in escrow policies can indicate an impending exit scam.

Conclusion: The Role of Escrow in OSINT & Cyber Investigations

Escrow systems play a critical role in Dark Web marketplaces, influencing how transactions are conducted, disputes are resolved, and scams unfold. Understanding these mechanisms helps investigators:

✅ Track cryptocurrency transactions tied to illegal activities.

✅ Identify scam vendors based on dispute patterns.

✅ Predict potential exit scams by monitoring escrow changes.

✅ Infiltrate and disrupt cybercriminal networks using dispute records.

7.6 Case Study: Tracking an Illegal Marketplace's Operators

Dark Web marketplaces are designed for anonymity, but no system is completely untraceable. Law enforcement agencies and OSINT analysts have successfully tracked, identified, and arrested marketplace operators using a mix of cryptocurrency tracing, metadata analysis, and human error exploitation.

In this case study, we will analyze how investigators tracked down and arrested the operators of a major illegal Dark Web marketplace, breaking down the techniques used and the key mistakes that led to their downfall.

1. The Target: A Major Dark Web Marketplace

In mid-2020, "DarkBay" (a fictional yet realistic name for this case study) emerged as a major Dark Web marketplace specializing in:

- Stolen financial data (credit cards, PayPal accounts)
- Hacked corporate databases
- Illegal drugs & weapons

Fraudulent identity documents

The platform operated similarly to AlphaBay, using:

✅ A Tor-based marketplace to anonymize access

✅ Escrow services for buyer-vendor transactions

✅ Cryptocurrency-only payments (primarily Bitcoin & Monero)

✅ An active forum for cybercriminals to discuss trade, tactics, and security

Despite its advanced security measures, law enforcement agencies and OSINT analysts began tracking its operators.

2. Identifying Marketplace Operators: The Investigation Begins

Investigators used a combination of OSINT, blockchain forensics, and operational security (OpSec) failures to track the individuals behind DarkBay.

2.1 Blockchain Analysis: Following the Money

Since DarkBay processed all transactions in Bitcoin and Monero, agencies began by analyzing the blockchain to track marketplace payments.

🔍 Key Findings:

- Bitcoin payments from DarkBay were funneled through known mixing services.
- Some funds were transferred to crypto exchanges that required KYC verification.
- A withdrawal from one exchange was linked to a real-world bank account.

📌 **Breakthrough**: A transaction from DarkBay's escrow wallet was traced to a personal wallet belonging to one of the suspected admins.

💡 **Tools Used**: Chainalysis, CipherTrace, Elliptic

2.2 Server Misconfiguration: The Hidden IP Leak

While DarkBay was hosted on the Tor network, investigators discovered that:

- The marketplace's backend server mistakenly exposed a real-world IP address for a fraction of a second during a maintenance update.
- Using network traffic analysis, OSINT analysts identified a hosting provider in Eastern Europe.
- Subpoenas to the hosting provider revealed that the server had been accessed from a residential IP address in Germany.

📌 **Breakthrough**: A single misconfigured connection allowed investigators to pinpoint the real-world location of one of the operators.

💡 **Tools Used**: Shodan, Censys, Wireshark

2.3 Username & Alias Reuse: The Human Mistake

DarkBay's main administrator, known as "ShadowAdmin", used:

- A PGP key to communicate with vendors

- A Bitcoin wallet for escrow transactions
- A hidden identity on cybercrime forums

Investigators searched for the same PGP key and alias across multiple platforms and found that:

- The PGP key had been used in older forum posts on a hacking site from 2015.
- An archived post from that forum linked "ShadowAdmin" to an email address.
- The email was then used to find an associated social media profile.

📌 **Breakthrough**: Investigators linked the marketplace admin to a real-world identity through OSINT and old forum data.

💡 **Tools Used**: Dehashed, IntelX, HaveIBeenPwned, Maltego

3. The Takedown: Coordinated Law Enforcement Action

After collecting sufficient intelligence, authorities:

- Coordinated raids in three countries (Germany, Netherlands, and Ukraine).
- Seized DarkBay's servers and cryptocurrency funds.
- Arrested three key marketplace operators.

📌 **Final Breakthrough**: During the arrest, one admin's laptop was open and logged into the marketplace's backend, giving law enforcement full access to user and vendor data.

4. Lessons Learned: How Investigators Track Dark Web Market Operators

🔎 **Common Mistakes by Marketplace Admins:**

Mistake	How It Led to Their Capture
Reusing usernames or PGP keys	Linked DarkBay admin to older forum posts.
Connecting to the server from a real IP	Exposed location due to a misconfiguration.
Using traceable cryptocurrency services	Bitcoin withdrawals linked to personal bank accounts.
Failing to use proper OpSec in personal life	Social media connections helped confirm identities.
Keeping a laptop unlocked at the time of arrest	Gave authorities access to marketplace operations.

💡 **OSINT Tip**: Searching for PGP key reuse, cryptocurrency wallet movements, and server metadata can expose hidden marketplace operators.

Conclusion: The Role of OSINT & Crypto Analysis in Dark Web Investigations

The takedown of DarkBay highlights the power of OSINT, blockchain forensics, and cyber threat intelligence in uncovering Dark Web marketplaces. By understanding these investigative methods, analysts can:

✅ Track crypto transactions and escrow systems to identify key players.

✅ Use PGP key analysis and alias tracking to uncover hidden identities.

✅ Analyze infrastructure weaknesses to find real-world IP leaks.

✅ Monitor forum activity and social media connections for additional clues.

8. Cryptocurrency Tracking in the Dark Web

In this chapter, we will explore the role of cryptocurrency in dark web transactions, particularly in the context of email breaches, data leaks, and cybercrime. Due to the anonymity cryptocurrencies provide, they have become the preferred method of payment for illicit activities conducted on dark web marketplaces. We will examine how cryptocurrencies like Bitcoin, Monero, and others are used to buy stolen data, including email addresses and credentials, and discuss the challenges investigators face when trying to trace these digital currencies. By learning how to track cryptocurrency transactions, investigators can uncover financial trails, link cybercriminals to specific breaches, and disrupt illegal operations. This chapter will provide essential techniques and tools for following the money behind cybercrime on the dark web, helping to connect cryptocurrency transactions to real-world criminal activities and furthering the investigation into email leaks and breaches.

8.1 How Cryptocurrencies Enable Anonymity in Cybercrime

Cryptocurrencies have revolutionized digital finance, but they have also become a key enabler for cybercrime. Unlike traditional banking systems, which require identity verification and centralized oversight, cryptocurrencies offer pseudonymity, decentralization, and cross-border transactions—features that criminals exploit for illicit activities.

This chapter explores:

✓ How cryptocurrencies provide anonymity

✓ Which cryptocurrencies are most used in cybercrime

✓ Common money laundering techniques used on the Dark Web

✓ How OSINT and blockchain forensics help track illicit transactions

1. Why Cryptocurrencies Are Popular in Cybercrime

Cybercriminals favor cryptocurrencies because they:

◆ Bypass traditional financial regulations (no need for banks or identity verification)

◆ Offer pseudonymity (transactions are recorded on a public ledger, but real identities are hidden)

◆ Enable rapid cross-border transfers (no oversight from governments or financial institutions)

◆ Facilitate escrow transactions (used in Dark Web marketplaces for safe trades)

◆ Are convertible to fiat currency (via crypto exchanges and peer-to-peer transactions)

📌 **Example**: Ransomware gangs demand Bitcoin or Monero payments because they can be received and laundered without detection.

📍 **OSINT Tip**: Tracking wallet addresses across multiple transactions can help de-anonymize criminals.

2. The Most Common Cryptocurrencies Used in Cybercrime

Not all cryptocurrencies offer the same level of anonymity. Some are easier to track than others.

Cryptocurrency	Why Cybercriminals Use It	Anonymity Level
Bitcoin (BTC)	Most accepted, widely used in Dark Web markets	✖ Low (all transactions are publicly recorded)
Monero (XMR)	Privacy-focused, hides sender/receiver details	✅ ✅ ✅ High
Ethereum (ETH)	Smart contracts enable automated cybercrime transactions	✖ Low
Zcash (ZEC)	Optional privacy features for untraceable payments	✅ ✅ Medium
Litecoin (LTC)	Fast transactions, used in scams and fraud	✖ Low
Tether (USDT)	Stable value, used for laundering money through DeFi	✖ Low

📌 **Example**: AlphaBay 2.0 (revived in 2021) dropped Bitcoin and only accepted Monero (XMR) due to its privacy features.

📍 **OSINT Tip**: Bitcoin remains traceable, but Monero transactions require different forensic techniques, such as timing analysis and wallet clustering.

3. How Cryptocurrencies Provide Anonymity

Cybercriminals use various techniques to obfuscate transactions and hide their identities.

3.1 Cryptocurrency Mixing Services (Tumblers)

Mixing services break the link between the sender and receiver by combining multiple transactions.

- A user sends Bitcoin to a mixer
- The mixer splits, shuffles, and redistributes coins to multiple wallets
- The user receives "cleaned" coins that are harder to trace

📌 **Example**: BestMixer.io was one of the largest Bitcoin mixers before it was shut down by Europol in 2019.

💡 **OSINT Tip**: Look for sudden fragmentation of funds into smaller amounts across multiple wallets—this is a sign of mixing.

3.2 Privacy Coins (Monero & Zcash)

Privacy coins like Monero (XMR) and Zcash (ZEC) make transactions untraceable by:

- Hiding sender and receiver addresses
- Obscuring transaction amounts
- Using cryptographic techniques (RingCT, zk-SNARKs)

📌 **Example**: The DarkSide ransomware gang demanded Monero payments because Bitcoin was too easily traceable.

💡 **OSINT Tip**: While Monero transactions are hidden, authorities track Monero usage by monitoring exchange points (where XMR is converted to BTC or fiat).

3.3 Chain Hopping

Cybercriminals move funds across multiple blockchains to break the tracking chain.

- Convert Bitcoin → Ethereum → Monero → Litecoin
- Use Decentralized Exchanges (DEXs) to swap tokens anonymously

◆ Withdraw funds in small amounts to avoid detection

✦ **Example**: The Lazarus Group (North Korean hackers) used chain hopping to launder stolen crypto from hacks.

💡 **OSINT Tip**: Monitor DEX activity for large-scale token swaps involving privacy coins.

3.4 Peer-to-Peer (P2P) Exchanges & Crypto ATMs

P2P marketplaces allow criminals to buy/sell cryptocurrency without identity verification.

◆ Paxful, LocalBitcoins, and Binance P2P allow anonymous trades
◆ Crypto ATMs let criminals withdraw cash without linking to a bank account

✦ **Example**: A cybercriminal in Canada used Bitcoin ATMs to withdraw ransomware payments before being arrested.

💡 **OSINT Tip**: Watch for multiple small transactions moving into P2P platforms—this often indicates money laundering.

4. How Cybercriminals Launder Stolen Crypto Funds

Once cybercriminals obtain illicit cryptocurrency, they need to launder it before cashing out.

4.1 Using Stolen or Fake IDs on Exchanges

◆ Criminals buy KYC-verified accounts from hackers to bypass exchange security.
◆ Some use fake documents to create new accounts.

✦ **Example**: In 2020, hackers sold verified Binance and Coinbase accounts on the Dark Web for $150 each.

💡 **OSINT Tip**: Monitor KYC account marketplaces on Dark Web forums to track criminals using fake identities.

4.2 Smurfing & Layering

◆ Criminals send small transactions across multiple wallets to avoid detection.

◆ Use Decentralized Finance (DeFi) protocols to shuffle funds.

📌 **Example**: The Ronin Network hackers laundered $540M through Tornado Cash, a DeFi privacy tool.

💡 **OSINT Tip**: Look for sudden patterns of small transactions moving through different DeFi services.

4.3 Converting to Gift Cards or Real Assets

◆ Buy Amazon, iTunes, or Google Play gift cards with crypto.
◆ Convert crypto into luxury items (cars, watches, NFTs).

📌 **Example**: A cybercriminal group used Bitcoin to buy Rolex watches, then resold them for cash.

💡 **OSINT Tip**: Track blockchain transactions leading to gift card resellers or high-value purchases.

5. OSINT & Law Enforcement: Tracking Cryptocurrency in Cybercrime

Despite efforts to remain anonymous, cybercriminals make mistakes that OSINT analysts and law enforcement exploit.

5.1 Tracking Bitcoin Transactions

Since Bitcoin transactions are recorded on a public ledger, investigators can:

✓ Identify wallet clusters to group addresses linked to the same user

✓ Track deposits & withdrawals on exchanges to find real identities

✓ Follow ransomware payments to cash-out points

📌 **Example**: The FBI tracked the Colonial Pipeline ransom payment by following Bitcoin transactions.

💡 **OSINT Tip**: Use blockchain explorers like Blockchain.com or BTCscan to analyze wallet movements.

5.2 Following Fiat Conversions

Cryptocurrency must eventually be converted to fiat (USD, EUR, etc.), which creates a vulnerability.

🔍 **Investigators look for:**

- Transfers to crypto exchanges that require KYC
- Connections to bank accounts or PayPal transactions
- Patterns of cash withdrawals from crypto ATMs

📌 **Example**: A darknet vendor was caught when he converted Bitcoin to USD via PayPal.

💡 **OSINT Tip**: Monitor known laundering points where criminals convert crypto to cash.

Conclusion: The Future of Crypto Crime & OSINT Investigations

Cryptocurrencies continue to evolve, and so do the methods criminals use to hide their activities. However, no system is perfect, and OSINT analysts can:

✓ Track Bitcoin transactions using blockchain forensics

✓ Identify money laundering tactics used on the Dark Web

✓ Monitor crypto-to-fiat conversion points for potential real-world identities

8.2 Using Blockchain Explorers to Track Bitcoin Transactions

Bitcoin transactions are pseudonymous, not anonymous—meaning that while identities are not directly linked to wallet addresses, all transactions are permanently recorded on the Bitcoin blockchain. By using blockchain explorers, OSINT analysts and law enforcement can trace Bitcoin movements, identify wallet clusters, and track funds linked to illicit activities.

This chapter covers:

✓ What blockchain explorers are and how they work

✅ How to track Bitcoin transactions step-by-step

✅ Common techniques criminals use to hide transactions

✅ How OSINT analysts de-anonymize Bitcoin wallets

1. What Are Blockchain Explorers?

A blockchain explorer is a search engine for blockchain transactions. It allows users to:

- View transaction histories for any Bitcoin address
- Track fund movements from one wallet to another
- Identify transaction timestamps and amounts
- Analyze inputs and outputs to find wallet connections

1.1 Popular Blockchain Explorers for Bitcoin

Blockchain Explorer	Website	Features
Blockchain.com	blockchain.com/explorer	Simple UI, wallet & transaction tracking
Blockchair	blockchair.com	Advanced search, filtering by text
BTCScan	btcscan.org	Analyzes wallet activity
OXT.me	oxt.me	Graph-based visualization of transactions
Bitquery	bitquery.io	API access for blockchain data

📌 **Example**: If you suspect a Bitcoin address is linked to a Dark Web marketplace, you can enter it into a blockchain explorer to view its full transaction history.

💡 **OSINT Tip**: If an address has multiple small incoming transactions followed by a large outgoing one, it may belong to a money launderer or mixer service.

2. Step-by-Step: Tracking a Bitcoin Transaction

Let's say an investigator is tracking 1BTC sent from a ransomware payment to an unknown wallet.

Step 1: Identify the Transaction Hash

A transaction hash (TXID) is a unique identifier for a Bitcoin transaction.

How to find it:

- The victim provides the Bitcoin address they sent funds to.
- Enter this address into a blockchain explorer.
- Locate the transaction hash for the payment.

📌 **Example**: TXID d3f0a2b1c4... links to a $50,000 ransomware payment.

Step 2: Analyze Inputs & Outputs

Bitcoin transactions have inputs (where funds come from) and outputs (where funds are sent).

What to look for:

- **Multiple inputs** → Suggests funds were combined from different sources (e.g., a hacker collecting payments).
- **Multiple outputs** → One may be the intended recipient, while the other could be change sent back to the sender.

📌 **Example**: If a hacker receives funds and immediately sends them to a mixing service, this is a red flag.

💡 **OSINT Tip**: Compare the input addresses to known ransomware or scam wallets using sites like BitcoinAbuse.

Step 3: Follow the Money Trail

Key techniques:

- Look for large transactions sent to exchanges (criminals cashing out).
- Check if funds were split into multiple smaller transactions (sign of laundering).
- Monitor if funds moved to privacy-focused coins like Monero (often done via decentralized exchanges).

📌 **Example**: A Dark Web vendor receives Bitcoin and converts it to Monero using a DEX, making further tracking difficult.

💡 **OSINT Tip**: If funds end up at a known exchange, subpoena requests can identify the account owner.

3. How Criminals Obfuscate Bitcoin Transactions

Cybercriminals use various techniques to break the traceability of Bitcoin transactions:

3.1 Bitcoin Mixing Services (Tumblers)

Mixers shuffle Bitcoin from multiple users, making transactions harder to trace.

- Criminals send BTC to a mixer
- The mixer sends "clean" BTC back from different wallets
- This breaks the connection between sender and receiver

📌 **Example**: ChipMixer, BestMixer (both shut down by law enforcement).

💡 **OSINT Tip**: Look for multiple small transactions merging into one large payout—this can indicate a mixer was used.

3.2 Chain Hopping

Criminals convert Bitcoin into other cryptocurrencies to disrupt tracking.

- BTC → Monero (XMR) → Ethereum (ETH) → USDT → Cash

📌 **Example**: North Korea's Lazarus Group used Chain Hopping to launder funds from crypto exchange hacks.

💡 **OSINT Tip**: Watch for sudden BTC withdrawals from exchanges into privacy coins.

3.3 Peel Chains

Criminals move Bitcoin through a series of small transactions to disguise the final destination.

📌 **Example**: A hacker sends 0.01 BTC to 100 different wallets before withdrawing to a crypto exchange.

💡 **OSINT Tip**: Identify patterns of repeated small transactions leading to a single exit point.

4. OSINT Techniques for De-Anonymizing Bitcoin Transactions

Despite obfuscation techniques, OSINT analysts can link Bitcoin transactions to real identities.

4.1 Identifying Exchange Deposit Points

🔍 Criminals must eventually convert Bitcoin to cash.

- Track funds entering regulated exchanges (Binance, Coinbase, Kraken).
- Subpoena the exchange to obtain KYC details of the user.

📌 **Example**: The FBI tracked Bitcoin ransom payments to a Coinbase wallet registered to a suspect's real identity.

💡 **OSINT Tip**: Use Whale Alert to monitor large transactions into exchanges.

4.2 Clustering Wallets to Find Hidden Connections

Even if criminals use multiple wallets, advanced blockchain analytics can link them together.

🔍 **How?**

- If two wallets regularly transact with the same address, they may belong to the same person.
- If a wallet sends small amounts to itself repeatedly, it could be consolidating funds.

📌 **Example**: Chainalysis helped law enforcement connect multiple Bitcoin wallets to a single ransomware operator.

💡 **OSINT Tip**: Use OXT.me to analyze wallet clusters.

4.3 Tracking Bitcoin to Real-World Assets

🔍 Criminals spend Bitcoin on real-world items that investigators can track.

- Luxury goods (cars, watches, real estate) purchased with Bitcoin
- Gift cards (Amazon, iTunes) resold for cash
- Crypto ATMs used to withdraw Bitcoin anonymously

📌 **Example**: A drug trafficker used Bitcoin to buy a Lamborghini, which led to his arrest.

💡 **OSINT Tip**: Monitor crypto-to-real-world transactions to find a suspect's location.

Conclusion: Using OSINT & Blockchain Forensics to Track Bitcoin Crime

While criminals use Bitcoin for its perceived anonymity, OSINT and forensic techniques make it possible to track, trace, and de-anonymize illicit transactions.

✅ Blockchain explorers reveal transaction histories and wallet movements

✅ Analyzing inputs/outputs can identify laundering techniques

✅ Tracking exchange deposits helps link wallets to real identities

✅ Clustering analysis connects multiple wallets to the same criminal group

8.3 Identifying Money Laundering Techniques on the Dark Web

The Dark Web serves as a hub for cybercriminals to launder illicit funds obtained from ransomware, fraud, drug trafficking, and data breaches. While Bitcoin and other cryptocurrencies offer a level of anonymity, they are not completely untraceable. Criminals use advanced laundering techniques to break the connection between illicit funds and their real-world identities.

This chapter will cover:

✅ How cybercriminals launder money on the Dark Web

✅ The role of mixing services, privacy coins, and peer-to-peer (P2P) trading

✅ OSINT techniques for tracking and de-anonymizing illicit transactions

✅ Real-world cases of Dark Web money laundering

1. The Role of Cryptocurrencies in Money Laundering

Cryptocurrencies are the preferred method of payment for cybercriminals on the Dark Web because they offer:

◆ **Pseudonymity** – Transactions are recorded on the blockchain, but wallets are not directly linked to real identities.

◆ **Global access** – No bank oversight or government restrictions.

◆ **Decentralization** – No central authority controlling transactions.

However, blockchain forensics tools and OSINT techniques can trace transactions and expose laundering schemes.

📌 **Example**: The FBI tracked ransomware payments in Bitcoin, leading to the seizure of millions of dollars from cybercriminals.

2. Common Money Laundering Techniques on the Dark Web

Cybercriminals use several techniques to obscure the origins of stolen or illicit funds.

2.1 Bitcoin Mixing Services (Tumblers)

A Bitcoin mixer (or tumbler) is a service that breaks the link between sender and receiver by mixing coins from multiple users.

🔍 **How it works:**

- Criminals send BTC to a mixer.
- The mixer shuffles the Bitcoin with other users' funds.
- The service returns "clean" BTC to different wallets.

📌 **Example**: BestMixer.io was one of the largest Dark Web tumblers before it was seized by Europol.

💡 **OSINT Tip:**

- Look for unusual transaction patterns, such as multiple small deposits followed by a single large withdrawal.
- Check blockchain explorers for transactions labeled as "mixer-related."

2.2 Chain Hopping (Cross-Blockchain Laundering)

Chain hopping (or cross-chain laundering) involves converting one cryptocurrency into another to break the tracking trail.

🔍 How it works:

- Criminals exchange Bitcoin for privacy coins like Monero (XMR) or Zcash (ZEC).
- They convert the Monero back to Bitcoin or Ethereum.
- The "cleaned" funds are moved to a legitimate crypto exchange and withdrawn as fiat.

📌 **Example**: The Lazarus Group (North Korean hackers) used chain hopping to launder funds stolen from crypto exchanges.

💡 OSINT Tip:

- Monitor transactions involving Monero (XMR) or privacy coins—these are red flags.
- Use crypto forensic tools like Chainalysis and CipherTrace to track cross-chain movements.

2.3 Peer-to-Peer (P2P) Exchanges & OTC Desks

P2P platforms allow criminals to trade crypto for cash or other assets without KYC (Know Your Customer) checks.

🔍 How it works:

- Criminals sell Bitcoin to a P2P buyer in exchange for cash, gift cards, or prepaid debit cards.
- They use over-the-counter (OTC) brokers who specialize in high-volume, no-ID transactions.
- The cash is then funneled into the traditional financial system.

📌 **Example**: The Hydra Marketplace (shut down by law enforcement) had an OTC service for laundering crypto.

💡 **OSINT Tip:**

- Investigate high-volume traders on P2P platforms like LocalBitcoins and Paxful.
- Search for Telegram and WhatsApp groups offering no-KYC crypto exchanges.

2.4 Gambling & Online Casinos

Criminals use crypto casinos to launder money by gambling illicit funds and withdrawing clean crypto.

🔍 **How it works:**

- Deposit dirty Bitcoin into an online casino.
- Place low-risk bets (or no bets at all).
- Withdraw the "winnings" into a new crypto wallet, making the funds appear legitimate.

📌 **Example**: Stake.com and Roobet are popular crypto casinos that have been exploited for money laundering.

💡 **OSINT Tip:**

- Check casino deposit and withdrawal patterns for irregular activity.
- Look for transactions moving between multiple casinos in short time frames.

2.5 NFT & Digital Art Laundering

Cybercriminals use Non-Fungible Tokens (NFTs) to move illicit funds under the guise of digital art transactions.

🔍 **How it works:**

- Criminals create and list an NFT.
- They "sell" the NFT to themselves using illicit crypto.
- The funds appear to be from a legitimate art sale.

📌 **Example**: In 2022, a report found that over $1 billion in illicit crypto was funneled through NFT marketplaces.

💡 **OSINT Tip:**

- Investigate suspicious NFT sales with no real artistic value.
- Check buyer-seller wallets for links to Dark Web markets.

3. OSINT Techniques to Identify Crypto Money Laundering

Despite criminals' attempts to hide their tracks, OSINT analysts can still uncover laundering schemes.

3.1 Using Blockchain Explorers

◈ Track suspicious wallets using tools like:

- Blockchain.com Explorer
- OXT.me (visual analysis)
- Bitquery (API tracking)

📌 **Example**: If a wallet receives funds from multiple ransomware victims, it is likely involved in laundering.

3.2 Analyzing Mixing Services

◈ Use whale alert tools to monitor large Bitcoin withdrawals into known mixers.

Websites like BitcoinWhosWho track flagged wallets.

📌 **Example**: If a wallet sends BTC to a mixer right after a ransom payment, it is likely laundering the funds.

3.3 Identifying High-Risk Crypto Exchanges

◈ Check if a suspect wallet transacts with high-risk exchanges like:

- Bitzlato (Russian laundering hub)
- BTC-e (linked to cybercrime)

📌 **Example**: If a wallet sends funds to Bitzlato, it may be involved in laundering operations.

3.4 Investigating P2P Traders

♦ Use Telegram, Reddit, and forums to find unregulated crypto traders offering no-KYC transactions.

Look for advertisements like "Cash for Bitcoin – No ID Required".

📌 **Example**: A trader offering $10,000+ Bitcoin cashouts with no verification is likely involved in laundering.

4. Case Study: How Law Enforcement Cracked a Dark Web Money Laundering Ring

📌 **Operation: The AlphaBay Takedown (2017)**

🔍 **What Happened?**

- AlphaBay, a major Dark Web marketplace, laundered over $1 billion in Bitcoin.
- Criminals used mixers, P2P trading, and Monero chain-hopping.
- The FBI tracked Bitcoin deposits into major exchanges.

🔍 **Outcome:**

- Authorities seized servers and traced transactions to real-world bank accounts.
- The marketplace admin was arrested, leading to further arrests in connected laundering networks.

💡 **OSINT Takeaway**: Even with laundering techniques, crypto transactions can still be traced with the right tools and investigative methods.

While the Dark Web provides a haven for money laundering, OSINT and blockchain forensics make it possible to trace illicit transactions and uncover laundering networks.

✅ Mixers, chain hopping, and P2P trading are key laundering methods

✅ OSINT tools can track suspicious wallets and transactions

✅ Following the money trail can lead to real-world arrests

8.4 Tracing Crypto Transactions Through Mixing Services

Cryptocurrency mixing services, also known as tumblers, are commonly used by cybercriminals to launder illicit funds and obscure transaction trails. These services mix tainted funds with clean ones, making it difficult to track the original source. However, with the right OSINT techniques and blockchain forensic tools, investigators can still uncover suspicious activity and trace transactions even after they have been "cleaned."

In this chapter, we will cover:

✅ How crypto mixing services work

✅ The different types of tumblers and their methods

✅ Tools and techniques for tracking mixed transactions

✅ Real-world case studies of authorities breaking mixing service anonymity

1. What Are Crypto Mixing Services?

Cryptocurrency transactions are recorded on a public blockchain, meaning that all transfers are visible. To break this transparency, criminals use mixing services that "wash" their funds before moving them to legitimate exchanges or wallets.

🔍 **How Mixing Services Work:**

- A user sends illicit crypto (Bitcoin, Ethereum, etc.) to a mixing service.
- The service splits and shuffles the funds across multiple wallets.
- The mixed funds are sent to new addresses, making it hard to link them to the original source.
- The user receives "clean" crypto, which appears untraceable.

💡 **Legitimate Use Case**: Some privacy-conscious users use mixing services to protect their financial information. However, the majority of mixing activity is linked to money laundering and cybercrime.

📌 **Example**: The Blender.io mixer was used by the Lazarus Group (North Korean hackers) to launder stolen cryptocurrency from ransomware attacks.

2. Types of Crypto Mixing Services

There are several types of mixers, each using different techniques to anonymize transactions.

2.1 Centralized Mixers

These are third-party services that take a fee (1-5%) in exchange for mixing crypto.

◆ **Examples:**

- BestMixer.io (shut down by Europol in 2019)
- Helix (seized by the FBI in 2021)

🔍 **Weakness**: If law enforcement seizes a centralized mixer, they can obtain logs of past transactions.

2.2 Decentralized Mixers (CoinJoin & CoinSwap)

Decentralized mixing protocols allow multiple users to combine their transactions, making tracking difficult.

◆ **CoinJoin** – Merges multiple transactions into a single one (used by wallets like Wasabi Wallet).
◆ **CoinSwap** – Allows users to swap coins across different blockchains to obfuscate origins.

📌 **Example**: The FBI traced a ransomware payment laundered through Wasabi Wallet's CoinJoin service by analyzing the blockchain.

2.3 Privacy Coin Mixers

Some cryptocurrencies have built-in mixing features, making tracking even harder.

◆ **Monero (XMR)** – Uses Ring Signatures to mix transactions.
◆ **Zcash (ZEC)** – Uses zk-SNARKs encryption to hide transaction details.

📌 **Example**: Dark Web markets prefer Monero over Bitcoin because it is nearly impossible to track.

3. Techniques for Tracing Mixed Crypto Transactions

Despite the anonymization techniques used by mixers, investigators can still uncover money laundering patterns.

3.1 Analyzing Transaction Clustering

◆ Mixers split large transactions into smaller amounts before sending them to new wallets.
◆ Blockchain analysis tools can detect unusual patterns, such as:

- Multiple deposits into a mixer from the same wallet
- Sudden distribution of funds to many new addresses

💡 **OSINT Tool:**

Chainalysis Reactor – Identifies clustering patterns and links suspicious transactions.

3.2 Identifying Known Mixer Wallets

◆ Many mixing services re-use the same Bitcoin addresses to handle multiple clients.
◆ Investigators can track wallets linked to past criminal activity and monitor their transactions.

💡 **OSINT Tool:**

BitcoinWhosWho – Identifies known Bitcoin addresses associated with mixers.

📌 **Example**: The Hydra Market (Dark Web) had wallets that were repeatedly linked to Bitcoin mixers.

3.3 Tracing Pre- and Post-Mix Transactions

◆ Even if a wallet uses a mixer, investigators can still track:

- Deposits into the mixing service
- Withdrawals from the mixer into clean wallets

◆ Some laundering operations send funds to crypto exchanges after mixing, which can be flagged.

💡 **OSINT Tool:**

Elliptic Forensics – Identifies mixing deposits and tracks post-mixer wallet activity.

📌 **Example**: In 2022, Interpol traced a Dark Web drug cartel's payments by following mixed Bitcoin funds that were later deposited into Binance and Coinbase accounts.

3.4 Timing Analysis: Mixer Withdrawals

◆ Mixers delay payouts to confuse blockchain analysis, but investigators can compare deposit timestamps to withdrawal activity.

📌 **Example**: A ransomware payment entered a mixer at 3:45 PM, and a similar-sized transaction exited at 3:52 PM—suggesting they are linked.

💡 **OSINT Tool:**

- **OXT.me** – Visualizes Bitcoin transaction flows and timing patterns.

4. Case Study: How Authorities Took Down a Major Bitcoin Mixer

📌 **Operation: The Fall of Helix Mixer (2021)**

🔍 **Background:**

- Helix was a Dark Web Bitcoin mixing service used to launder funds from AlphaBay, Silk Road, and ransomware attacks.
- It processed over $300 million in illicit Bitcoin transactions.

🔍 **How Investigators Cracked It:**

- Blockchain forensics linked Helix transactions to known cybercriminal wallets.
- Undercover agents sent Bitcoin through Helix and traced its movement.

- The FBI obtained server logs, revealing real-world identities of Helix users.
- Helix's founder was arrested, and the service was shut down.

💡 **Takeaway**: Even with mixing services, law enforcement can track illicit funds using OSINT and blockchain analytics.

5. Best Practices for OSINT Analysts Investigating Mixers

🔍 To effectively trace mixed cryptocurrency, OSINT analysts should:

✅ Monitor known mixing wallets using blockchain explorers.

✅ Track deposits and withdrawals around mixer timestamps.

✅ Look for patterns of large transactions being split into smaller ones.

✅ Follow post-mix transactions to see where "clean" crypto ends up.

✅ Use darknet intelligence to identify new mixing services.

While crypto mixers help cybercriminals launder funds, they are not 100% untraceable. With the right OSINT techniques, analysts can:

✓ Detect suspicious transaction patterns

✓ Identify known mixer wallets and clusters

✓ Trace post-mix activity to real-world exchanges

✓ Assist law enforcement in uncovering Dark Web money laundering operations

8.5 Investigating Ransomware & Extortion Payments

Ransomware attacks have become one of the most lucrative cybercrime operations, costing businesses, governments, and individuals billions of dollars annually. Threat actors encrypt victims' files and demand cryptocurrency payments, typically in Bitcoin (BTC) or Monero (XMR), to restore access.

Investigating these payments is critical to identifying ransomware groups, uncovering laundering networks, and tracking down the operators behind these attacks.

In this chapter, we will explore:

✅ How ransomware payments work

✅ Techniques for tracing Bitcoin ransom transactions

✅ How Monero complicates tracking efforts

✅ Case studies of law enforcement tracking ransom payments

1. How Ransomware & Extortion Payments Work

Ransomware gangs typically follow a structured process when executing attacks and collecting payments.

1.1 The Ransomware Payment Process

♦ **Step 1**: Victim's files are encrypted, and a ransom note appears.
♦ **Step 2**: The note provides a crypto wallet address for payment (usually BTC or XMR).
♦ **Step 3**: Victim sends the ransom payment.
♦ **Step 4**: The attacker transfers the funds to laundering services (mixers, P2P exchanges, privacy coins).
♦ **Step 5**: Funds are eventually withdrawn via crypto exchanges or converted into cash.

💡 **Example**: The REvil ransomware gang demanded Bitcoin payments from corporate victims, using laundering networks to obfuscate the transaction trail.

1.2 Ransomware-as-a-Service (RaaS)

Some groups operate Ransomware-as-a-Service (RaaS), where affiliates deploy ransomware in exchange for a cut of the ransom payments.

📌 **Example**: The Conti ransomware group provided ransomware tools to affiliates who received 70% of the ransom, while Conti retained 30%.

💡 **OSINT** Tip:

- Monitor known ransom payment wallets associated with RaaS groups.
- Track BTC addresses listed in leaked ransomware group communications (e.g., Conti leaks).

2. Techniques for Tracking Ransomware Payments

2.1 Identifying Ransom Payment Wallets

⬥ Where to find ransom payment wallets:

- On ransom notes (displayed on the victim's computer).
- In darknet forums or leak sites where gangs post payment instructions.
- Blockchain explorers tracking transactions associated with ransomware groups.

💡 **OSINT Tool:**

- **Bitcoin Abuse Database** – Lists BTC addresses linked to ransomware.
- **Ransomwhere** – Open-source ransomware payment tracking project.

📌 **Example**: The Ryuk ransomware gang used a few dozen BTC wallets, which were identified and monitored by OSINT analysts.

2.2 Following Bitcoin Transactions on the Blockchain

Once a ransom is paid, investigators can trace the movement of funds through the blockchain.

🔍 **How to track BTC ransom payments:**

- Identify the victim's transaction (from ransom note or blockchain records).
- Follow outgoing transactions from the attacker's wallet.
- Look for transactions moving through:
- Mixing services (attempts to launder funds).
- Crypto exchanges (potential off-ramp to fiat).
- Known criminal wallets (linked to past ransomware cases).

💡 **OSINT Tool:**

- **Chainalysis Reactor** – Detects transactions linked to ransomware groups.
- **Elliptic Forensics** – Tracks BTC movements and laundering patterns.

📌 **Example**: The Colonial Pipeline attack (2021) involved a BTC ransom payment that the FBI later recovered by tracing blockchain transactions.

2.3 How Monero (XMR) Obscures Ransom Payments

Unlike Bitcoin, Monero transactions are virtually untraceable due to:

- ◆ **Ring signatures** – Mixes a transaction with others, making it impossible to track.
- ◆ **Stealth addresses** – Generates a one-time address for each transaction.
- ◆ **No public ledger** – Transaction details are hidden.

📌 **Example**: The DarkSide ransomware gang (behind the Colonial Pipeline attack) encouraged Monero payments to avoid detection.

💡 **OSINT Tip:**

- Monitor Monero discussions on darknet forums for laundering tactics.
- Check crypto-to-Monero exchange services where ransom payments might be converted.

3. Case Study: How the FBI Recovered a Bitcoin Ransom Payment

📌 **Operation: Colonial Pipeline Ransomware Attack (2021)**

🔍 **What Happened?**

- DarkSide ransomware shut down a major U.S. fuel pipeline.
- The company paid a $4.4 million Bitcoin ransom to regain access.

🔍 **How Investigators Tracked the Funds:**

- The FBI identified the Bitcoin ransom payment on the blockchain.
- They monitored wallet movements, following BTC through multiple transfers.
- The funds were eventually sent to a crypto exchange wallet under FBI surveillance.
- The FBI seized $2.3 million of the ransom before it could be fully laundered.

💡 **Takeaway**: Even after being transferred through multiple wallets, ransom payments can still be traced using blockchain analysis.

4. Best Practices for OSINT Analysts Investigating Ransom Payments

✓ Monitor public ransom payment tracking databases like Bitcoin Abuse DB.

✓ Use blockchain explorers to trace known ransomware wallet transactions.

✓ Identify laundering tactics such as mixers, chain hopping, and Monero conversions.

✓ Look for ransom payment discussions on darknet forums and Telegram groups.

✓ Use leaked ransomware gang communications to map payment structures.

Despite cybercriminals' efforts to hide ransom payments, OSINT analysts and law enforcement agencies can still track Bitcoin transactions, identify laundering networks, and even recover stolen funds.

8.6 Case Study: Unmasking a Dark Web Drug Dealer Through Crypto Analysis

Cryptocurrency has become the preferred payment method for illegal transactions on the dark web, especially in drug markets. While Bitcoin and other cryptocurrencies offer a degree of anonymity, advanced blockchain forensic techniques can still expose criminals who believe they are untraceable.

In this case study, we will analyze how OSINT investigators and law enforcement used blockchain analytics to identify and arrest a major dark web drug dealer.

1. Background: The Dark Web Drug Trade & Crypto Payments

Dark web marketplaces such as Silk Road, AlphaBay, and Hydra have facilitated billions of dollars in illegal drug sales, with payments almost exclusively made in Bitcoin (BTC), Monero (XMR), and other cryptocurrencies.

◆ Why Drug Dealers Prefer Crypto

✓ No need for traditional banking (avoids detection).

✓ Transactions can be pseudonymous.

✓ Easily converted into cash using crypto exchanges or P2P markets.

📌 **Example**: The Hydra Market (shut down in 2022) processed over $1.3 billion in Bitcoin transactions before being taken down.

💡 **OSINT Tip:**

- Monitor cryptocurrency transactions linked to known dark web markets.
- Analyze deposit and withdrawal patterns to identify potential laundering techniques.

2. The Target: A High-Profile Dark Web Drug Vendor

Authorities were investigating a major fentanyl and methamphetamine vendor operating under the alias "DarkPharma" on a darknet marketplace.

◆ **Key Observations from Market Activity:**

- "DarkPharma" only accepted Bitcoin for transactions.
- The vendor's BTC wallet address was listed in buyer reviews.
- Orders were shipped using fake return addresses on packages.

💡 **OSINT Tip:**

- Dark web vendor feedback pages often contain wallet addresses used for payments.
- Tracking these addresses on the blockchain can expose transaction patterns.

3. How Investigators Tracked the Drug Dealer's Bitcoin Transactions

3.1 Identifying the Suspect's Crypto Wallet

Using blockchain analysis tools, investigators located Bitcoin transactions associated with the vendor's wallet.

🔍 **Techniques Used:**

- Blockchain explorers (e.g., Blockchair, OXT.me) were used to analyze wallet activity.
- Dark web intelligence gathering helped correlate vendor usernames with transactions.
- Forum scraping identified discussions about cashing out BTC earnings.

📌 **Findings:**

Investigators identified a cluster of Bitcoin wallets linked to the vendor, suggesting a laundering operation.

💡 **OSINT Tip:**

- Look for BTC wallet reuse across multiple darknet marketplaces.
- Cross-reference vendor usernames with crypto transaction histories.

3.2 Tracking Bitcoin Laundering Techniques

The suspect attempted to launder funds through common crypto anonymization methods:

◈ **Use of Mixers & Tumblers**: Sent BTC through multiple wallets to break transaction links.
◈ **Crypto-to-Crypto Swaps**: Converted BTC into Monero (XMR) for added privacy.
◈ **Off-Ramping to Exchanges**: Cashed out BTC using major exchanges.

💡 **OSINT Tools Used:**

- **Chainalysis Reactor** – Identified Bitcoin wallet clusters.
- **Elliptic Forensics** – Traced BTC through mixing services.
- **BitcoinWhosWho** – Flagged wallets associated with past darknet drug cases.

📌 **Example**: The suspect used a well-known Bitcoin mixer, but blockchain clustering techniques linked his deposits and withdrawals, revealing connections between transactions.

💡 **OSINT Tip:**

- Monitor transactions entering and exiting known mixing services.
- Use blockchain forensics to detect reoccurring laundering patterns.

3.3 Identifying a Crypto Exchange Cash-Out

After laundering the funds, the dealer withdrew Bitcoin into fiat currency via a centralized exchange.

🔍 How Investigators Found the Cash-Out:

- The suspect withdrew BTC from a mixer and deposited it into an exchange wallet.
- The exchange required KYC (Know Your Customer) verification.
- Investigators subpoenaed exchange records, revealing the suspect's real identity.

📌 **Breakthrough**: The exchange records revealed a registered email, phone number, and a withdrawal to a linked bank account, unmasking the real identity behind "DarkPharma."

💡 OSINT Tip:

- Track deposits into exchanges that enforce KYC verification.
- Look for connections between anonymous wallets and real-world bank transactions.

4. Arrest & Legal Action

🔍 Final Steps Taken by Law Enforcement:

✅ Linked Bitcoin transactions to drug shipments.

✅ Tracked laundering activity to identify real-world cash-out points.

✅ Subpoenaed exchange records, exposing the suspect's real identity.

📌 Outcome:

- The suspect was arrested at his home, where authorities found drugs, cash, and transaction records linking him to darknet drug sales.
- The seized BTC funds were used as evidence in court.
- The darknet marketplace was shut down following additional arrests.

💡 Case Takeaway:

Even though Bitcoin provides some level of anonymity, transaction tracking can still expose real-world identities, especially when criminals cash out through regulated exchanges.

5. Best Practices for OSINT Analysts Investigating Crypto Transactions

✅ Monitor known darknet vendor wallets and transaction histories.

✅ Use blockchain forensics tools to detect laundering attempts.

✅ Look for links between Bitcoin transactions and real-world identities.

✅ Analyze crypto exchange withdrawals to find cash-out points.

✅ Scrape darknet markets and forums for vendor wallet addresses.

This case study highlights how OSINT and blockchain analytics can be used to unmask darknet criminals, even when they attempt to launder funds through complex crypto schemes.

9. OSINT on Ransomware Groups & Threat Actors

In this chapter, we will focus on utilizing OSINT techniques to investigate ransomware groups and other threat actors responsible for cyberattacks targeting email systems and sensitive data. Ransomware attacks, often involving the encryption of critical data and demanding payment in cryptocurrency, have become one of the most damaging forms of cybercrime. We will examine how to identify and track the actors behind these attacks, from their tactics and infrastructure to their communication methods and ransom demands. By gathering intelligence from open sources, including dark web forums, public leaks, and social media channels, investigators can trace the movements of ransomware groups and their affiliates. This chapter will equip you with the tools to identify patterns, track specific threat actors, and understand the broader context of ransomware campaigns, all essential for preventing or mitigating the impact of these sophisticated cyber threats.

9.1 Understanding How Ransomware Groups Operate

Ransomware groups have evolved into highly organized cybercriminal enterprises, targeting corporations, governments, and individuals for financial gain. These groups use sophisticated malware, extortion tactics, and underground networks to maximize their profits while evading law enforcement.

In this chapter, we will explore:

✅ The structure of ransomware groups

✅ How Ransomware-as-a-Service (RaaS) works

✅ The tactics used to spread ransomware

✅ How ransomware gangs extort their victims

✅ How these groups avoid detection and prosecution

Understanding how ransomware groups operate is critical for OSINT analysts, cybersecurity professionals, and law enforcement in combating this global cyber threat.

1. The Structure of Ransomware Groups

Modern ransomware groups function like businesses, often with:

- **Developers** – Create and update ransomware strains
- **Affiliates** – Distribute ransomware and launch attacks
- **Negotiators** – Communicate with victims and demand ransoms
- **Money Launderers** – Convert crypto ransoms into cash
- **Access Brokers** – Sell stolen credentials and initial network access

📌 **Example**: The REvil ransomware gang operated as a hierarchical organization, offering ransomware tools to affiliates and splitting ransom payments.

💡 **OSINT Tip:**

- Monitor darknet forums for job postings from ransomware groups.
- Track ransom payment transactions to uncover laundering networks.

2. How Ransomware-as-a-Service (RaaS) Works

2.1 What is RaaS?

Ransomware-as-a-Service (RaaS) is a subscription-based model where cybercriminals rent ransomware tools from developers and share profits.

🔍 **RaaS Model Workflow:**

1️⃣ Developers create and maintain ransomware strains

2️⃣ Affiliates pay to use the ransomware

3️⃣ Affiliates launch attacks (via phishing, exploits, or RDP attacks)

4️⃣ Victims pay ransoms

5️⃣ Revenue is split (affiliates keep 70-80%, developers take 20-30%)

📌 **Example**: The Conti ransomware gang ran a highly structured RaaS operation, with affiliates receiving training, support, and scripts to launch attacks.

💡 **OSINT Tip:**

- Look for leaked RaaS contracts or affiliate communications on dark web forums.
- Monitor forums for new ransomware strains being advertised.

3. Common Ransomware Attack Vectors

3.1 Phishing Emails & Malicious Attachments

📌 Attackers send fake emails with malware-laden attachments or links.

💡 **Example**: The Emotet botnet spread ransomware via phishing emails with infected Word documents.

3.2 Exploiting Remote Desktop Protocol (RDP) Weaknesses

📌 Hackers brute-force RDP credentials to gain access to corporate networks.

💡 **Example**: The Ryuk ransomware gang used RDP attacks to compromise hospitals and city governments.

3.3 Software Vulnerabilities & Zero-Day Exploits

📌 Attackers exploit unpatched software vulnerabilities to deploy ransomware.

💡 **Example**: The WannaCry ransomware attack (2017) used an SMB exploit (EternalBlue) to infect thousands of computers.

💡 **OSINT Tip:**

- Monitor leaked credential databases for stolen RDP logins.
- Track exploit discussions on cybercrime forums.

4. Ransomware Extortion Tactics

4.1 Double Extortion

◆ Attackers steal sensitive data before encrypting files.
◆ Victims must pay to decrypt data AND prevent public leaks.

📌 **Example**: The Maze ransomware group pioneered double extortion by threatening to leak corporate data.

4.2 Triple Extortion

◆ Attackers steal data, encrypt files, and threaten DDoS attacks if victims refuse to pay.

📌 **Example**: The SunCrypt ransomware gang combined data theft with DDoS threats.

💡 **OSINT Tip:**

- Monitor leak sites for ransomware groups posting stolen data.
- Analyze ransom notes for common extortion techniques.

5. How Ransomware Groups Evade Detection

5.1 Using Cryptocurrency for Payments

📌 Most ransoms are paid in Bitcoin (BTC) or Monero (XMR).
💡 **Example**: The DarkSide ransomware gang (Colonial Pipeline attack) preferred Monero due to its anonymity.

5.2 Hosting Operations on the Dark Web

📌 Ransomware groups use .onion leak sites to publish stolen data.
💡 **Example**: The LockBit ransomware group has a dark web leak site listing victims who refuse to pay.

5.3 Using Bulletproof Hosting & Fast Flux Networks

📌 Attackers use bulletproof hosting providers and rotating IP addresses to avoid takedowns.
💡 **Example**: The REvil ransomware group used hidden servers and VPNs to avoid tracking.

💡 **OSINT Tip:**

- Use dark web monitoring tools to track ransomware leak sites.
- Analyze blockchain transactions for laundering patterns.

6. Case Study: The REvil Ransomware Group

🔍 Background:

- REvil was a notorious RaaS group, responsible for multi-million dollar attacks.
- They targeted corporations, IT providers, and government agencies.

🔍 Key Events:

📌 **2021**: REvil hacked Kaseya, affecting 1,500+ companies.
📌 **2021**: REvil extorted JBS Foods for $11 million in Bitcoin.
📌 **2021**: REvil's servers were taken offline by international law enforcement.

🔍 Investigation Techniques Used:

✅ Blockchain tracking tools identified ransom payments.

✅ Dark web monitoring located REvil's leak sites and forums.

✅ Undercover agents infiltrated RaaS forums to track affiliate operations.

📌 Outcome:

- Several REvil members were arrested in Russia and the US.
- Millions in ransom payments were seized by authorities.

💡 **Case Takeaway**: Even sophisticated ransomware groups can be tracked and dismantled through OSINT and blockchain forensics.

7. Best Practices for OSINT Analysts Investigating Ransomware Groups

✅ Monitor dark web forums for RaaS advertisements.

✅ Track blockchain transactions linked to ransom payments.

✅ Scrape ransomware leak sites for new victim announcements.

✅ Analyze phishing campaigns to detect early-stage ransomware attacks.

✅ Collaborate with cybersecurity and law enforcement agencies.

Ransomware groups operate like cybercriminal corporations, leveraging RaaS models, extortion tactics, and crypto laundering to generate massive profits. However, through

OSINT investigations, blockchain analysis, and dark web monitoring, analysts can expose and disrupt their operations.

9.2 Investigating Ransomware Victim Data Leaks

Ransomware attacks have evolved from simple file encryption schemes into high-stakes extortion operations. Today, most ransomware groups use "double extortion"—stealing sensitive data before encrypting files and threatening to leak it if the victim refuses to pay. This tactic forces organizations into public relations crises, regulatory scrutiny, and financial losses.

For OSINT analysts, cybersecurity professionals, and law enforcement, investigating ransomware victim data leaks is crucial for:

✅ Identifying compromised organizations and individuals.

✅ Tracing stolen data across the dark web, forums, and leak sites.

✅ Understanding the tactics, techniques, and procedures (TTPs) used by ransomware groups.

✅ Assisting victims in mitigating the damage and securing exposed assets.

This chapter will cover how to track, analyze, and investigate ransomware victim data leaks using OSINT techniques, forensic tools, and dark web intelligence gathering.

1. Understanding How Ransomware Victim Data is Leaked

1.1 The Role of Dark Web Leak Sites

Most ransomware gangs operate dedicated dark web leak sites where they:

◆ List hacked companies that refuse to pay the ransom.
◆ Provide sample files to prove they have stolen data.
◆ Gradually release full datasets if victims don't comply.

📌 **Example:**

- The LockBit gang maintains a dark web site where victim data is leaked in stages to pressure payments.
- The Conti ransomware group publicly released corporate emails and financial records of Costa Rica's government after a ransom was refused.

💡 OSINT Tip:

- Use dark web monitoring tools (e.g., DarkTracer, OnionScan) to track active ransomware leak sites.
- Look for announcements on underground forums where ransomware groups advertise new leaks.

1.2 Common Data Types Exposed in Ransomware Leaks

Ransomware victim data leaks often include:

- **Personal Identifiable Information (PII)** – Names, addresses, phone numbers.
- **Financial Records** – Bank statements, payroll data, invoices.
- **Corporate Emails & Internal Documents** – Business strategies, legal files.
- **Medical Data** – Patient records, insurance details.
- **Login Credentials** – Username-password pairs from breached systems.

📌 Example:

The Cl0p ransomware group leaked millions of private medical records from the MOVEit hack, affecting hospitals and healthcare firms.

💡 OSINT Tip:

- Cross-reference leaked email credentials with breach notification sites (e.g., Have I Been Pwned?).
- Check if financial records appear on underground data broker sites like Genesis Market (before its takedown).

2. Tracking Ransomware Leak Sites & Forums

2.1 Using Dark Web Monitoring Tools

Since ransomware leak sites are hosted on the Tor network (.onion domains), traditional search engines won't index them. Instead, analysts can use:

🔍 **Tools for Monitoring Leak Sites:**

✅ **Dark.fail** – Directory of active darknet sites.
✅ **Onion.live** – Search engine for .onion domains.
✅ **IntelX & DarkTracer** – Monitors ransomware groups' leak activity.
✅ **Hunchly** – Helps archive and analyze dark web pages.

📌 **Example:**

Cybersecurity firms and journalists regularly scrape LockBit's dark web site to identify newly leaked corporate documents.

💡 **OSINT Tip:**

- Use a virtual machine and Tor browser when accessing ransomware leak sites for safety.
- Monitor GitHub and Telegram OSINT groups for updates on new ransomware leaks.

2.2 Investigating Ransomware Leak Announcements on Forums

Many ransomware groups first announce their data leaks on cybercrime forums before posting them on their dark web leak sites.

🔍 **Where to Look:**

✅ **Exploit & BreachForums** – Hackers discuss stolen data availability.
✅ **RAMP Forum** – RaaS affiliates coordinate and leak samples.
✅ **Telegram Channels** – Some ransomware groups use Telegram to share links to leaks.

📌 **Example:**

The Babuk ransomware gang leaked law enforcement data on Russian Telegram channels before it spread to dark web forums.

- Search for keywords like "ransomware dump" + company name on cybercrime forums.
- Look for threat actors selling access to leaked data, indicating a potential data broker operation.

3. Analyzing Ransomware-Leaked Data

3.1 Verifying the Authenticity of a Leak

Before assuming leaked data is real, OSINT analysts should:

✓ Check sample files for metadata (e.g., creation dates, email addresses).

✓ Cross-check file hashes with previously leaked data to detect duplicates.

✓ Look at past ransomware group claims—some gangs exaggerate leak contents.

📌 **Example:**

The Hive ransomware group falsely claimed to have 1TB of corporate data, but investigators found only 50GB of relevant files.

💡 **OSINT Tip:**

Use file analysis tools like CyberChef to extract metadata from leaked PDFs, Word documents, and Excel files.

3.2 Investigating How Leaked Data is Used

Once ransomware groups leak victim data, it often spreads to:

◆ **Dark Web Marketplaces** – Sold in bulk to identity thieves.
◆ **Public Torrent Sites** – Some ransomware groups release data via torrents.
◆ **Phishing & Fraud Schemes** – Criminals use stolen emails and credentials to scam victims.

📌 **Example:**

Colonial Pipeline ransomware attack – Leaked credentials were later used in secondary phishing campaigns.

💡 OSINT Tip:

- Check breached credential marketplaces (e.g., Snusbase, DeHashed) to see if leaked passwords reappear.
- Monitor scam forums for fraudsters using leaked data to commit identity theft and business email compromise (BEC) fraud.

4. Legal & Ethical Considerations in Investigating Data Leaks

4.1 What Investigators Can & Cannot Do

✅ You Can:

- Use OSINT techniques to analyze publicly available leaks.
- Report findings to victims, cybersecurity teams, or law enforcement.
- Monitor ransomware leak announcements and discussion forums.

✖ You Cannot:

- Pay for stolen data on darknet marketplaces.
- Hack into ransomware leak sites (illegal and unethical).
- Distribute stolen data unless authorized for research or disclosure purposes.

📌 Example:

Security researchers investigating the REvil ransomware leaks had to follow strict ethical guidelines to avoid legal repercussions.

💡 OSINT Tip:

Always document investigative steps to ensure compliance with cybersecurity laws.

5. Best Practices for OSINT Analysts Investigating Ransomware Leaks

✅ Use dark web monitoring tools to track active ransomware leak sites.

✅ Archive leaked data for analysis but avoid distributing it.

✅ Cross-check leaked credentials with public breach databases.

✅ Monitor cybercrime forums for early leak announcements.

✅ Report findings to affected organizations or authorities when possible.

Investigating ransomware victim data leaks requires a combination of OSINT skills, forensic tools, and ethical considerations. By tracking leak sites, analyzing leaked data, and understanding how ransomware groups operate, analysts can help victims mitigate damage and disrupt cybercriminal operations.

9.3 Tracking Communications Between Attackers & Victims

Ransomware attacks often involve direct communication between cybercriminals and their victims. These interactions typically occur via ransom notes, dark web chat portals, encrypted messaging services, and email. For OSINT analysts and cybersecurity professionals, tracking these communications can:

✅ Provide insights into ransomware group operations

✅ Reveal affiliated threat actors and their negotiation tactics

✅ Help law enforcement identify and disrupt ransomware networks

✅ Assist victims in responding strategically to extortion demands

This chapter will cover how to track, analyze, and investigate ransomware-related communications using OSINT tools, blockchain intelligence, and forensic techniques.

1. Common Communication Channels in Ransomware Attacks

1.1 Ransom Notes & Payment Instructions

◆ Found in encrypted files, desktop backgrounds, or text documents after an attack
◆ Typically contain:

✅ Instructions on how to contact the attackers

✅ Bitcoin or Monero wallet addresses for ransom payments

✅ Threats about data leaks if payment isn't made

📌 **Example:**

REvil ransomware placed ransom notes in each encrypted folder, directing victims to a dark web payment portal.

💡 **OSINT Tip:**

Use forensic tools like FTK Imager or Autopsy to extract hidden ransom notes from infected systems.
Search for similar ransom note templates in malware databases like MalwareBazaar or VX Underground.

1.2 Dark Web Chat Portals & Ransom Negotiation Sites

◆ Most ransomware groups provide a dark web portal where victims can:

✅ Chat anonymously with attackers

✅ Negotiate ransom amounts

✅ Receive decryption test files

📌 **Example:**

The LockBit ransomware group operates an automated dark web chat system where victims can communicate securely.

💡 **OSINT Tip:**

- Use Tor and dark web monitoring tools (e.g., DarkTracer) to track active ransom chat portals.
- Look for reused phrasing or unique negotiation tactics that might link multiple attacks to the same ransomware group.

1.3 Encrypted Messaging Apps & Email Correspondence

◆ Some ransomware gangs prefer secure messaging apps (e.g., Tox, Telegram, ProtonMail) for negotiations.

◆ Attackers may use burner email accounts with services like Tutanota or Mailfence.

📌 **Example:**

The Ryuk ransomware group used ProtonMail accounts to communicate with victims and deliver decryption keys.

💡 **OSINT Tip:**

Search leaked ransomware communications in data breach dumps to find reused email addresses or aliases.

Use email header analysis (e.g., MXToolbox) to identify attacker IP locations and mail servers.

2. Analyzing Ransomware Communications for Attribution

2.1 Identifying Ransomware Group Signatures

Each ransomware group follows specific communication patterns, including:

✅ Preferred languages (e.g., Russian, English, Mandarin)

✅ Unique ransom note wording (e.g., "Your network has been compromised")

✅ Specific payment demands (e.g., percentage-based vs. fixed amount)

📌 **Example:**

The Black Basta ransomware group always demands ransom in Bitcoin and refers to itself as "The Corporation" in negotiations.

💡 **OSINT Tip:**

Compare ransom notes from different attacks to detect common wording patterns using NLP tools like Aleph or Logarynth.

2.2 Investigating Cryptocurrency Wallets from Ransom Notes

Since attackers provide crypto wallet addresses for ransom payments, tracking these transactions can reveal:

✓ Money laundering networks

✓ Connections to other ransomware groups

✓ Exchanges where funds are cashed out

📌 **Example:**

The DarkSide ransomware group (Colonial Pipeline attack) used Bitcoin wallets that were later traced to exchanges with weak KYC policies.

💡 **OSINT Tip:**

- Use blockchain explorers (e.g., BitcoinWhosWho, Chainalysis, CipherTrace) to analyze ransom payments.
- Look for wallet reuse across multiple ransomware attacks to identify linked groups.

3. Monitoring Victim Responses & Negotiation Strategies

3.1 How Companies Handle Ransom Demands

Victims often:

✓ Negotiate for lower ransoms

✓ Refuse to pay (and risk data leaks)

✓ Hire ransomware negotiators

✓ Engage law enforcement

📌 **Example:**

Travelex (2020 ransomware attack) initially refused to pay but later negotiated a reduced ransom of $2.3 million in Bitcoin.

💡 **OSINT Tip:**

Monitor ransomware negotiation firms (e.g., Coveware) for insights into current ransom trends.
Analyze public breach disclosures to determine if companies are paying or resisting attackers.

3.2 Tracking Leaked Negotiation Transcripts

◆ Some ransomware groups publish victim negotiations on their dark web sites to pressure companies.

◆ These transcripts often expose:

✓ How companies respond to ransom demands

✓ The level of desperation in victim responses

✓ Tactics used by attackers to manipulate victims

📌 Example:

The Conti ransomware group leaked full negotiation logs, revealing how victims try to stall payments while consulting cybersecurity experts.

💡 OSINT Tip:

- Look for leaked chat logs on dark web sites (e.g., DDoSSecrets, RAMP forum).
- Compare past negotiations to find repeat victims or targeted industries.

4. Case Study: Tracking Ransomware Communications in the Colonial Pipeline Attack

🔍 Background:

- In May 2021, the DarkSide ransomware gang attacked Colonial Pipeline, disrupting fuel supply across the U.S.
- Colonial Pipeline paid a $4.4 million ransom in Bitcoin.

🔍 How Communications Were Tracked:

✓ DarkSide's dark web portal contained victim instructions.

✓ Investigators monitored Bitcoin transactions linked to the ransom payment.

✓ FBI cyber teams tracked the ransom wallet, ultimately recovering $2.3 million in stolen funds.

🔍 Key Takeaways:

- Ransomware groups prefer direct communication via dark web portals.
- Crypto transaction tracking helped recover stolen funds.
- Law enforcement can infiltrate and disrupt attacker networks by analyzing ransom negotiations.

5. Best Practices for OSINT Analysts Investigating Ransomware Communications

✓ Archive ransom notes & dark web chat screenshots for pattern analysis.

✓ Monitor blockchain transactions linked to ransom payments.

✓ Search for leaked negotiation logs to understand attacker tactics.

✓ Analyze email headers & metadata to identify attacker infrastructure.

✓ Collaborate with cybersecurity firms to track emerging ransomware threats.

Tracking ransomware communications is critical for OSINT analysts looking to expose, disrupt, and attribute ransomware attacks. By investigating ransom notes, dark web portals, crypto payments, and leaked negotiations, investigators can gain valuable intelligence on ransomware gangs and their operations.

9.4 Analyzing Ransomware-as-a-Service (RaaS) Operations

Ransomware has evolved into a highly organized cybercriminal business model known as Ransomware-as-a-Service (RaaS). Instead of a single hacker executing an attack, RaaS operations function like legitimate businesses, where developers create ransomware strains and lease them to affiliates who carry out the actual attacks.

For OSINT analysts, cybersecurity professionals, and law enforcement, understanding RaaS ecosystems is crucial to:

⊘ Identifying key ransomware groups and their tactics.

⊘ Tracking affiliates and their attack campaigns.

⊘ Disrupting payment and infrastructure networks.

⊘ Predicting future ransomware threats before they escalate.

This chapter will provide a deep dive into how RaaS operations work, how they recruit affiliates, and how analysts can investigate them using OSINT techniques.

1. How Ransomware-as-a-Service (RaaS) Works

1.1 The RaaS Business Model

RaaS follows a subscription-based or profit-sharing model, much like legal Software-as-a-Service (SaaS) companies. A typical RaaS structure includes:

- **Ransomware Developers** – Create and maintain the ransomware malware.
- **Administrators** – Operate dark web portals, manage affiliates, and provide support.
- **Affiliates** – Rent the ransomware and execute attacks.
- **Money Launderers** – Handle ransom payments and convert cryptocurrency.

📌 **Example:**

Conti RaaS functioned like a corporate structure, with HR policies, recruitment documents, and even performance-based bonuses for affiliates.

💡 **OSINT Tip:**

Monitor dark web forums like Exploit and RAMP for RaaS advertisements targeting new affiliates.

1.2 The Affiliate System: Who Launches the Attacks?

Unlike traditional hacking groups, RaaS developers rarely execute attacks themselves. Instead, they:

⊘ Sell or lease ransomware to affiliates.

⊘ Offer tech support for affiliates struggling to deploy malware.

☑ Manage ransom negotiations through automated dark web portals.

Affiliates, on the other hand, are responsible for:

◆ Target selection (corporations, hospitals, government agencies).
◆ Deploying the ransomware (via phishing, RDP brute force, or supply chain attacks).
◆ Interacting with victims and pressuring them to pay.

📌 **Example:**

The BlackCat/ALPHV RaaS model allows affiliates to keep 80-90% of ransom payments, while developers take a cut.

💡 **OSINT Tip:**

Look for affiliate discussions on hacker forums where they review different RaaS platforms like a marketplace.

2. Investigating RaaS Recruitment & Operations on the Dark Web

2.1 Where RaaS Operators Recruit Affiliates

Ransomware gangs recruit affiliates via:

☑ **Dark web forums** – Cybercrime forums like Exploit, RAMP, and XSS feature job postings.
☑ **Telegram channels** – Private groups for vetted cybercriminals.
☑ **ICQ & Tox messaging** – Secure platforms for negotiations.

📌 **Example:**

The REvil RaaS program openly recruited hackers on Exploit.in, advertising "high payouts" for affiliates.

💡 **OSINT Tip:**

Use keyword searches like "RaaS partnership" or "RaaS affiliates needed" on dark web marketplaces.

2.2 How RaaS Groups Advertise Their Services

RaaS groups market their ransomware using:

- ◈ Demo videos showcasing encryption speed and efficiency.
- ◈ Testimonials from past affiliates who made large profits.
- ◈ Screenshots of successful ransom negotiations to prove legitimacy.

📌 Example:

The DarkSide RaaS operators posted "client testimonials" on cybercrime forums to attract new affiliates.

💡 OSINT Tip:

Analyze leaked RaaS advertisements to understand their target demographics and recruitment strategies.

3. Identifying RaaS Payment Structures & Money Laundering Tactics

3.1 How RaaS Revenue is Distributed

Once a ransom is paid, the funds are split between:
✓ The affiliate (70-90%)
✓ The RaaS developers (10-30%)

Payments are processed through:

- ◈ Bitcoin (BTC) and Monero (XMR) for anonymity.
- ◈ Mixing services & tumblers to obscure transaction history.
- ◈ Cash-out services via crypto exchanges or underground brokers.

📌 Example:

The DarkSide RaaS required affiliates to use specific Bitcoin wallets that were pre-approved for laundering.

💡 OSINT Tip:

Use blockchain explorers like Chainalysis or BitcoinWhosWho to trace ransom payments across wallets.

3.2 Tracing Cryptocurrency Flow in RaaS Operations

Tracking crypto transactions can:

✅ Identify wallets used in multiple ransomware attacks.

✅ Reveal money laundering networks.

✅ Expose weak points where law enforcement can intervene.

📌 Example:

FBI tracked REvil's Bitcoin transactions, leading to the seizure of $6.1 million in ransom payments.

💡 OSINT Tip:

Use heuristics like wallet reuse, transaction timing, and cluster analysis to link affiliates to RaaS groups.

4. Case Study: The Conti Ransomware Leak & RaaS Exposure

🔍 Background:

In February 2022, a Ukrainian security researcher leaked over 60,000 internal Conti ransomware messages, exposing:

✅ The internal RaaS structure (hierarchies, payments, and development).

✅ Chat logs between Conti operators and affiliates.

✅ Crypto transactions linked to ransom payments.

🔍 Key Takeaways:

- Conti ran its RaaS like a corporation, with HR departments, affiliate recruitment, and employee performance tracking.
- Chat leaks revealed rivalries among RaaS groups, indicating that affiliates often switch between services.
- Some Conti developers previously worked for other ransomware groups, proving crossover between major RaaS networks.

💡 OSINT Tip:

Cross-reference leaked RaaS chat logs with known cybercrime forum aliases to link threat actors across multiple attacks.

5. Best Practices for OSINT Analysts Investigating RaaS

✅ Monitor dark web forums for new RaaS recruitment campaigns.

✅ Track affiliate discussions to understand RaaS market shifts.

✅ Analyze leaked RaaS chat logs for organizational insights.

✅ Trace cryptocurrency transactions to follow ransom payments.

✅ Use language and phrasing analysis to link multiple attacks to the same RaaS group.

Ransomware-as-a-Service (RaaS) has transformed cybercrime into a scalable, profitable industry. By investigating recruitment methods, financial transactions, and affiliate operations, OSINT analysts can expose and disrupt RaaS networks.

9.5 Identifying Common Tactics, Techniques & Procedures (TTPs)

Ransomware groups follow a structured approach to infiltrate, encrypt, and extort victims. Their Tactics, Techniques, and Procedures (TTPs) provide valuable insight into how these cybercriminals operate, allowing investigators to detect, attribute, and mitigate threats effectively.

By analyzing these TTPs, OSINT analysts, cybersecurity professionals, and law enforcement can:

✅ Recognize patterns used by different ransomware gangs.

✅ Track Ransomware-as-a-Service (RaaS) affiliates.

✅ Develop countermeasures to prevent future attacks.

✅ Link multiple incidents to the same operators.

This chapter will break down the common TTPs used by ransomware groups, how to track them using OSINT, and how to leverage frameworks like MITRE ATT&CK for investigations.

1. Understanding TTPs in the Ransomware Kill Chain

1.1 What Are TTPs?

◆ **Tactics** – The overarching goals or strategies attackers use (e.g., initial access, lateral movement).
◆ **Techniques** – The methods used to achieve a tactic (e.g., phishing, RDP brute force).
◆ **Procedures** – The specific implementations of a technique (e.g., using Emotet malware for initial access).

📌 Example:

The Ryuk ransomware gang uses spear phishing (technique) to steal credentials and gain initial access (tactic).

💡 OSINT Tip:

Use MITRE ATT&CK to map out ransomware behavior and compare it to known adversaries.

1.2 The Ransomware Kill Chain

Ransomware attacks follow a typical progression, which includes:

Phase Tactic Example

Phase	Tactic	Example
1 Initial Access	Phishing, RDP brute force	TrickBot, Emotet
2 Execution	PowerShell scripts, malware loaders	Cobalt Strike
3 Persistence	Registry keys, scheduled tasks	GPO hijacking
4 Privilege Escalation	Credential dumping	Mimikatz
5 Lateral Movement	RDP, SMB exploitation	PsExec
6 Data Exfiltration	Cloud sync abuse, FTP	Mega, Rclone
7 Encryption & Ransom Note	File encryption	AES-256
8 Extortion & Payment	Dark web leaks	Tor payment sites

📌 Example:

The Conti ransomware group follows this exact sequence, often using Cobalt Strike for lateral movement before deploying their payload.

💡 OSINT Tip:

Monitor leaked ransomware playbooks from cybercriminal forums to see their step-by-step attack methods.

2. Common TTPs Used by Ransomware Gangs

2.1 Initial Access: How Ransomware Gets In

◆ **Phishing Emails** – Malicious attachments or links.
◆ **Exploiting RDP (Remote Desktop Protocol)** – Brute-force attacks on exposed RDP ports.
◆ **Supply Chain Attacks** – Infecting trusted software updates (e.g., Kaseya attack).

📌 Example:

Emotet malware delivered via phishing is a major initial access vector for ransomware groups like Ryuk.

💡 OSINT Tip:

Search VirusTotal for known phishing email samples related to ransomware campaigns.

2.2 Privilege Escalation & Lateral Movement

◆ **Credential Dumping** – Using Mimikatz or LSASS dumps to steal Windows credentials.
◆ **Pass-the-Hash Attacks** – Moving laterally without passwords.
◆ **Exploiting Windows Admin Tools** – Using PsExec, WMI, and PowerShell.

📌 Example:

The Maze ransomware group used legitimate Windows tools (LOLBins) to avoid detection.

💡 OSINT Tip:

Use Shodan to scan for exposed RDP services that attackers could exploit.

2.3 Data Exfiltration & Double Extortion

◆ Exfiltrating sensitive data before encryption.
◆ Threatening public leaks on dark web sites if ransom isn't paid.
◆ Using Mega, Rclone, or FTP for data transfers.

📌 Example:

The BlackMatter ransomware gang used Rclone to upload stolen data to cloud storage.

💡 OSINT Tip:

Monitor leak sites on the dark web (e.g., DarkTracer) to track stolen data dumps.

2.4 Encryption & Ransomware Deployment

◆ Encrypting files with AES-256 & RSA keys.
◆ Renaming files with extensions like .lock, .crypted, .conti.
◆ Dropping ransom notes (e.g., README.txt).

📌 Example:

LockBit ransomware appends .lockbit to all encrypted files.

💡 OSINT Tip:

Look for unique file extensions & ransom note signatures in malware repositories.

3. Investigating Ransomware TTPs Using OSINT

3.1 Tracking Ransomware Group Signatures

Each ransomware gang has a distinct TTP pattern, including:

✅ Preferred malware droppers (TrickBot, QakBot).

✅ Encryption algorithms (ChaCha20, AES-256).

✅ Dark web payment sites.

📌 Example:

The Hive ransomware gang only accepts Monero (XMR) for payments to ensure anonymity.

💡 OSINT Tip:

Use blockchain explorers to track known ransomware Bitcoin wallets.

3.2 Leveraging MITRE ATT&CK for Ransomware Analysis

MITRE ATT&CK helps map specific TTPs to known ransomware groups.

📌 Example:

The REvil ransomware group matches the T1486 (Data Encrypted for Impact) technique in MITRE ATT&CK.

💡 OSINT Tip:

Use ATT&CK Navigator to visualize TTP overlaps between different ransomware families.

4. Case Study: How Tracking TTPs Led to the REvil Takedown

🔍 Background:

- REvil (Sodinokibi) ransomware was one of the most prolific RaaS groups.
- They used initial access brokers to buy compromised credentials.
- After the Kaseya supply chain attack, law enforcement analyzed their TTPs and disrupted their infrastructure.

🔍 How OSINT Helped:

✅ Dark web monitoring revealed recruitment ads for REvil affiliates.

✅ MITRE ATT&CK mapping linked multiple attacks to the same TTPs.

✅ Blockchain analysis traced ransom payments to centralized exchanges.

🔍 Outcome:

In 2021, law enforcement seized REvil's servers and arrested affiliates.

💡 OSINT Tip:

Compare past ransomware TTPs to emerging threats to predict new attack waves.

5. Best Practices for OSINT Analysts Tracking Ransomware TTPs

✅ Monitor dark web forums for new TTP discussions.

✅ Track ransomware-specific indicators (file extensions, note signatures).

✅ Analyze phishing email metadata for common sender patterns.

✅ Map ransomware behaviors using MITRE ATT&CK.

✅ Investigate blockchain transactions linked to ransom payments.

Understanding ransomware TTPs is crucial for attributing attacks, predicting future threats, and preventing infections. By mapping out common techniques, tracking ransomware behavior, and leveraging OSINT tools, analysts can proactively defend against ransomware threats.

9.6 Case Study: How OSINT Helped Disrupt a Ransomware Group

Ransomware groups operate in secrecy, often relying on anonymous communication channels, cryptocurrency transactions, and underground networks to evade law enforcement. However, Open-Source Intelligence (OSINT) techniques have played a significant role in tracking, exposing, and dismantling some of these cybercriminal organizations.

In this case study, we will explore how OSINT investigators, cybersecurity researchers, and law enforcement unmasked members of a ransomware gang, leading to their disruption and arrests. This real-world investigation demonstrates how publicly available data, blockchain tracking, and dark web monitoring can be leveraged to identify ransomware operators and affiliates.

1. Background: The Ransomware Group & Its Operations

In mid-2021, a high-profile ransomware group, which we will refer to as "DarkMaze", emerged on underground forums. DarkMaze operated as a Ransomware-as-a-Service (RaaS) model, where:

- Developers created the ransomware and managed the encryption/decryption process.
- Affiliates conducted the attacks, often using phishing, RDP brute-force, or supply chain compromises.
- Operators handled ransom negotiations and money laundering.

DarkMaze was responsible for multiple attacks on corporations, hospitals, and government agencies, demanding ransoms in Bitcoin (BTC) and Monero (XMR). Their operations followed a double extortion strategy, where victims were threatened with public data leaks if they refused to pay.

📌 **Key Observations:**

✅ DarkMaze used a dedicated leak site on the dark web to publish stolen data.

✅ They demanded payments via Bitcoin, but also accepted Monero for added anonymity.

✅ Their ransomware payloads were distributed via affiliated hacking groups.

✅ DarkMaze was active on cybercrime forums, advertising partnerships for initial access brokers.

💡 **OSINT Tip:**

Monitoring dark web marketplaces and forums can reveal cybercriminal activity and recruitment patterns.

2. OSINT Investigation Begins

2.1 Tracking the Dark Web Presence

Investigators started by analyzing DarkMaze's ransomware leak site hosted on Tor.

🔍 **Findings:**

- The site listed dozens of victims, with stolen data samples.
- Each victim had a ransom note, including a Bitcoin address for payment.
- The site contained contact details for negotiations, including a Tox ID and a ProtonMail address.

💡 **OSINT Tip:**

Extract metadata from ransom notes to identify common email domains, usernames, and crypto wallets.

📌 **Key Breakthrough:**

Investigators linked DarkMaze's Tor site to multiple forum usernames across cybercrime marketplaces. Using OSINT correlation techniques, they discovered:

✅ The same PGP key was used for signing messages across different forums.

✅ An old forum post from 2019 contained an early version of the ransomware.

✅ A username linked to a GitHub repository where similar malware samples were stored.

🚀 **Result:**

The OSINT team identified multiple aliases used by DarkMaze affiliates across hacking forums.

2.2 Blockchain Analysis: Tracing Ransom Payments

Since DarkMaze demanded Bitcoin payments, analysts used blockchain forensics tools to trace transactions.

🔎 Findings:

- Multiple Bitcoin wallets were linked to DarkMaze's ransom payments.
- Some transactions were sent to known cryptocurrency exchanges.
- A pattern of "peeling" transactions was identified—funds were moved through multiple wallets to obscure their origin.

📌 Key Breakthrough:

Investigators tracked ransom payments to an exchange that required KYC (Know Your Customer) verification.

✅ A Bitcoin wallet connected to DarkMaze received funds from multiple victims.

✅ The wallet converted Bitcoin to Monero using a mixing service.

✅ A withdrawal from the exchange led to an IP address in Eastern Europe.

🚀 Result:

This intelligence was shared with law enforcement agencies, leading to a request for account holder information from the exchange.

💡 OSINT Tip:

Use blockchain explorers like Blockchair or Chainalysis to track Bitcoin ransom transactions.

2.3 Identifying the Ransomware Operators

As part of the investigation, researchers monitored hacker recruitment forums where ransomware affiliates and initial access brokers (IABs) operate.

🔎 Findings:

- A forum user known as "XCrypt0" was actively recruiting penetration testers for a "profitable project."
- The same user had advertised malware development services in the past.
- Through forum footprinting, investigators linked XCrypt0's account to a personal email address.

📌 Key Breakthrough:

Cross-referencing with previous data breaches, researchers found that XCrypt0's email was exposed in a leaked database from an old hacking forum breach.

✅ The leaked data contained an IP address linked to previous cyber activities.

✅ The email address was used to register a domain tied to malware distribution.

✅ The domain hosted a server with ransomware payloads, connecting XCrypt0 to DarkMaze.

🚀 Result:

This evidence helped law enforcement pinpoint the real identity of one of DarkMaze's core members.

💡 OSINT Tip:

Use breach databases like "Have I Been Pwned" to find compromised emails of cybercriminals.

3. The Takedown: Law Enforcement Action

By compiling OSINT findings, blockchain analysis, and forum tracking, the investigators handed over a detailed intelligence dossier to law enforcement.

📌 Key Actions:

✅ Law enforcement coordinated with crypto exchanges to freeze DarkMaze-linked accounts.

✅ Authorities seized DarkMaze's infrastructure, including command-and-control servers.

✅ Several ransomware operators were arrested in Eastern Europe based on IP address logs and financial transactions.

🚀 Final Outcome:

- DarkMaze's leak site was taken offline.
- Multiple affiliates were arrested, significantly disrupting their operations.
- Victims were given decryption keys, allowing them to recover files without paying ransom.

💡 OSINT Tip:

Cooperation between cybersecurity firms, OSINT researchers, and law enforcement is key to dismantling ransomware operations.

4. Key Takeaways for OSINT Investigators

🔎 How OSINT Helped Disrupt DarkMaze:

✅ **Dark Web Monitoring** – Analyzing ransom notes, leak sites, and cybercrime forums.
✅ **Blockchain Analysis** – Tracking Bitcoin ransom payments to identify laundering techniques.
✅ **Forum Intelligence** – Linking ransomware operators to usernames and past activity.
✅ **Data Breach Analysis** – Using leaked credentials to uncover cybercriminals' real identities.

💡 Lessons Learned:

✔️ Monitor cybercrime forums for recruitment activity.
✔️ Use blockchain analysis to track ransom payments and laundering techniques.
✔️ Leverage past data breaches to find links to cybercriminal identities.
✔️ Work with law enforcement and cybersecurity firms to take action.

This case study highlights how OSINT techniques played a crucial role in identifying and dismantling a ransomware group. By analyzing dark web activity, tracking cryptocurrency payments, and uncovering hidden identities, OSINT investigators helped disrupt a major cybercriminal operation.

As ransomware threats continue to evolve, OSINT will remain a critical tool in the fight against cybercrime.

10. De-anonymizing Dark Web Users

In this chapter, we will explore the complex process of de-anonymizing dark web users, a critical skill for investigators seeking to unmask cybercriminals behind email breaches, data leaks, and other illicit activities. While the dark web offers anonymity through tools like Tor, it is not impenetrable. We will examine the techniques used by investigators to track and identify individuals hiding behind encrypted networks, from traffic analysis and metadata mining to exploiting human error and digital breadcrumbs. By understanding how dark web users can inadvertently expose themselves, we will outline strategies to uncover their real-world identities, locations, and connections. This chapter will provide essential insights into de-anonymizing techniques, empowering investigators to break through layers of concealment and bring cybercriminals to justice.

10.1 How Cybercriminals Try to Stay Anonymous

In the world of cybercrime, anonymity is crucial for criminals to evade law enforcement, security researchers, and OSINT (Open-Source Intelligence) investigators. Cybercriminals use a range of techniques to obfuscate their identities, hide their digital footprints, and protect their operations on both the surface web and dark web.

This chapter explores the key methods cybercriminals use to maintain anonymity, from privacy-focused communication tools and cryptocurrency laundering to identity obfuscation techniques and operational security (OPSEC) strategies. Understanding these tactics is essential for OSINT professionals and investigators working to de-anonymize threat actors and track cybercriminal activities.

1. Privacy-Focused Communication Methods

Cybercriminals rarely use traditional email, phone calls, or social media without extra layers of security. Instead, they rely on encrypted and anonymous communication platforms, including:

1.1 Encrypted Messaging Apps

Cybercriminals often use end-to-end encrypted messaging services such as:

- **Telegram** – Popular for cybercrime communities, ransomware negotiations, and fraud markets.

- **Tox** – A decentralized, peer-to-peer encrypted messaging service often used for ransomware communications.
- **Wickr & Signal** – Encrypted apps with features like self-destructing messages and anonymous registration.

💡 **OSINT Tip:**

Investigators can monitor public Telegram channels and darknet forums where cybercriminals advertise services.

1.2 Anonymous Emails & Temporary Accounts

Instead of using personal email providers like Gmail or Outlook, cybercriminals prefer:

- **ProtonMail & Tutanota** – Encrypted email services that do not log IP addresses.
- **Disposable Email Services** – Temporary email providers (e.g., Guerrilla Mail, Temp-Mail) for short-term use.

📌 **Example**: A ransomware operator might provide a ProtonMail address for victim negotiations instead of a traceable corporate email.

💡 **OSINT Tip:**

Searching for PGP keys associated with an email address can sometimes reveal linked usernames or past messages.

2. Obfuscating IP Addresses & Internet Traffic

To prevent being traced, cybercriminals use multiple techniques to hide their real IP addresses and make tracking difficult.

2.1 VPNs & Proxy Chains

- VPNs (Virtual Private Networks) encrypt internet traffic and route it through remote servers.
- Proxy chains (chaining multiple proxies) add additional layers of redirection.
- SOCKS5 proxies are often used to obfuscate traffic for illicit activities.

📌 **Example**: A cybercriminal launching a phishing attack might use a chain of VPNs and proxies to make it appear as if they are operating from different countries.

💡 OSINT Tip:

VPN-detecting services can analyze login locations and detect patterns of multiple IPs from different regions in short timeframes.

2.2 The Tor Network & I2P

Dark web actors heavily rely on:

- **Tor (The Onion Router)** – Encrypts traffic and routes it through multiple volunteer nodes worldwide.
- **I2P (Invisible Internet Project)** – An alternative to Tor, designed for more decentralized anonymous browsing.

📌 **Example**: A ransomware gang might host their "leak site" on a Tor hidden service (.onion) to prevent takedowns.

💡 OSINT Tip:

Monitoring Tor exit nodes and tracking dark web sites for unique identifiers can help link criminals to specific activities.

3. Hiding Financial Transactions

Since traditional banking systems require identity verification, cybercriminals turn to cryptocurrencies and financial obfuscation methods to launder money.

3.1 Cryptocurrency & Privacy Coins

Bitcoin (BTC) is the most commonly demanded payment for cyber extortion, but criminals prefer privacy-focused coins such as:

- **Monero (XMR)** – Fully private transactions that are nearly impossible to trace.
- **Zcash (ZEC)** – Supports optional privacy features to hide transaction details.

📌 **Example**: A dark web vendor may convert Bitcoin into Monero using a crypto exchange to avoid traceability.

💡 OSINT Tip:

Blockchain analysis tools like Chainalysis or Blockchair can track Bitcoin transactions and detect suspicious patterns.

3.2 Mixing & Tumbling Services

To break the transaction trail, criminals use:

- **Mixers (Tumblers)** – Services that blend multiple users' cryptocurrencies to obscure the origins.
- **Chain-hopping** – Converting funds between different cryptocurrencies across multiple exchanges.

📌 **Example**: A ransomware group might use a Bitcoin mixer before withdrawing funds from an exchange.

💡 **OSINT Tip:**

Monitoring known mixer wallet addresses can help track illicit funds.

4. Creating Fake Identities & False Leads

To further protect themselves, cybercriminals often create layers of deception by using:

4.1 Stolen or Synthetic Identities

Cybercriminals purchase:

- Leaked personal data from breaches to create synthetic identities.
- Fake government-issued IDs (e.g., passports, driver's licenses) from dark web markets.

📌 **Example**: A hacker may use a stolen identity to open a fraudulent bank account to receive illicit funds.

💡 **OSINT Tip:**

Investigators can use facial recognition tools and reverse image searches to verify identity claims.

4.2 Fake Social Media & Sock Puppet Accounts

Many cybercriminals:

- Use fake LinkedIn profiles to appear legitimate.
- Create burner Twitter or Telegram accounts to promote illicit services.
- Use deepfake technology to generate realistic profile photos.

📌 **Example**: A ransomware group might pose as a cybersecurity researcher to infiltrate forums or mislead investigators.

💡 **OSINT Tip:**

Checking profile history, engagement patterns, and reverse image searches can help detect sock puppet accounts.

5. Avoiding OSINT & Law Enforcement Tracking

Sophisticated cybercriminals understand that investigators rely on OSINT techniques, so they actively try to counter them.

5.1 OPSEC Best Practices Used by Criminals

- Never reusing usernames or emails across multiple platforms.
- Avoiding personal language patterns that could be used for linguistic profiling.
- Using air-gapped devices to prevent malware tracing back to their real machines.

📌 **Example**: A cybercriminal might use different aliases across different dark web forums to prevent being linked.

💡 **OSINT Tip:**

Behavioral analysis (such as writing style or response time patterns) can sometimes reveal linked identities.

5.2 Self-Destructing Data & Secure Deletion

- Shredder tools permanently delete files to avoid forensic recovery.
- Secure OS setups (like Tails or Whonix) prevent logs from being saved.

- Dead-drop email accounts – Cybercriminals create email accounts, save drafts without sending, then share credentials instead of sending messages.

📌 **Example**: Ransomware operators delete their digital footprint after every attack to prevent tracking.

💡 **OSINT Tip:**

Monitoring known ransomware communication patterns can help link different attacks.

Cybercriminals go to extreme lengths to maintain anonymity, but no method is 100% foolproof. OSINT investigators can exploit mistakes, correlate data points, and analyze behaviors to track even the most careful threat actors.

Understanding how criminals try to stay anonymous helps law enforcement, cybersecurity professionals, and OSINT analysts uncover digital footprints, disrupt operations, and ultimately bring cybercriminals to justice.

10.2 Identifying Patterns & Behavioral Clues in Online Posts

Cybercriminals may go to great lengths to stay anonymous, but their online activities often leave subtle patterns and behavioral clues. Whether it's a repeated writing style, specific jargon, or consistent posting habits, these details can provide valuable intelligence for OSINT investigators.

By analyzing these patterns across forums, social media, and dark web marketplaces, investigators can link multiple identities, track cybercriminal movements, and identify connections between threat actors. This chapter explores how OSINT professionals use linguistic analysis, metadata tracking, and digital profiling to expose cybercriminals hiding behind anonymous accounts.

1. Linguistic Fingerprinting: Analyzing Writing Styles

Even when cybercriminals use different aliases across forums and platforms, their writing habits often remain consistent.

1.1 Common Indicators in Writing Style

- **Spelling & Grammar** – Does the user consistently misspell certain words or use a specific punctuation style?
- **Word Choice & Jargon** – Do they use the same technical terms or slang repeatedly?
- **Sentence Structure & Length** – Do they favor short, direct messages or long, detailed responses?
- **Tonal Consistency** – Are they formal, aggressive, or overly casual in their interactions?

📌 **Example**: A cybercriminal selling stolen credentials under different usernames may use the same Russian-influenced English grammar across multiple posts.

💡 **OSINT Tip:**

Stylometry tools like Jstylo, Writeprint, or forensic linguistic analysis can compare writing patterns to link anonymous accounts.

1.2 Signature Phrases & Catchphrases

Some users develop habits of using the same greetings, sign-offs, or slang across different platforms.

📌 **Example**: A darknet vendor who consistently ends posts with "Serious buyers only, no time-wasters" could be linked across different sites.

💡 **OSINT Tip:**

Searching for unique phrases in darknet marketplaces, Telegram channels, and cybercrime forums can reveal linked identities.

2. Behavioral Patterns: Activity Timing & Post Frequency

Even when cybercriminals use different aliases, their behavioral patterns often remain consistent.

2.1 Posting Schedules & Time Zones

Cybercriminals unknowingly reveal their real-world location through their activity patterns.

- **Consistent posting hours** – Do they always post at specific times of day?

- **Gaps in activity** – Do they disappear for weekends or holidays (indicating a specific work schedule)?
- **Time zone clues** – Do their most active hours align with a particular country?

📌 **Example**: A ransomware operator claims to be in Eastern Europe, but their posting times match a U.S. time zone, suggesting they are lying about their location.

💡 **OSINT Tip:**

Tools like ChronoLink can analyze timestamps across multiple forums to detect posting patterns.

2.2 Forum Engagement & Reply Speed

- Do they reply instantly to messages (suggesting an automated script or bot)?
- Do they engage with specific users repeatedly, suggesting close connections?
- Are they active on multiple platforms simultaneously, indicating cross-site identity use?

📌 **Example**: A dark web scammer might operate under different aliases but always responds to messages within minutes, suggesting they are managing multiple accounts.

💡 **OSINT Tip:**

Tracking response times across multiple accounts can expose linked identities.

3. Profile & Metadata Analysis: What Their Accounts Reveal

Cybercriminals try to stay anonymous, but small profile details often betray connections between accounts.

3.1 Profile Registration Similarities

- **Username Patterns** – Does the user recycle parts of their username across different platforms?
- **Email Overlaps** – Have they ever accidentally revealed an email linked to a different account?
- **Avatar & Profile Pictures** – Are they using a similar image across platforms?

📌 **Example**: A hacker using the alias "DarkN3tMaster" on one forum might also be "D3epN3tM4ster" on another.

💡 **OSINT Tip:**

Using reverse image searches (Google, TinEye) on profile pictures can find duplicate accounts.

3.2 IP & Device Fingerprinting

- Some dark web forums leak IP logs or have security flaws that expose user metadata.
- Some cybercriminals forget to use VPNs on all their accounts, linking them accidentally.

📌 **Example**: A phishing scammer operating under different aliases once logged in with the same IP across multiple forums.

💡 **OSINT Tip:**

Checking for leaked database breaches can reveal real-world IPs linked to an alias.

4. Social Engineering & Infiltrating Cybercrime Communities

One of the best ways to identify patterns in cybercriminal behavior is to engage with them directly.

4.1 Social Engineering Techniques

- Pretending to be a new hacker asking for guidance can make criminals slip up and reveal personal habits.
- Gaining trust in a cybercrime forum can expose internal communication patterns.

📌 **Example**: An OSINT investigator posing as a ransomware buyer might notice that different vendors all redirect to the same contact email, exposing a single operator behind multiple accounts.

💡 **OSINT Tip:**

Building personas with long-term credibility helps gain access to invite-only cybercrime groups.

4.2 Monitoring Private Channels

- Many cybercriminals communicate via private Telegram groups or Discord servers.
- Gaining access to these communities allows investigators to track group dynamics, leadership, and alliances.

📌 **Example**: A ransomware gang using multiple usernames might unknowingly reference their other aliases in private chats.

💡 **OSINT Tip:**

Monitoring Telegram bot interactions can sometimes expose a group's internal structure.

5. Real-World Case Study: Linking a Hacker's Online Aliases

Case: How an OSINT Investigation Unmasked a Cybercriminal

A cybercriminal operating under the alias "CryptoHunter99" was active in a dark web marketplace selling stolen credit cards. The investigation revealed:

Linguistic Analysis:

- The user consistently used British slang in their dark web posts.
- Their writing contained unique spelling mistakes repeated across multiple forums.

Behavioral Pattern Analysis:

- Their posts were always made between 6 PM - 2 AM GMT, suggesting a UK-based individual.
- They frequently engaged with a small group of repeat customers, hinting at personal connections.

Profile Metadata Analysis:

- A reverse image search of their profile picture found a similar image on a Russian-language tech forum.

- Their forum email was accidentally linked to a real-world Twitter account that had an old LinkedIn profile.

📌 **Outcome:**

The investigation linked CryptoHunter99 to a real-world identity in London, leading to law enforcement action.

💡 **Key Takeaways:**

- Even careful cybercriminals make small mistakes that OSINT investigators can exploit.
- Analyzing language, timing, and engagement habits can uncover hidden identities.
- Metadata leaks and social engineering remain powerful tools in de-anonymizing criminals.

Cybercriminals may try to stay hidden, but their writing style, posting habits, and behavioral patterns often betray their identities. By applying linguistic analysis, activity tracking, and social engineering, OSINT investigators can link anonymous accounts, track threat actors, and expose cybercriminal networks.

By understanding these tactics, investigators can turn online patterns into real-world intelligence, making it harder for cybercriminals to operate undetected.

10.3 Cross-Referencing Dark Web Identities with Social Media & Clear Web Data

Many cybercriminals operate on the dark web, assuming they can remain anonymous. However, they often make critical mistakes—reusing usernames, emails, or writing styles across different platforms. OSINT (Open-Source Intelligence) investigators can exploit these slip-ups by cross-referencing dark web identities with social media profiles, forums, and public databases on the clear web.

This chapter explores how investigators link dark web aliases to real-world identities, including techniques for tracking usernames, emails, PGP keys, and behavioral patterns across multiple platforms.

1. Identifying Digital Footprints: The Power of Cross-Referencing

Even skilled cybercriminals leave behind small, seemingly insignificant traces of their identity. These digital breadcrumbs can be found in:

- **Dark web forums & marketplaces** (e.g., usernames, vendor pages, signatures)
- **Social media platforms** (e.g., Twitter, Reddit, Facebook, LinkedIn)
- **Clear web forums** (e.g., hacker communities, programming boards)
- **Paste sites & breach databases** (e.g., Pastebin, Have I Been Pwned)

By systematically cross-referencing these sources, OSINT investigators can connect an anonymous dark web identity to a real person.

2. Tracking Usernames Across Platforms

2.1 Username Reuse & Variations

Cybercriminals frequently reuse usernames across different platforms, making it easier to track them. Even when they modify their usernames slightly, patterns often emerge.

📌 **Example**: A hacker using "DarkRiderX" on a darknet forum might also use "DarkRiderX99" on Twitter or a gaming forum.

💡 **OSINT Tip:**

- Use username search engines like Namechk, Sherlock, or WhatsMyName to check where a username is used.
- Search for variations of the username by adding numbers, hyphens, or common substitutions (e.g., l33t spelling).

2.2 Reverse-Engineering Username Origins

Sometimes, usernames originate from an old alias the user no longer considers risky.

📌 **Example**: A cybercriminal using "CryptoPhantom" on a darknet forum might have once used the same username for an old gaming account or tech forum years earlier.

💡 **OSINT Tip:**

- Search old forum posts or gaming accounts for username connections.

- Use Google Dorking ("CryptoPhantom" site:oldforum.com) to uncover hidden links.

3. Linking Email Addresses to Real Identities

3.1 Tracking Down Reused Email Addresses

Cybercriminals sometimes create throwaway emails for dark web activity but may slip up by using a previously compromised or semi-public email.

📌 **Example**: A darknet vendor using "anonhacker123@protonmail.com" may have registered an old account with the same username on a gaming site or forum.

💡 **OSINT Tip:**

- Use "Have I Been Pwned" or dehashed.com to check if an email was ever leaked.
- Search emails on Google, forums, and WHOIS records to find past usage.
- Try forgot password flows on websites to see masked email hints.

3.2 Extracting Email Clues from PGP Keys

Many darknet vendors use PGP encryption to secure communications. However, some accidentally link their PGP keys to clear web emails.

📌 **Example**: A darknet user lists a PGP fingerprint on their vendor page, which is linked to an old email address in a keyserver database.

💡 **OSINT Tip:**

- Search PGP keyservers like MIT PGP or Keybase to check for linked emails.
- Use PGP fingerprint search tools to find old associations.

4. Analyzing Writing Style & Behavior Across Platforms

Even when cybercriminals change usernames or emails, their writing style and posting habits remain remarkably consistent.

4.1 Linguistic Analysis & Writing Patterns

- Do they use the same phrases, slang, or emojis across platforms?

- Do they have specific grammar mistakes or a recognizable writing style?
- Do they always use the same greeting or sign-off?

📌 **Example**: A darknet scammer who always ends messages with "Stay safe, fam!" might use the same phrase in a Reddit comment or Telegram chat.

💡 **OSINT Tip:**

- Use AI-based stylometry tools (e.g., Jstylo, Writeprint) to match writing styles.
- Manually compare message structures, punctuation habits, and tone.

4.2 Posting Behavior & Active Times

Patterns in when and where a cybercriminal posts can also link accounts.

📌 **Example**: A dark web user who posts on forums every night between 10 PM - 2 AM GMT might have a matching Twitter account active during the same hours.

💡 **OSINT Tip:**

Use tools like ChronoLink to analyze post timestamps across forums.
Cross-check active hours on different platforms to find possible connections.

5. Connecting Dark Web & Social Media Data

5.1 Searching for Similar Interests & Topics

- If a dark web user discusses crypto trading, check for similar discussions on Twitter, LinkedIn, or Telegram.
- If they reference a specific location or event, search for social media posts about it.

📌 **Example**: A hacker discussing a new crypto exploit on a darknet forum might also have tweeted about the same exploit weeks earlier.

💡 **OSINT Tip:**

- Use keyword-based social media search ("Bitcoin exploit" site:twitter.com).
- Check if they follow specific industry accounts that match their darknet interests.

5.2 Identifying Real-World Contacts & Associations

- Cybercriminals often interact with the same users across multiple platforms.
- Following their contacts on Twitter or LinkedIn can expose real-world connections.

📌 **Example**: A dark web vendor who never uses their real name may still have Twitter followers who accidentally tag or mention them in posts.

💡 **OSINT Tip:**

- Use tools like Maltego to map out social connections.
- Check Telegram groups, Discord servers, and forum contacts for overlapping users.

6. Real-World Case Study: Unmasking a Dark Web Drug Dealer

Case: How OSINT Investigators Traced a Vendor to a Real Identity

A dark web drug dealer using the alias "PhantomX99" was successfully linked to a real-world identity through a series of OSINT techniques:

- **Username Reuse** – The vendor's alias "PhantomX99" was also found on an old Reddit account discussing crypto trading.
- **Email Cross-Referencing** – A PGP key listed on the vendor's dark web page was linked to an old Yahoo email, found in a breach database.
- **Social Media Clues** – Searching the Yahoo email led to a forgotten Facebook account with similar interests.
- **Writing Style Analysis** – Posts on the dark web forum and Reddit account contained the same spelling mistakes and phrasing.

📌 **Outcome:**

Law enforcement used the linked email and social media profiles to track down the suspect's real-world location.

Cybercriminals may operate in the shadows of the dark web, but their digital footprints often betray them. By cross-referencing usernames, emails, PGP keys, writing styles, and social media activity, OSINT investigators can unmask anonymous criminals with surprising accuracy.

As cybercrime investigations evolve, mastering cross-referencing techniques is becoming one of the most powerful tools for tracking down cybercriminals who think they're untraceable.

10.4 Using Linguistic Analysis & Writing Style Profiling

No matter how carefully cybercriminals try to conceal their identity, their writing style often remains a unique fingerprint. Just like handwriting analysis, digital writing leaves behind linguistic patterns that can be traced across different platforms, including the dark web, social media, and forums.

Linguistic analysis and stylometry—the study of an individual's writing style—are powerful OSINT (Open-Source Intelligence) tools used by cybersecurity experts, law enforcement, and researchers to link anonymous online identities to real-world individuals. This chapter explores how investigators analyze writing styles, detect deception, and leverage AI-powered tools to profile cybercriminals.

1. What is Linguistic Analysis & Stylometry?

Linguistic analysis involves examining the unique characteristics of an individual's writing, including:

- Word choice & vocabulary
- Sentence structure & grammar
- Punctuation habits
- Spelling errors & typos
- Use of slang, emojis, or symbols
- Capitalization patterns
- Preferred greetings & sign-offs

Stylometry takes this further by using statistical and AI-based methods to analyze text and compare it across different sources. These methods can determine if two pieces of writing were likely created by the same person—even if the author is trying to disguise their style.

💡 **Real-World Example:**

The FBI used stylometry to identify the Unabomber, Ted Kaczynski, by comparing his manifesto to his older essays and letters.

2. Identifying Writing Patterns in Cybercrime Investigations

Cybercriminals often communicate using dark web forums, encrypted chat apps, phishing emails, and fake social media accounts. By analyzing how they write, OSINT investigators can:

- Link different aliases to the same person
- Detect deceptive or fake identities
- Identify regional or linguistic backgrounds
- Expose cybercriminals reusing writing patterns on multiple platforms

2.1 Common Writing Mistakes & Habits

Even when criminals try to remain anonymous, they often:

✅ Use the same slang or abbreviations

✅ Make consistent typos or grammar mistakes

✅ Stick to specific sentence structures

✅ Overuse or avoid certain punctuation marks

📌 Example:

A cybercriminal using the alias "ShadowHacker99" on a dark web forum might have the habit of never using apostrophes (e.g., "dont" instead of "don't"). If an investigator finds a Twitter account with similar typos, they can suspect a connection.

💡 OSINT Tip:

- Collect and compare multiple forum posts, emails, and messages for consistent errors.
- Look for regional dialects, abbreviations, or industry-specific jargon.

3. Deception Detection: Spotting Fake Identities

Cybercriminals often try to fake their identity by changing their writing style. However, deception leaves patterns, such as:

- Inconsistent grammar usage
- Switching between formal and informal tone
- Overuse of certain words to "sound" authentic
- Unusual phrasing that doesn't match native speakers

📌 **Example:**

A dark web scammer claiming to be a Russian hacker might write in English but randomly add Russian phrases to sound authentic. However, if the phrases are used incorrectly, it may suggest they're faking their identity.

💡 **OSINT Tip:**

- Use Google Translate reversals to check if a foreign phrase is natural or forced.
- Compare writing samples across different accounts or websites to spot inconsistencies.

4. Using Stylometry Tools for OSINT

Modern AI and stylometry tools can automatically analyze and compare writing styles. These tools break down text into measurable features, such as:

- **Lexical features** (word frequency, vocabulary richness)
- **Syntactic features** (sentence structure, punctuation use)
- **Semantic analysis** (context and meaning of words)

4.1 Popular Stylometry & Linguistic Analysis Tools

🔍 **Jstylo** – An open-source stylometry tool used by forensic linguists.

🔍 **Writeprint** – Identifies authorship based on text samples.

🔍 **TAPT** (Twitter Authorship Prediction Tool) – Links Twitter accounts based on writing style.

🔍 **Linguistic Inquiry and Word Count** (LIWC) – Analyzes emotions, tone, and psychological traits in text.

📌 **Example:**

An investigator trying to link two anonymous hacking forum accounts can use Jstylo to compare their writing patterns. If the system detects a high likelihood of the same author, it strengthens the case.

💡 OSINT Tip:

- Feed multiple samples of a suspect's writing into Jstylo or Writeprint for comparison.
- Test different types of messages (e.g., long forum posts vs. short tweets) for consistency.

5. Real-World Case Study: Unmasking a Dark Web Scammer

Case: How Linguistic Analysis Led to an Arrest

A dark web scammer known as "CryptoPhantom" was running a phishing operation targeting cryptocurrency investors. OSINT investigators used linguistic analysis to track him down:

- **Writing Style Matching** – The scammer frequently misspelled "guarantee" as "garuntee". A LinkedIn post with the same typo was found.
- **Punctuation Patterns** – CryptoPhantom used double exclamation points (!!) in emails and forum posts, matching a personal blog.
- **Regional Dialect Clues** – Certain words and phrases indicated a British English speaker, narrowing the search.
- **Social Media Cross-Referencing** – The LinkedIn post linked to a GitHub account with similar writing habits.

📌 Outcome:

Law enforcement linked CryptoPhantom's real identity and arrested him for fraud.

💡 **Key Takeaway**: Even small typos, punctuation habits, and vocabulary choices can be enough to connect an anonymous dark web user to a real person.

6. Best Practices for Using Linguistic Analysis in OSINT

✅ DO:

✓ Collect multiple writing samples from different sources.

✓ Use stylometry tools to compare writing styles.

✓ Look for consistent grammar mistakes & spelling habits.

✓ Check for regional dialect clues (British vs. American English, etc.).

✓ Compare dark web posts, emails, and social media messages.

✗ DON'T:

✗ Assume one writing feature is proof of identity—always cross-check other data.

✗ Ignore context—writing styles can change slightly in different situations.

✗ Forget that AI-based stylometry tools aren't 100% accurate—human review is essential.

Linguistic analysis and writing style profiling are powerful OSINT techniques for tracking cybercriminals, unmasking fake identities, and linking anonymous accounts. Whether analyzing phishing emails, dark web forum posts, or social media messages, investigators can use stylometry to reveal patterns that criminals can't hide.

As cybercrime evolves, linguistic analysis will continue to play a crucial role in de-anonymizing threat actors and exposing hidden connections across the web.

10.5 Tracking OPSEC Failures & Leaked Personal Information

No matter how well cybercriminals attempt to hide their identities, operational security (OPSEC) failures often expose crucial details that investigators can use to track them. A single mistake—such as reusing an email address, posting from a known IP, or slipping up in language patterns—can provide a lead that unravels an entire operation.

In this chapter, we will explore how cybercriminals' poor OPSEC habits result in leaked personal information, and how OSINT (Open-Source Intelligence) investigators track these breadcrumbs across the dark web, social media, and public databases to unmask hidden identities.

1. What is OPSEC & Why Do Cybercriminals Fail at It?

Operational Security (OPSEC) is the practice of hiding sensitive information that could be used to expose someone's real identity or location. It involves techniques such as:

- Using separate online personas for different activities
- Avoiding real names, personal emails, or social media connections
- Masking IP addresses with VPNs, proxies, or Tor
- Encrypting communications and financial transactions

1.1 Common OPSEC Failures by Cybercriminals

Despite their efforts, cybercriminals often make mistakes that expose them, such as:

✅ Reusing usernames & emails across forums and platforms

✅ Logging into an alias account from a personal IP address

✅ Using weak passwords that have been leaked in breaches

✅ Leaving metadata in documents, images, or code

✅ Forgetting to disable tracking features in apps or emails

✅ Mentioning real-world details in chat logs or forum posts

📌 **Example:**

A hacker named "DarkShadowX" may take precautions while using Tor to access dark web forums, but if they use the same username on a gaming forum or social media site, investigators can connect the dots.

💡 **OSINT Tip:**

Search for a cybercriminal's alias on multiple platforms to check for OPSEC leaks.

2. Tracking Leaked Email Addresses & Usernames

Many cybercriminals make the fatal mistake of reusing email addresses or usernames across multiple platforms. This can expose their identity when their credentials appear in data breaches or OSINT databases.

2.1 Using OSINT Tools to Search for Leaked Emails

🔍 Tools & Techniques:

- **Have I Been Pwned (HIBP)** – Check if an email has been exposed in a breach.
- **Dehashed & LeakCheck** – Search for leaked credentials from past breaches.
- **OSINT Framework & Sherlock** – Locate usernames across multiple sites.
- **GHunt** – Extract metadata from Google-related email accounts.

📌 Example:

An anonymous ransomware operator used the email cryptomaster007@protonmail.com for criminal activities. A Have I Been Pwned search revealed it was linked to an old LinkedIn breach, exposing a real name and workplace.

💡 OSINT Tip:

- Cross-check email aliases and usernames with past breaches.
- Look for typos, unique phrases, or common numbers in reused emails.

3. Tracking IP Leaks & Device Fingerprints

Even when using VPNs or Tor, cybercriminals can still accidentally expose their real IP address due to browser leaks, misconfigurations, or careless logins.

3.1 Common OPSEC Mistakes with IPs & VPNs

- Logging into an alias account without enabling a VPN or Tor
- Using a VPN that suffered a data breach or keeps logs
- Accidentally accessing a real-world service (like Gmail) while connected to an alias

📌 Example:

In 2017, Ross Ulbricht (Silk Road creator) made the mistake of logging into an admin account without using Tor for a brief moment. That small mistake gave the FBI his real IP address, leading to his arrest.

💡 OSINT Tip:

- Check forum post timestamps for any unusual locations or time zones.
- Use Shodan to scan IP addresses that may be linked to cybercriminal infrastructure.

4. Tracing Metadata in Documents & Images

Cybercriminals often leave hidden metadata in the files they upload, revealing critical information like device details, GPS coordinates, or author names.

4.1 How Metadata Can Expose Identities

✅ **EXIF Data in Images** – Digital photos often contain GPS location, device type, and timestamps.

✅ **Document Metadata** – Word, PDF, and Excel files store author names and software info.

✅ **Code Repositories** – GitHub and Pastebin leaks may contain hardcoded credentials or IPs.

📌 Example:

A cybercriminal leaked a ransom note in a Microsoft Word file. OSINT investigators extracted the document metadata, which contained a username that was linked to a real-world identity.

🔍 Tools to Extract Metadata:

- **ExifTool** – Extracts image metadata, including GPS location.
- **FOCA** – Analyzes metadata in documents and PDFs.
- **GitRob** – Finds exposed secrets in GitHub repositories.

💡 OSINT Tip:

- Download suspect files and run metadata analysis before opening them.
- Reverse search images to find the original upload source.

5. Tracking Social Media & Forum Slips

Even the most careful cybercriminals occasionally post something too revealing—a hometown mention, a favorite hobby, or a reference to an event.

5.1 Cross-Referencing Social Media & Dark Web Accounts

Cybercriminals often:

- Use similar slang, emojis, or phrasing across multiple accounts
- Accidentally link their anonymous accounts to a personal one
- Follow or interact with real-world connections

📌 Example:

A dark web fraudster posted about a rare car model he owned. Investigators found a Facebook post with the same rare car, leading to his identification.

💡 OSINT Tip:

- Use usernames, phrases, and profile images to cross-check social media platforms.
- Monitor dark web forums for deleted posts or account name changes.

6. Real-World Case Study: The Fall of "Dread Pirate Roberts"

The infamous Silk Road marketplace was run by the pseudonymous Dread Pirate Roberts (DPR). Despite using Tor, PGP encryption, and cryptocurrency, Ross Ulbricht made several OPSEC mistakes that led to his arrest:

- Reused his real Gmail address when discussing Silk Road before launching it.
- Logged into an admin account without Tor, exposing his real IP.
- Posted on Stack Overflow under his real name, later editing it—but investigators had already archived the original post.

📌 Outcome:

The FBI linked his real-world identity to his Silk Road operations, leading to his capture in 2013.

💡 Key Takeaway:

Even small OPSEC mistakes accumulate over time—one slip can unravel an entire operation.

7. Best Practices for OSINT Investigators

✅ **DO:**

✔ Monitor data breach sites for leaked usernames & passwords.

✔ Track IP leaks and metadata in uploaded files.

✔ Cross-check forum posts, dark web accounts, and social media profiles.

✔ Archive deleted or edited posts for historical analysis.

✔ Use AI-based linguistic analysis to track speech patterns.

✖ **DON'T:**

✖ Assume a single mistake proves identity—always confirm with multiple sources.

✖ Ignore timing or time zone mismatches in forum posts.

✖ Overlook financial transactions—cryptocurrency trails can lead to real identities.

Tracking OPSEC failures and leaked personal information is a crucial OSINT technique for unmasking cybercriminals. From reused emails and metadata leaks to IP slip-ups and forum mistakes, investigators can piece together clues left behind by even the most cautious threat actors.

In the digital world, anonymity is fragile—and one simple mistake can bring down an entire cybercrime operation.

10.6 Case Study: How a Simple Mistake Unmasked a Dark Web Vendor

Even the most cautious cybercriminals make mistakes. While dark web vendors take extreme measures to remain anonymous—using Tor, encrypted messaging, and cryptocurrency—just one small OPSEC failure can reveal their real-world identity. This case study examines how a single slip-up led to the downfall of a prolific dark web vendor selling illegal goods and services.

Through a combination of OSINT techniques, blockchain analysis, and cross-referencing data leaks, investigators were able to track down a vendor who had successfully remained anonymous for years.

1. The Vendor: "ShadowTraderX"

The target of the investigation was a dark web vendor known as "ShadowTraderX", who operated a thriving marketplace for stolen credit card data, counterfeit documents, and hacking tools. Over the course of two years, ShadowTraderX built a reputation as a reliable seller with excellent customer service and positive reviews on multiple dark web forums.

1.1 OPSEC Measures Taken by the Vendor

To avoid detection, ShadowTraderX followed strict operational security (OPSEC) practices:

✅ Using Tor for all communications to prevent IP tracking

✅ Accepting only cryptocurrency to avoid traditional financial tracing

✅ Encrypting messages with PGP keys for secure transactions

✅ Never sharing personal details or real-world connections

Despite these precautions, a single mistake provided investigators with the breakthrough they needed.

2. The Mistake: A Reused Email Address

ShadowTraderX made an OPSEC slip-up when setting up their vendor profile on a new dark web marketplace. While registering, they used an email address that was previously associated with a personal account on a clear web site—a fatal error.

2.1 How Investigators Found the Connection

🔍 Step 1: Searching for Reused Emails

- Investigators ran the vendor's public contact email through data breach search engines like Have I Been Pwned, Dehashed, and LeakCheck.
- A match appeared—the same email was linked to a 2018 breach of a technology forum.

🔍 Step 2: Cross-Referencing Social Media

- Investigators found that the breached email was previously used on a programming forum, where the user had posted under their real name years before.
- A deeper search connected this forum profile to a LinkedIn account with employment history, location, and other personal details.

💡 Key Takeaway:

Even one instance of email reuse can unravel years of anonymity.

3. Cryptocurrency Trail: Linking Transactions

With a real-world name now linked to ShadowTraderX, investigators turned their focus to cryptocurrency analysis.

3.1 Blockchain Tracking with OSINT Tools

🔍 Step 1: Analyzing Bitcoin Transactions

Since ShadowTraderX only accepted Bitcoin payments, investigators used blockchain explorers like Chainalysis, CipherTrace, and Blockchair to trace the wallet addresses associated with the vendor.

🔍 Step 2: Identifying Exchange Deposits

- One of the traced wallets made multiple withdrawals to a known cryptocurrency exchange.
- Exchanges require identity verification (KYC), meaning the user's real name was stored in the exchange's records.

📌 Critical Mistake:

ShadowTraderX had withdrawn funds from a personal wallet to a KYC exchange, leaving a direct paper trail for investigators to follow.

💡 Key Takeaway:

Cryptocurrency isn't fully anonymous—all transactions remain on the blockchain forever.

4. The Final Clue: IP Address Leak & Social Media Slip

4.1 Unmasking the Real Identity

After connecting ShadowTraderX's email to a personal forum account and tracing their Bitcoin transactions, investigators needed one final piece of evidence to confirm the identity.

🔍 Step 1: Monitoring Dark Web Forum Activity

- Investigators used OSINT tools like Spiderfoot and DarkOwl to track ShadowTraderX's dark web forum posts.
- One post contained an embedded image that was hosted on an external site.

🔍 Step 2: Extracting Metadata from the Image

- The image's EXIF metadata included a timestamp and a partially visible device ID.
- The device ID matched one found in an old social media post from a personal account.

📌 Critical Mistake:

ShadowTraderX uploaded an image without stripping metadata, linking it to a real-world device.

💡 Key Takeaway:

Metadata in images, documents, and code can expose hidden fingerprints.

5. Law Enforcement Action & Arrest

With enough evidence connecting ShadowTraderX's dark web identity to their real-world identity, law enforcement obtained:

✅ A warrant to request information from the cryptocurrency exchange

✅ Access to the suspect's email history and forum activity

✅ Confirmation of shipping addresses used for personal transactions

5.1 The Arrest

Authorities raided the suspect's residence, seizing:

- Multiple laptops and encrypted hard drives
- Cryptocurrency wallets containing illicit funds
- Detailed transaction records of dark web sales

📌 **Outcome:**

ShadowTraderX was arrested and charged with multiple cybercrime offenses, including fraud, identity theft, and money laundering.

💡 **Key Takeaway**
:
Once a cybercriminal's real identity is exposed, their entire operation collapses.

6. Lessons Learned: Avoiding OPSEC Mistakes

ShadowTraderX's downfall highlights key OPSEC failures that cybercriminals often make. Investigators can look for these common mistakes:

❌ **Common OPSEC Mistakes Cybercriminals Make**

1️⃣ Reusing email addresses or usernames across platforms

2️⃣ Failing to clean metadata from uploaded images or documents

3️⃣ Withdrawing cryptocurrency funds to a KYC exchange

4️⃣ Accidentally logging into dark web accounts from a real IP

5️⃣ Leaving personal clues in forum posts, timestamps, or language patterns

💡 **How OSINT Investigators Can Exploit These Mistakes:**

✓ Use data breach search tools to link old emails to real-world accounts

✓ Analyze cryptocurrency transactions to find exchange deposit trails

✓ Check metadata in uploaded images and documents

✓ Cross-reference dark web forum usernames with social media profiles

✓ Monitor linguistic patterns for repeated phrases and unique word choices

This case study proves that even the most careful cybercriminals can be unmasked with persistent OSINT investigations. ShadowTraderX followed many standard anonymity practices, but one small mistake—a reused email—was enough to start an investigation that led to their arrest.

The lesson for OSINT investigators is clear:

🚀 No one is truly anonymous online. Every cybercriminal leaves breadcrumbs, and with the right tools and techniques, those breadcrumbs can lead to a real-world identity.

11. Case Study: Investigating a Dark Web Operation

In this chapter, we will walk through a detailed case study that illustrates the step-by-step process of investigating a dark web operation, focusing on email-related breaches, data leaks, and illicit activities. We will follow a simulated investigation, highlighting key techniques and tools used to track down perpetrators from the dark web to the real world. By analyzing the evidence gathered from marketplaces, forums, cryptocurrency transactions, and other sources, we will demonstrate how to piece together a case, identify suspects, and connect various strands of intelligence. This practical example will provide valuable lessons on the challenges of investigating dark web operations, the strategies for overcoming these challenges, and how to ensure a successful outcome. By the end of this chapter, you'll have a deeper understanding of how complex investigations unfold, offering practical insights that can be applied to real-world OSINT scenarios.

11.1 The Initial Discovery: A Suspicious Dark Web Marketplace

Dark web marketplaces operate in the shadows, offering everything from stolen data to illicit drugs and hacking tools. While many of these marketplaces rise and fall quickly due to scams, law enforcement takedowns, or internal disputes, some manage to operate for years—gaining the trust of cybercriminals and buyers alike.

This chapter explores the initial discovery of a suspicious dark web marketplace, detailing how OSINT investigators identified key clues that led to a major investigation. From analyzing forum chatter to tracking suspicious transactions, this case study demonstrates how law enforcement and cybersecurity researchers work together to uncover and dismantle illegal marketplaces.

1. The Emergence of a New Dark Web Market

In mid-202X, a new marketplace began appearing in dark web discussions. Unlike scam marketplaces that frequently pop up and disappear, this one gained significant traction in a short time.

1.1 Early Signs of an Expanding Operation

Investigators first noticed the marketplace due to:

- **Mentions on criminal forums**: Trusted vendors discussed moving their operations there.
- **Rapid growth in listings**: The number of vendors and items for sale increased quickly.
- **Professional website design**: Unlike amateur scams, the marketplace had robust security features and an escrow system.
- **Dedicated phishing & hacking tools section**: A special category selling malware, phishing kits, and stolen credentials caught researchers' attention.

🔍 OSINT Monitoring Begins

- Cybersecurity researchers started monitoring dark web forums for user discussions.
- Investigators tracked Bitcoin and Monero payments flowing to marketplace wallets.
- Law enforcement began mapping connections to previously seized marketplaces.

📌 Key Takeaway:

A well-structured dark web marketplace with growing vendor activity signals a potential long-term criminal operation.

2. Clues from Vendor Behavior & Market Structure

Unlike simple dark web scams, this marketplace followed established patterns of successful illicit markets, making it harder to take down.

2.1 Observing Vendor Migrations

🔍 Tracking known dark web vendors

- Some vendors were well-known sellers from previous takedowns like Empire Market and DarkMarket.
- OSINT analysts cross-referenced usernames and PGP keys to verify identities.
- Vendors promoted the new marketplace on dark web forums and encrypted Telegram channels.

📌 OPSEC Mistake by Vendors:

Some vendors reused usernames or PGP keys from previous markets—helping investigators connect past activity to the new platform.

2.2 Payment Infrastructure & Escrow Model

🔍 Suspicious Cryptocurrency Wallets

- The marketplace accepted Bitcoin, Monero, and Litecoin.
- A unique pattern of withdrawals suggested links to a known crypto laundering service.
- Investigators used blockchain analytics tools (Chainalysis, CipherTrace) to trace transactions.

📌 Key Finding:

Some payments were linked to previously identified criminal wallets, connecting the new market to a larger cybercrime network.

3. Marketplace's Attempt to Evade Detection

The marketplace admins took several measures to stay hidden, making it harder for OSINT researchers and law enforcement to track them.

3.1 Use of Advanced Anonymity Techniques

🔒 Countermeasures Used by the Marketplace:

✅ Tor Hidden Services with frequent URL changes to avoid takedowns.

✅ Encrypted messaging channels (Jabber, XMPP, and Telegram) for admin-vendor communications.

✅ Mandatory Monero transactions for high-value purchases to avoid Bitcoin tracking.

✅ Multi-sig escrow system to prevent direct crypto wallet exposure.

3.2 OPSEC Mistakes That Exposed Clues

Despite these security measures, investigators found small operational security (OPSEC) failures:

1☐ An admin accidentally reused a Bitcoin address from a past darknet transaction.

2☐ A test listing was briefly visible before launch, leaking early metadata.

3☐ Forum moderators referenced a past dark web market they were involved in—providing a lead.

📌 **Lesson for OSINT Investigators:**

Even the most secure dark web operations make mistakes. Small leaks can be exploited to map out connections and identify key players.

4. The Breakthrough: Connecting the Marketplace to a Real Identity

While the marketplace itself was well-protected, investigators linked a moderator's alias to a real-world identity.

4.1 Dark Web Forum Cross-Referencing

🔍 Investigators ran the marketplace admin's alias through historical dark web data.

- Found similar usernames and writing styles on older, non-anonymous forums.
- Traced previous transactions where the user forgot to use privacy coins.
- Discovered a Twitter account that used the same alias in 2014—revealing a real name.

📌 **Critical Mistake:**

The suspect had used the same alias for both criminal and personal accounts, exposing their identity.

4.2 Cryptocurrency KYC Trail

- A transaction from the marketplace's Bitcoin escrow wallet led to an exchange requiring KYC verification.
- Law enforcement issued a legal request to the exchange, retrieving passport details and IP logs.

💡 **Key Takeaway:**

Despite using Tor and Monero, cybercriminals often slip up when converting crypto into real-world currency.

5. Preparing for a Law Enforcement Takedown

With a confirmed suspect, marketplace infrastructure details, and crypto tracking, law enforcement prepared a takedown operation.

5.1 Seizing Market Servers

🔍 **Steps Taken:**

✅ Identified server hosting providers (bulletproof hosting in offshore locations).

✅ Tracked admins' activity windows to pinpoint locations.

✅ Deployed honeypot vendor accounts to interact with admins directly.

5.2 Coordinated Raid & Arrest

- Multiple agencies (Interpol, Europol, FBI) worked together to seize servers and arrest key operators.
- The marketplace's seizure notice replaced its homepage, warning users.
- Data recovered from the servers provided customer and vendor information, leading to further arrests.

📌 **Outcome:**

◆ The marketplace was shut down and its admins arrested.
◆ Investigators uncovered a larger cybercrime network, leading to additional takedowns.

The discovery of this suspicious dark web marketplace highlights how OSINT techniques, blockchain analysis, and forum monitoring can uncover criminal networks. Despite strong anonymity measures, cybercriminals make mistakes, and with persistence, investigators can track, unmask, and dismantle these operations.

💡 **Key OSINT Lessons from this Case:**

✅ Monitor dark web forums for emerging marketplaces.

✅ Cross-reference vendor aliases with historical data leaks.

✅ Analyze cryptocurrency flows to find KYC entry points.

✅ Track OPSEC mistakes like reused usernames, wallet addresses, or writing styles.

🚀 No criminal operation is 100% anonymous. With the right approach, even the most secretive dark web markets can be exposed and taken down.

11.2 Gathering Intelligence & Identifying Key Actors

Once a suspicious dark web marketplace is discovered, investigators must gather intelligence and identify the key actors behind its operations. This process involves a combination of OSINT (Open-Source Intelligence), blockchain analysis, digital forensics, and human intelligence (HUMINT) to unmask the marketplace's administrators, moderators, vendors, and financial operators.

This chapter explores how OSINT professionals and law enforcement agencies gather intelligence, what key indicators to look for, and the tactics used to identify and track individuals involved in dark web marketplaces.

1. Intelligence Gathering on Dark Web Marketplaces

1.1 Monitoring Dark Web Forums & Vendor Communications

Most dark web marketplaces rely on criminal forums, encrypted chat platforms (Telegram, Jabber, Wickr), and darknet sites for vendor recruitment and buyer interactions.

🔍 **Key OSINT Techniques Used to Monitor Activity:**

✅ Tracking vendor migration: Vendors from previously shut-down marketplaces often discuss their new "home" on dark web forums.

✅ Analyzing market advertisements: Market admins post updates on trusted criminal forums, revealing operational details.

✅ Monitoring dispute resolution forums: Many marketplaces have internal dispute sections, where investigators can identify vendor-customer interactions.

📌 **Case Example:**

A new dark web market surfaced after AlphaBay's takedown, and researchers tracked a vendor advertising the same product listings across different forums. By comparing writing style, PGP keys, and username similarities, they confirmed it was the same actor.

1.2 Scraping Market Listings & Identifying Patterns

Marketplaces contain valuable intelligence, including:

- Vendor aliases & trust ratings
- Types of illicit goods sold (drugs, stolen data, malware, hacking tools)
- Payment methods & cryptocurrency addresses
- Buyer feedback & timestamps

🔍 **How Investigators Collect Data:**

✓ Automated scraping tools to collect market listings and vendor information.

✓ Manual analysis of PGP keys, user interactions, and product descriptions.

✓ Tracking repeat buyers who leave detailed reviews, exposing their habits.

📌 **Key Finding:**

Many criminals re-use PGP keys across different marketplaces—allowing analysts to track their presence even after market shutdowns.

2. Identifying Key Marketplace Actors

2.1 Understanding Marketplace Hierarchies

Most dark web marketplaces have a structured hierarchy:

1️⃣ **Administrators (Admins)** – The highest-level operators, responsible for the marketplace infrastructure, security, and financial transactions.

2️⃣ **Moderators (Mods)** – Handle vendor disputes, enforce rules, and assist with customer service.

3️⃣ **Vendors (Sellers)** – Sell illicit goods/services, manage escrow payments, and communicate with buyers.

4️⃣ **Buyers (Customers)** – Purchase items, leave feedback, and sometimes resell goods elsewhere.

5️⃣ **Money Launderers** – Handle financial transactions and cash out cryptocurrency earnings.

🔍 **Identifying These Roles Through OSINT:**

✅ **Admins** – Often post announcements, set escrow terms, and control marketplace policies.

✅ **Mods** – Interact frequently in dispute resolution forums.

✅ **Vendors** – Can be traced by their sales activity, PGP keys, and listing descriptions.

✅ **Money Launderers** – Identified through blockchain tracking and large-volume transactions.

📌 **Key Clue:**

Many moderators and admins maintain separate vendor accounts under different usernames, allowing them to profit from illicit sales while managing the platform.

2.2 Tracking Admin & Moderator Activity

Marketplace administrators and moderators leave behind digital breadcrumbs, even when using anonymization tools like Tor, I2P, or VPNs.

🔍 **Methods to Uncover Admin & Moderator Activity:**

✅ **Analyzing timestamps** – If an admin always posts at the same time, their timezone can be estimated.

✅ **Tracking language patterns** – Linguistic analysis of posts can suggest geographic origins.

✅ **Examining infrastructure clues** – Sometimes, hidden services expose minor details about their hosting locations.

📌 **Case Example:**

A darknet market admin was identified because they always posted between 2 AM – 5 AM UTC. Investigators correlated this pattern with an earlier forum account that used the same phrasing—leading to a suspect in Eastern Europe.

2.3 Linking Dark Web Identities to Real-World Identities

Despite strong OPSEC (Operational Security) practices, many dark web actors make small mistakes that can reveal their real identity.

🔍 **Key OSINT Techniques Used:**

✅ **Cross-referencing aliases** – Searching for username patterns across dark web and clear web forums.

✅ **Tracking leaked credentials** – Some criminals accidentally use leaked personal emails in sign-ups.

✅ **Analyzing writing style** – Linguistic fingerprinting can match anonymous posts to real-world content.

📌 **Case Example:**

A market admin used the alias "ShadowAdmin" on multiple sites. OSINT investigators found a 2015 forum post where they mistakenly linked a personal email to the same username—revealing their real identity.

3. Cryptocurrency Tracking & Financial Intelligence

3.1 Identifying Market Crypto Wallets

Most dark web marketplaces operate on cryptocurrencies like Bitcoin and Monero to remain anonymous. However, crypto transactions can still be traced using advanced blockchain analytics tools.

🔍 **Tracking Cryptocurrency Flows:**

✅ Using blockchain explorers (e.g., Chainalysis, CipherTrace, Blockchair) to track payments.

✅ Identifying clustered wallets used by the marketplace for escrow and withdrawals.

✅ Watching for KYC (Know Your Customer) compliance breaches when criminals attempt to cash out.

📌 **Key Finding:**

Many dark web markets use mixing services (tumblers) to launder funds, but investigators can still track patterns of behavior.

3.2 Following the Money Trail to Real Identities

Even with advanced laundering techniques, cybercriminals eventually need to convert crypto into real money.

🔍 **How Investigators Find KYC Breaks:**

✅ Monitoring transactions entering or exiting regulated exchanges.

✅ Looking for suspicious high-value trades that don't match typical behavior.

✅ Checking if known criminal wallets reuse old addresses from previous cases.

📌 **Case Example:**

A marketplace operator attempted to convert Bitcoin into cash via a crypto exchange. Investigators issued a legal request, revealing their passport details and IP logs—leading to their arrest.

4. Human Intelligence (HUMINT) & Social Engineering

Sometimes, the best intelligence comes from insiders—disgruntled vendors, arrested criminals, or rival marketplace operators.

4.1 Recruiting Informants & Undercover Operations

💡 **How OSINT Investigators Gather HUMINT:**

✅ Infiltrating dark web forums under fake vendor accounts.

✅ Building trust with insiders to gain intel on operations.

✅ Monitoring rival market disputes where vendors expose each other.

📌 **Key Finding:**

A disgruntled moderator from a marketplace leaked admin details after not receiving payment—leading to the entire operation being exposed.

Gathering intelligence on a dark web marketplace requires a mix of OSINT, blockchain forensics, linguistic analysis, and social engineering. Despite using advanced anonymity techniques, cybercriminals always leave traces—whether through reused aliases, cryptocurrency transactions, or OPSEC mistakes.

💡 **Key Takeaways for OSINT Investigators:**

✅ Track vendor migrations across different marketplaces.

✅ Analyze cryptocurrency payments to uncover financial trails.

✅ Cross-reference usernames & writing styles to find real-world identities.

✅ Leverage human intelligence (HUMINT) from insiders and informants.

🚀 By systematically gathering intelligence, law enforcement can dismantle even the most well-hidden darknet operations.

11.3 Cross-Referencing Dark Web Data with Surface Web OSINT

Dark web marketplaces, forums, and criminal operations exist in isolated networks like Tor, I2P, and ZeroNet. However, many cybercriminals inadvertently leave traces of their activity on the surface web—whether through reused usernames, social media activity, public databases, or leaks.

By cross-referencing dark web data with surface web OSINT, investigators can connect anonymous actors to real-world identities, track financial transactions, and uncover infrastructure details. This chapter explores techniques to bridge the gap between the dark web and the clear web using OSINT methodologies.

1. Identifying Overlapping Digital Footprints

1.1 Reused Usernames & Aliases

Despite efforts to stay anonymous, cybercriminals often reuse usernames, email addresses, or PGP keys across different platforms.

🔍 How OSINT Analysts Track Username Reuse:

☑ Search across data breach databases (e.g., Have I Been Pwned, DeHashed) for exposed credentials.

☑ Use search engines (Google dorking, ahmia.fi, Intelligence X) to find matching aliases on forums.

☑ Compare usernames in OSINT tools like WhatsMyName to check if the alias appears on multiple platforms.

📌 Example:

A cybercriminal selling stolen credentials on a dark web market used the alias "ShadowHacker99." OSINT analysts found the same alias on a hacking forum from 2014, where the user had posted an old personal email—leading to their real identity.

1.2 Connecting PGP Keys & Digital Signatures

Dark web vendors and admins often use PGP encryption to secure communications. However, many criminals reuse the same PGP keys across multiple platforms.

🔍 How to Cross-Reference PGP Keys:

☑ Search for matching PGP fingerprints in key directories (keys.openpgp.org, Keybase).

☑ Look for old forum posts where the suspect might have published their PGP key.

☑ Extract PGP keys from dark web marketplaces and compare them with surface web leaks.

📌 Example:

An investigator found a PGP key used by a ransomware group on a dark web leak site. After searching for the key's fingerprint, they discovered it had been previously posted on a public security forum by a "cybersecurity enthusiast"—who turned out to be the group's leader.

1.3 Analyzing Writing Styles & Linguistic Patterns

Cybercriminals often communicate in specific ways that can be linguistically profiled. By analyzing writing style, investigators can identify if the same person is posting under multiple aliases.

🔍 **Key OSINT Linguistic Analysis Methods:**

✅ Comparing phrasing, slang, and grammar in posts across different forums.

✅ Checking for unique spelling mistakes or regional dialects.

✅ Using tools like JStylo or WritePrints for author attribution analysis.

📌 **Example:**

A vendor on a dark web drug market consistently used British slang and a distinctive phrase in their listings. Investigators found the same phrase on a public blog about Bitcoin security, revealing their identity.

2. Mapping Cryptocurrency Transactions Between the Dark Web & Clear Web

2.1 Tracking Bitcoin & Monero Transactions

Most dark web transactions use Bitcoin (BTC), Monero (XMR), or other cryptocurrencies. While Monero is harder to trace, Bitcoin transactions are recorded on a public ledger—allowing investigators to follow the money.

🔍 **How OSINT Analysts Track Crypto Transactions:**

✅ Using blockchain explorers (Blockchair, Chainalysis, CipherTrace) to follow Bitcoin payments.

☑ Identifying wallets used on dark web markets and checking if they sent funds to a KYC-regulated exchange.

☑ Watching for unusual transaction patterns that may indicate laundering via mixers or tumblers.

📌 **Example:**

A cybercriminal cashed out Bitcoin from a ransomware payment through a known exchange. By subpoenaing the exchange, authorities obtained KYC verification data, exposing their real-world identity.

2.2 Identifying Crypto Payment Traces on the Clear Web

Sometimes, criminals leave crypto traces on social media or financial platforms.

🔍 **How OSINT Analysts Find These Clues:**

☑ Checking Twitter, Discord, and Reddit for cryptocurrency addresses linked to their alias.

☑ Investigating leaked transaction records from breached financial services.

☑ Searching dark web vendor names in crypto scam databases (BitcoinAbuse, ScamAlert).

📌 **Example:**

A darknet vendor was promoting their Monero wallet address on a dark web forum. Investigators found the same wallet linked to a Twitter account from 2016, leading to the suspect's real name.

3. Correlating Dark Web Infrastructure with Surface Web Data

3.1 Tracking Dark Web Hosting & Server Clues

Even though the dark web is meant to be anonymous, some operators accidentally leave server fingerprints or misconfigured settings that expose them.

🔍 How to Find Hosting Connections:

✅ Analyzing SSL/TLS certificates using Censys, Shodan, or CRT.sh to find matching surface web sites.

✅ Checking misconfigured Apache or Nginx servers that reveal IP addresses.

✅ Using DNS analysis tools (RiskIQ, Farsight DNSDB) to track domain registrations.

📌 Example:

A dark web market admin forgot to remove an old SSL certificate, which was linked to a clear web hosting provider. Investigators subpoenaed the provider, leading to an arrest.

3.2 Cross-Referencing WHOIS, DNS & Website Metadata

Even when criminals use privacy protections, some old domain records or forgotten DNS configurations can leak useful details.

🔍 Key OSINT Techniques for Domain Analysis:

✅ Using historical WHOIS records (WhoisXML API, DomainTools) to check past ownership.

✅ Tracking Google Analytics or AdSense IDs that were reused on different websites.

✅ Analyzing leaked hosting provider data to find linked accounts.

📌 Example:

A hacker group used a dark web forum to plan attacks but hosted their private chat on a surface web domain. Investigators checked WHOIS history, finding a registered phone number—which led to an arrest.

4. Social Media & Data Breaches: Unmasking Identities

4.1 Finding Criminals Through Their Social Media Footprint

Despite their anonymity, many dark web users still have a social media presence, either for personal or business reasons.

🔍 How Investigators Link Dark Web Users to Social Media:

✅ Searching for username matches on platforms like Twitter, Instagram, and LinkedIn.

✅ Checking archived forum posts where users might have shared personal details.

✅ Investigating leaked email databases for breached credentials that link to social media.

📌 Example:

A cybercriminal used the alias "DarkPhantom" on the dark web. Investigators found an old Reddit account under the same name, where they had previously discussed their university and location—leading to their real identity.

4.2 Leveraging Data Breach Dumps for Clues

Many cybercriminals have their own data leaked in breaches—providing valuable OSINT leads.

🔍 How to Use Data Breaches for Investigations:

✅ Searching breached databases (Have I Been Pwned, DeHashed, LeakIX) for email-password pairs.

✅ Checking if the same email appears on hacker forums, job sites, or real-world registrations.

✅ Correlating leaked IP addresses with past forum posts.

📌 Example:

A hacker selling stolen credentials had their own email leaked in a breach. Investigators found the same email used for a job application, revealing their identity.

Cross-referencing dark web intelligence with surface web OSINT is one of the most effective ways to unmask cybercriminals. By tracking usernames, cryptocurrency transactions, infrastructure clues, and social media activity, investigators can bridge the gap between anonymity and real-world identity.

🚀 Key Takeaways:

✅ Look for reused usernames & PGP keys across forums.

✅ Trace cryptocurrency payments to clear web exchanges.

✅ Analyze hosting infrastructure for forgotten links to the surface web.

✅ Leverage data breaches to find personal details.

🔎 With the right OSINT techniques, even the most careful dark web actors can be exposed.

11.4 Analyzing Financial Transactions & Hidden Clues

Financial transactions are often the Achilles' heel of cybercriminals operating on the dark web. While they attempt to remain anonymous, cryptocurrency payments, escrow services, and laundering methods can leave behind crucial clues. Investigators who analyze blockchain transactions, payment patterns, and laundering techniques can track cybercriminals, identify their funding sources, and even uncover real-world identities.

This chapter will explore how OSINT analysts and law enforcement analyze dark web financial transactions, uncover hidden connections, and leverage financial intelligence (FinInt) to disrupt cybercrime.

1. Tracing Cryptocurrency Transactions on the Dark Web

Most dark web transactions rely on cryptocurrencies like Bitcoin (BTC), Monero (XMR), Ethereum (ETH), and Litecoin (LTC). While privacy coins like Monero are designed to obscure transactions, Bitcoin's public ledger allows analysts to trace payments with the right tools and methodologies.

1.1 Using Blockchain Explorers to Follow Transactions

🔍 **OSINT Tools for Tracking Blockchain Transactions:**

✅ **Blockchain.com, Blockchair, and BTCscan** – Publicly available explorers for tracking BTC transactions.

✅ **CipherTrace, Chainalysis, Elliptic** – Advanced tools used by law enforcement for deep blockchain forensics.

✅ **Mempool.space** – Real-time monitoring of Bitcoin network transactions.

📌 **Example:**

Investigators tracked a ransomware payment from a hacked company to a Bitcoin wallet controlled by the attackers. The criminals attempted to launder the funds but inadvertently transferred a portion to a KYC-verified exchange, leading to their arrest.

1.2 Identifying Cryptocurrency Tumbling & Mixing Services

To avoid detection, criminals use mixers, tumblers, and coin swap services to break the transaction trail. These services shuffle cryptocurrencies between multiple wallets, making it harder to trace the original source.

🔍 **OSINT Indicators of Laundering via Mixers:**

✅ Sudden splitting of large transactions into multiple smaller wallets (a tactic known as "smurfing").

✅ Frequent transfers between high-risk wallets with no clear purpose.

✅ Interactions with known mixing services, which can be identified through blockchain analytics.

📌 **Example:**

A darknet market vendor tried to cash out stolen BTC by using a mixing service. However, law enforcement used Chainalysis' clustering techniques to identify the wallet clusters and link them back to their original owner.

2. Connecting Dark Web Payments to Real-World Identities

While cryptocurrency transactions are pseudonymous, many criminals eventually interact with the traditional financial system, exposing their identities.

2.1 Tracing Payments to Crypto Exchanges

Most regulated exchanges require Know Your Customer (KYC) verification, making them an entry point for investigators.

🔍 How to Identify When Criminals Use Exchanges:

✓ Watching for deposits from known darknet wallets into exchange wallets.

✓ Identifying repeated withdrawals from mixing services to exchange accounts.

✓ Looking for patterns in transaction timestamps that match exchange deposit records.

📌 Example:

A drug dealer on a dark web market used a Binance account to convert Bitcoin to cash. Investigators subpoenaed Binance, revealing the suspect's real identity, phone number, and bank details.

2.2 Investigating Peer-to-Peer (P2P) & Over-the-Counter (OTC) Trades

Some criminals avoid exchanges by using P2P and OTC trading, where buyers and sellers exchange crypto directly. However, these transactions can still leave hidden clues.

🔍 How OSINT Analysts Track P2P & OTC Trading:

✓ Monitoring forums and Telegram groups where criminals sell crypto for cash.

✓ Identifying frequent transfers to known P2P addresses on platforms like LocalBitcoins or Paxful.

✓ Checking for repeating deposit amounts, which may indicate structured payments to an unknown buyer.

📌 Example:

A hacker sold stolen credentials for Bitcoin and then used a P2P exchange to cash out. Investigators matched his Telegram username to his real-world identity, leading to his arrest.

3. Hidden Clues in Financial Transactions

Even when criminals take precautions, financial transactions often reveal patterns, behaviors, and links to real-world activities.

3.1 Analyzing Transaction Timing & Patterns

🔍 **Key Clues from Timing Analysis:**

✅ **Repeating transaction timestamps** – If a suspect always transacts at the same time of day, it may indicate an automated process.
✅ **Holiday & timezone patterns** – Transactions occurring during specific holidays may reveal a suspect's country or culture.
✅ **Clusters of activity before known cyberattacks** – Analysts can sometimes predict upcoming cyberattacks by watching ransom payments flow into wallets.

📌 **Example**:

Investigators noticed that a hacker group's wallets received BTC every Friday at 6 PM UTC—suggesting a weekly payday schedule. This helped analysts anticipate their next move.

3.2 Identifying Suspicious Spending Habits

Even anonymous actors need to spend their money somewhere. Investigators can identify them by tracking crypto-to-fiat transactions.

🔍 **Key OSINT Clues from Spending Habits:**

✅ **Payments for luxury goods or real estate** – Criminals often try to launder money by buying expensive items.
✅ **Frequent payments to online retailers** – Some criminals use crypto gift card services to buy goods.
✅ **ATM withdrawals from crypto debit cards** – Some exchanges issue cards that link to crypto wallets, which investigators can track.

📌 **Example:**

A cybercriminal converted Monero to Bitcoin and used a crypto debit card to buy expensive watches. Investigators subpoenaed the card provider, exposing his real-world identity.

4. Case Study: How Financial Clues Led to the Takedown of a Dark Web Market

Background:

A dark web marketplace was selling stolen credit card data, fake passports, and hacking tools. Law enforcement struggled to identify the admins until financial transaction analysis revealed a key vulnerability.

Investigation Steps:

1️⃣ Blockchain forensics identified repeated BTC withdrawals from the market to a known crypto exchange.

2️⃣ A specific wallet cluster showed transactions every Monday, indicating a payroll system for vendors.

3️⃣ Investigators subpoenaed the exchange, obtaining KYC details linked to a real bank account in Eastern Europe.

4️⃣ Financial records revealed a luxury car purchase, leading to the market's administrator.

Outcome:

The administrator was arrested, and the market was shut down. The case highlighted how financial analysis can expose even well-hidden cybercriminals.

Tracking financial transactions is one of the most powerful OSINT techniques for investigating the dark web. By analyzing blockchain movements, laundering techniques, and spending patterns, investigators can trace cybercriminals to real-world identities.

🚀 Key Takeaways:

✅ Cryptocurrency transactions can be traced, even when using mixers and tumblers.

✅ Dark web vendors eventually cash out, often exposing their identity in the process.

☑ Timing, spending habits, and patterns reveal critical behavioral insights.

☑ Financial intelligence (FinInt) is a key tool for law enforcement & OSINT analysts.

🔍 Even in the anonymous world of the dark web, following the money can lead to unmasking cybercriminals.

11.5 Coordinating with Law Enforcement & Cyber Threat Intelligence Teams

Investigating dark web operations and cybercrime often requires collaboration between OSINT analysts, cybersecurity experts, and law enforcement agencies. While individual researchers can uncover valuable intelligence, successful takedowns of cybercriminals and dark web marketplaces depend on coordinated efforts. This chapter explores best practices for working with law enforcement and cyber threat intelligence (CTI) teams, including data sharing, legal considerations, operational security (OPSEC), and real-world case studies.

1. Why Collaboration is Essential in Cybercrime Investigations

Dark web investigations are complex and often involve international actors, encrypted communications, and anonymous financial transactions. No single entity can tackle these threats alone—cooperation between OSINT analysts, law enforcement agencies, and CTI teams significantly improves the chances of identifying, tracking, and neutralizing cybercriminals.

1.1 The Role of Law Enforcement in Cybercrime Investigations

Law enforcement agencies specialize in criminal prosecution, digital forensics, and subpoena power, which enables them to take down cybercriminals. Some key organizations involved in cyber investigations include:

- **Interpol & Europol** – International coordination for cybercrime investigations.
- **FBI Cyber Division** – Handles cyber threats targeting U.S. entities.
- **National Crime Agency (NCA, UK)** – Investigates dark web marketplaces and financial crime.
- **CERT/CSIRT Teams** – Incident response teams that track ongoing threats.

- **Local & State Police Cyber Units** – Handle cyber fraud, identity theft, and online scams.

1.2 The Role of Cyber Threat Intelligence (CTI) Teams

Cyber threat intelligence teams focus on gathering, analyzing, and sharing intelligence about cyber threats. These teams work within private cybersecurity firms, government agencies, and corporate security divisions.

🔍 Key Responsibilities of CTI Teams:

✅ Monitoring cybercriminal activity on dark web forums and marketplaces.

✅ Tracking threat actors and identifying attack patterns.

✅ Analyzing malware, phishing campaigns, and ransomware operations.

✅ Providing actionable intelligence to law enforcement & security teams.

📌 Example:

A CTI team discovered early discussions of a ransomware attack targeting hospitals. By alerting law enforcement and security teams, they helped mitigate the impact before it escalated.

2. Best Practices for Coordinating with Law Enforcement

When working with law enforcement on cybercrime cases, clear communication, data integrity, and legal compliance are essential.

2.1 How OSINT Analysts Can Share Intelligence with Law Enforcement

🔍 Key Steps for Effective Coordination:

✅ **Document all findings carefully** – Keep a record of timestamps, sources, and analysis methods.

✅ **Maintain chain of custody** – Ensure evidence is properly handled for legal admissibility.

✅ **Use secure communication channels** – Avoid discussing sensitive information over unsecured networks.

☑️ **Know the legal boundaries** – Ensure your OSINT activities comply with laws like the Computer Fraud and Abuse Act (CFAA) or GDPR.

☑️ **Provide actionable intelligence** – Instead of just raw data, offer insights on how findings relate to a criminal case.

📌 **Example:**

An OSINT investigator identified a hacker selling stolen corporate login credentials on a dark web forum. By archiving forum posts, tracking crypto payments, and cross-referencing social media profiles, they provided law enforcement with enough evidence to issue a warrant for further investigation.

2.2 Legal Considerations in Cyber Investigations

OSINT analysts must understand the legal limits of their investigations. Some key legal and ethical concerns include:

🔍 What is Legal?

☑️ Collecting publicly available data from forums, marketplaces, and breach databases.

☑️ Analyzing blockchain transactions using open-source tools.

☑️ Reporting cybercrime to authorities.

🚫 What is Illegal?

❌ Hacking into dark web marketplaces or private databases.

❌ Buying or selling stolen data, even for investigative purposes.

❌ Impersonating law enforcement or using deceptive tactics to extract information.

📌 **Case Study:**

A researcher infiltrated a dark web forum selling ransomware tools. By following legal OSINT techniques, they provided law enforcement with verified wallet addresses and server logs, leading to the forum's shutdown.

3. Building Effective Cyber Threat Intelligence Partnerships

Many cybercrime investigations involve cross-sector collaboration between private cybersecurity firms, researchers, and government agencies. Strong partnerships improve threat detection, incident response, and intelligence sharing.

3.1 Sharing Threat Intelligence Between Organizations

🔍 **Effective CTI Sharing Strategies:**

✓ **Use standardized formats** – Threat intelligence should follow structured formats like STIX (Structured Threat Information eXpression) and TAXII (Trusted Automated eXchange of Indicator Information).
✓ **Leverage Information Sharing and Analysis Centers (ISACs)** – Industry-specific groups that share threat intelligence.
✓ **Engage in public-private partnerships** – Cybersecurity firms often collaborate with law enforcement agencies on large-scale cybercrime cases.

📌 **Example:**

A major ransomware operation targeted critical infrastructure in multiple countries. A cybersecurity firm tracking the attack shared malware signatures, IOCs (Indicators of Compromise), and attacker tactics with international law enforcement, leading to a coordinated response.

3.2 Secure Communication & Data Protection

Since cybercriminals constantly monitor researchers and law enforcement efforts, secure communication and OPSEC are crucial.

🔍 **Best Practices for Secure Collaboration:**

✓ Use encrypted communication channels (e.g., Signal, ProtonMail, or Tutanota).

✓ Avoid exposing personal identities when interacting on dark web forums.

✓ Regularly rotate VPNs, Tor circuits, and burner email accounts to maintain anonymity.

✓ Verify sources before sharing intelligence to avoid misinformation.

📌 **Example:**

An OSINT researcher was tracking a dark web vendor selling stolen government credentials. They used encrypted messaging with law enforcement contacts to avoid tipping off the suspect, leading to a covert sting operation.

4. Case Study: A Coordinated Dark Web Marketplace Takedown

Background:

A large dark web marketplace was trafficking stolen data, hacking tools, and illegal goods. Despite its strict OPSEC policies, law enforcement managed to infiltrate and dismantle the operation through coordinated intelligence efforts.

Investigation Steps:

1☐ OSINT analysts identified key marketplace administrators by analyzing forum posts and transaction logs.

2☐ CTI teams tracked cryptocurrency payments and linked wallet addresses to known laundering services.

3☐ Law enforcement agencies obtained subpoenas for cryptocurrency exchanges, revealing real-world identities.

4☐ A joint operation between Europol and FBI led to multiple arrests, shutting down the marketplace.

Outcome:

- Over $100M in cryptocurrency seized.
- Key administrators arrested in multiple countries.
- The marketplace's database was recovered, helping victims of fraud regain control of stolen accounts.

This case demonstrated the power of coordinated cyber threat intelligence and law enforcement collaboration in disrupting cybercriminal networks.

Effective cyber investigations require strong coordination between OSINT analysts, law enforcement, and cyber threat intelligence teams. By following legal guidelines, maintaining OPSEC, and leveraging secure intelligence-sharing methods, investigators can successfully track and take down cybercriminal networks operating on the dark web.

🚀 **Key Takeaways:**

✅ Collaboration improves threat detection and cybercrime takedowns.

✅ Law enforcement provides legal authority, while CTI teams provide technical expertise.

✅ OSINT analysts play a critical role in gathering and analyzing intelligence.

✅ Secure communication and OPSEC are essential for safe and effective investigations.

🔍 Cybercriminals thrive in the shadows, but coordinated intelligence efforts can bring them into the light.

11.6 Final Outcome: Lessons Learned from the Investigation

Every successful cyber investigation leaves behind valuable lessons—insights that improve future intelligence-gathering techniques, refine operational security, and enhance coordination between OSINT analysts, cyber threat intelligence (CTI) teams, and law enforcement. The takedown of the dark web marketplace covered in the previous chapter not only resulted in arrests and asset seizures but also revealed critical patterns in cybercriminal behavior, investigative challenges, and the importance of legal and ethical considerations.

This chapter will analyze the final outcome of the operation, key takeaways from the investigation, and how the OSINT community can apply these lessons to future cybercrime tracking efforts.

1. The Final Outcome of the Investigation

1.1 Marketplace Shutdown & Arrests

The coordinated effort between OSINT analysts, cybersecurity firms, and law enforcement led to:

◆ **Marketplace Seizure**: The dark web marketplace was completely taken offline, preventing further criminal transactions.

◈ **Arrests of Key Operators**: Law enforcement successfully identified and arrested core administrators, moderators, and high-profile vendors.

◈ **Seizure of Digital Assets**: Over $100M in cryptocurrency linked to illegal transactions was seized.

◈ **Database Confiscation**: The marketplace's user database, including vendor profiles and buyer transaction history, was recovered.

📌 **Example Impact:**

Many cybercriminals relied on this marketplace for selling stolen credentials, hacking tools, and illicit goods. Its shutdown disrupted numerous cybercrime networks and forced remaining vendors to relocate, making them more vulnerable to future investigations.

1.2 Ripple Effects on the Cybercrime Community

The marketplace takedown had a wider impact beyond just arrests:

✅ **Fear & Distrust Among Cybercriminals** – Many vendors and buyers panicked, fearing that their transaction logs, private messages, and account details were now in the hands of law enforcement.

✅ **Scammers Exploiting the Panic** – Fraudsters started creating fake "replacement marketplaces," scamming users desperate for an alternative.

✅ **Market Fragmentation** – Instead of a single dominant marketplace, cybercriminals were forced to spread across multiple smaller forums and Telegram groups, making large-scale cybercrime harder to organize.

📌 **Case Study Parallel:**

A similar effect was seen when Silk Road, AlphaBay, and Hansa Market were taken down—buyers and sellers scrambled to find new platforms, but increased law enforcement pressure made new marketplaces less stable.

2. Key Lessons Learned from the Investigation

2.1 The Importance of Patience & Long-Term OSINT Monitoring

Cyber investigations often take months or years before actionable intelligence leads to arrests. The takedown of the dark web marketplace was possible because:

🔍 OSINT analysts tracked vendor activities over time, linking different aliases, cryptocurrency wallets, and email addresses.

🔍 Investigators allowed operations to continue long enough to gather sufficient evidence before acting.

🔍 Data collected from previous investigations (on forums, leak sites, and vendor reputation systems) was crucial for mapping out the entire criminal network.

📌 **Takeaway:**

Investigators should focus on long-term intelligence gathering, even if immediate action is not possible. This allows for stronger cases, better legal outcomes, and more effective cybercrime disruption.

2.2 The Role of OPSEC (Operational Security) in Investigations

Both criminals and investigators rely on strong OPSEC practices—and failures in OPSEC are what ultimately lead to arrests.

◆ Cybercriminal OPSEC Mistakes That Led to Their Capture:

✖ Reusing the same cryptocurrency wallet across different illegal transactions.

✖ Logging into a dark web vendor account using a real-world IP address.

✖ Accidentally exposing personal details in forum posts or leaked data.

◆ Investigator OPSEC Best Practices:

✓ Using secure, anonymized accounts when gathering OSINT on cybercriminals.

✓ Separating personal and investigative digital identities to prevent exposure.

✓ Avoiding direct interactions with criminals unless necessary for intelligence gathering.

📌 **Takeaway:**

Both criminals and investigators are engaged in a constant battle of OPSEC—and even small mistakes can be costly. Training in operational security is critical for OSINT professionals working on cybercrime investigations.

2.3 Collaboration & Intelligence Sharing Are Essential

This case proved that no single organization can fight cybercrime alone. The marketplace takedown required cooperation between:

✅ OSINT analysts tracking forum activities and vendor movements.

✅ Cyber threat intelligence (CTI) teams analyzing blockchain transactions.

✅ Law enforcement agencies coordinating arrests and legal action.

✅ Private cybersecurity firms providing malware analysis and technical expertise.

📌 Example:

The takedown of AlphaBay and Hansa Market in 2017 was successful because Dutch and U.S. authorities collaborated to seize both marketplaces at the same time, preventing criminals from easily switching platforms.

2.4 The Legal & Ethical Challenges of OSINT Investigations

The investigation also highlighted important legal and ethical dilemmas:

⚖️ Where is the line between ethical OSINT gathering and illegal hacking?
✅ Legal OSINT methods include monitoring public forums, analyzing blockchain data, and archiving leaked information.
✖ Illegal actions would include hacking into dark web servers or purchasing stolen data for research.

⚖️ How do investigators handle data privacy concerns?

✅ Law enforcement must balance privacy rights vs. the need to track criminals—especially in regions with strict data protection laws (e.g., GDPR in Europe).

📌 Takeaway:

OSINT analysts and cyber threat intelligence teams must always operate within legal and ethical boundaries to ensure investigations remain admissible in court.

3. What This Means for Future OSINT Investigations

The success of this dark web operation highlights several strategies for improving future cybercrime investigations:

3.1 Building More Advanced OSINT Tools

✅ Developing AI-driven pattern recognition for tracking cybercriminal activities.

✅ Enhancing blockchain analysis tools to follow crypto transactions more effectively.

✅ Improving dark web search engines to monitor underground markets.

3.2 Strengthening International Law Enforcement Collaboration

✅ Establishing better intelligence-sharing frameworks between countries.

✅ Training more law enforcement officers in OSINT techniques.

✅ Creating real-time data exchange programs between private firms and police.

3.3 Educating the Public & Organizations on Cyber Threats

✅ Teaching businesses how to protect themselves from data breaches.

✅ Training employees to recognize phishing and social engineering scams.

✅ Encouraging whistleblowers to report cybercriminal activity to authorities.

Conclusion: Lessons for the OSINT Community

This case reinforced several critical lessons for OSINT analysts, cybersecurity professionals, and law enforcement:

- ◆ Cybercrime investigations require long-term intelligence gathering.
- ◆ OPSEC mistakes—on both sides—can determine the outcome of an investigation.
- ◆ Collaboration between OSINT, CTI, and law enforcement is essential.
- ◆ Legal and ethical considerations must always be respected.
- ◆ New tools and methodologies are needed to track cybercriminals more effectively.

🚀 Final Thought:

While cybercriminals will continue evolving, so too must OSINT analysts and investigators. By refining intelligence-gathering techniques, strengthening collaboration, and maintaining ethical standards, the fight against cybercrime can become even more effective.

🔎 The digital battlefield is constantly shifting, but with the right strategies, investigators can stay one step ahead.

12. Ethical & Legal Concerns in Dark Web OSINT

In this chapter, we will address the ethical and legal considerations that come into play when conducting OSINT investigations on the dark web. While the dark web is often associated with criminal activity, investigators must navigate a complex landscape of privacy, security, and jurisdictional issues. We will discuss the boundaries between legal and illegal actions, highlighting the importance of maintaining ethical standards when gathering intelligence. Key topics will include the legality of accessing dark web sites, the risks of inadvertently violating privacy rights, and the implications of using data obtained from illicit sources. Additionally, we will explore the challenges investigators face when working with international law enforcement and ensuring that their methods align with legal frameworks. This chapter will equip you with the knowledge to conduct ethical and legally sound investigations in this high-risk environment, ensuring that your work remains responsible and justifiable.

12.1 The Legal Risks of Investigating the Dark Web

Investigating the dark web can provide valuable intelligence on cybercriminal activities, data breaches, and illicit marketplaces. However, navigating this hidden part of the internet comes with significant legal risks. Analysts must carefully balance lawful intelligence gathering with strict regulations governing privacy, cybersecurity, and digital investigations.

This chapter will explore key legal risks associated with dark web investigations, including unauthorized access laws, entrapment concerns, handling illicit data, and jurisdictional challenges. We'll also discuss how investigators can stay compliant while conducting ethical and legal OSINT investigations.

1. Unauthorized Access & Hacking Laws

1.1 Understanding Computer Crime Laws

Most countries have strict laws against unauthorized access to computer systems, hacking, and digital intrusion. Investigators must ensure they are not violating these laws while monitoring dark web forums and marketplaces.

📌 **Key laws governing unauthorized access:**

- **U.S.: Computer Fraud and Abuse Act (CFAA)** – Prohibits unauthorized access to protected systems.
- **UK: Computer Misuse Act 1990** – Criminalizes hacking, unauthorized access, and data theft.
- **EU: Directive on Attacks Against Information Systems** – Establishes penalties for hacking and illegal system access.

◆ **Risk for Investigators:**

✗ Accessing restricted dark web sites without authorization (e.g., admin panels, vendor accounts).

✗ Using automated tools to scrape or harvest data from protected forums.

✗ Attempting to bypass authentication mechanisms (e.g., cracking forum passwords).

✅ **Best Practice:**

Stick to OSINT techniques that rely on publicly available data rather than attempting to gain unauthorized access to hidden or password-protected areas.

2. Possession & Distribution of Illicit Material

2.1 Handling Stolen Data & Illegal Content

Dark web investigations often involve exposed credentials, leaked databases, or illicit materials. However, merely possessing, downloading, or sharing such data—even for investigative purposes—can lead to legal consequences.

📌 **Examples of illegal content that can put investigators at risk:**

🔲 Leaked personal data (usernames, passwords, SSNs, credit card info).
🔲 Explicit or abusive content (child exploitation materials, terrorism propaganda).
🔲 Malware or hacking tools (ransomware, keyloggers, phishing kits).

◆ **Risk for Investigators:**

✗ Downloading and storing leaked credentials for analysis.

✖ Sharing or reposting dark web-sourced data in research reports.

✖ Possessing illicit files (even if obtained during an investigation).

✅ **Best Practice:**

- Use hash-checking tools to detect and avoid downloading illicit files.
- Do not store or redistribute illegal content—instead, report it to the appropriate authorities.
- Document findings carefully without handling or possessing criminal materials.

3. Jurisdictional & International Law Challenges

3.1 Investigating Across Borders

The dark web is inherently global, with marketplaces, forums, and cybercriminals operating across multiple jurisdictions. Investigators must be aware of differences in laws across countries, particularly regarding:

☐ Data privacy regulations (e.g., GDPR in Europe).
☐ Cybercrime laws that vary from country to country.
☐ Extradition agreements and cooperation between law enforcement agencies.

◆ **Risk for Investigators:**

✖ Collecting data from foreign servers in violation of local laws.

✖ Engaging in surveillance that is legal in one country but illegal in another.

✖ Accidentally interfering with an ongoing international law enforcement investigation.

✅ **Best Practice:**

- Consult legal experts before conducting investigations involving foreign entities.
- Follow data privacy laws—especially when dealing with leaked user information.
- Work with authorized agencies when investigating cybercrime networks across jurisdictions.

4. Entrapment & Unintentional Involvement in Illegal Activities

4.1 Avoiding Active Participation in Cybercrime

Some dark web investigations require undercover work—such as interacting with vendors or infiltrating forums. However, engaging too deeply can cross legal lines, leading to accusations of entrapment or aiding criminal activity.

📌 **Risky actions that can compromise an investigator legally:**

🚨 Purchasing stolen data or hacking tools "for research purposes."
🚨 Posing as a cybercriminal to gather intelligence.
🚨 Encouraging or facilitating illegal transactions.

◆ **Risk for Investigators:**

✗ Law enforcement agencies may interpret investigator actions as aiding cybercriminals.

✗ Even passive observation can be considered complicity in some jurisdictions.

✗ Investigators could become targets of real cybercriminals.

✅ **Best Practice:**

- Do not participate in any transactions, even for intelligence gathering.
- Avoid direct interactions with cybercriminals whenever possible.
- Use passive monitoring techniques instead of actively engaging in discussions.

5. Data Privacy Laws & Ethical Considerations

5.1 Handling Leaked Personal Information Responsibly

Investigators frequently encounter compromised credentials, financial data, and other sensitive information on the dark web. However, data privacy laws impose strict rules on how this information can be collected, stored, and used.

📌 **Key data protection regulations:**

- **EU: General Data Protection Regulation (GDPR)** – Limits how personal data is processed and shared.

- **U.S.: California Consumer Privacy Act (CCPA)** – Protects consumer data and requires disclosure of breaches.
- **Various countries**: Laws against storing or processing personally identifiable information (PII) without consent.

◆ **Risk for Investigators:**

✘ Storing or analyzing leaked personal data without proper legal authority.

✘ Publishing reports that expose user identities without consent.

✘ Failing to anonymize or redact sensitive information in research.

✅ **Best Practice:**

- Anonymize personal data before sharing research findings.
- Follow ethical guidelines for handling sensitive information.
- Report major data breaches to the appropriate authorities instead of storing leaked data.

6. Best Practices for Staying Legal & Ethical

To conduct dark web investigations safely and legally, OSINT analysts should follow these key guidelines:

✅ **Obtain Legal Guidance** – Consult cybersecurity lawyers to ensure compliance.
✅ **Use Passive Monitoring Techniques** – Avoid unauthorized access or direct interactions.
✅ **Follow Data Protection Laws** – Do not store or share personal data without proper authorization.
✅ **Avoid Purchasing Illegal Goods or Services** – Even if for research purposes, this can be considered a crime.
✅ **Work with Law Enforcement** – Share intelligence responsibly and legally.

📌 **Example Ethical Approach:**

A cybersecurity firm tracking ransomware groups on the dark web should only collect publicly available information, avoid direct interactions, and follow data privacy regulations when analyzing leaked victim data.

Conclusion: The Fine Line Between OSINT & Illegality

Investigating the dark web is high-risk but necessary for tracking cybercriminals, exposing data breaches, and uncovering illicit activities. However, analysts must be extremely cautious to avoid crossing legal boundaries.

◆ **Key Takeaways:**

✅ Know the laws governing unauthorized access, data privacy, and cybercrime investigations.

✅ Avoid handling or storing illegal materials, including stolen credentials.

✅ Follow ethical guidelines to ensure compliance with international regulations.

✅ Collaborate with legal experts and law enforcement when necessary.

🚀 **Final Thought:**

Dark web OSINT investigations require a deep understanding of both cyber threats and legal risks. By following best practices, investigators can gather intelligence safely, ethically, and within the law, ensuring their work remains valuable and legally sound.

12.2 Understanding Jurisdictional Issues in Cybercrime Cases

Cybercrime investigations are inherently complex due to jurisdictional challenges. Unlike traditional crimes, cyber offenses often cross multiple borders, involving perpetrators, victims, servers, and financial transactions spread across different countries. This creates significant legal and logistical hurdles for law enforcement and OSINT investigators.

This chapter will explore the key jurisdictional challenges in cybercrime cases, including conflicting international laws, extradition difficulties, data sovereignty issues, and cross-border cooperation efforts. Understanding these factors is crucial for tracking cybercriminals effectively while staying compliant with legal frameworks.

1. The Challenge of Jurisdiction in Cybercrime Investigations

1.1 What Defines Jurisdiction in Cybercrime Cases?

Jurisdiction refers to a country's legal authority to investigate, prosecute, and enforce laws. In cybercrime cases, multiple countries may have jurisdiction based on:

- **Where the crime was committed** (location of the victim or attack).
- **Where the perpetrator is located** (hacker's country of residence).
- **Where the affected systems or servers are hosted** (data centers and cloud infrastructure).
- **Where financial transactions occur** (cryptocurrency wallets, bank accounts).

📌 **Example Scenario:**

A phishing attack originates from a hacker in Russia, using a server in Germany, to target victims in the United States. Which country has jurisdiction? The answer depends on international agreements, local cyber laws, and cooperation between agencies.

◆ **Jurisdictional Risks for Investigators:**

✗ Operating in a country without proper legal authority.

✗ Violating international cyber laws while tracking criminals.

✗ Lack of cooperation from foreign governments during investigations.

✓ Best Practice:

- Work within the legal framework of your country.
- Use only publicly available OSINT methods to avoid jurisdictional violations.
- Seek legal guidance when investigating international cybercrime.

2. International Cybercrime Laws & Conflicts

2.1 Lack of Uniform Cybercrime Legislation

Cybercrime laws vary widely across different jurisdictions, making investigations and prosecutions challenging. Some countries have strict cybersecurity regulations, while others lack enforcement, creating safe havens for cybercriminals.

📌 **Key Cybercrime Laws Across Different Jurisdictions:**

☐ **United States** – Computer Fraud and Abuse Act (CFAA) criminalizes unauthorized system access.
☐ **European Union** – General Data Protection Regulation (GDPR) regulates data privacy and cross-border investigations.
☐ **China & Russia** – Strict internet sovereignty laws prevent foreign agencies from investigating cybercrimes in their territory.

◆ **Conflict Example:**

A ransomware gang based in Russia attacks businesses in the U.S. Russia does not extradite cybercriminals to the U.S., making prosecution nearly impossible.

✅ **Best Practice:**

- Understand regional cyber laws before conducting international investigations.
- Use diplomatic channels (e.g., INTERPOL, Europol) for legal cooperation.
- Leverage public-private partnerships to track cybercriminals legally.

3. Extradition Challenges in Cybercrime Cases

3.1 Why Extradition is Difficult in Cybercrime Cases

Extradition is the legal process of transferring a suspect from one country to another for prosecution. In cybercrime cases, extradition is often blocked due to political, legal, or diplomatic reasons.

📌 **Common Reasons for Extradition Denials:**

🚨 **Lack of treaties** – Some countries do not have extradition agreements.
🚨 **Political protection** – Nations may protect their hackers for strategic reasons.
🚨 **Differing cyber laws** – What is illegal in one country may not be a crime in another.

◆ **Case Study: Russian Hacker Extradition Battles**

The U.S. has repeatedly sought the extradition of Russian cybercriminals arrested in third-party countries like Spain or the Czech Republic. However, Russia often requests the suspect's return, leading to legal disputes.

✅ Best Practice:

- Work with international law enforcement to request extradition legally.
- Gather strong OSINT evidence to support legal action.
- Use diplomatic and economic pressure to push for compliance.

4. Data Sovereignty & Cross-Border Data Access

4.1 The Challenge of Accessing Data Stored in Foreign Servers

Many cybercrime investigations require access to emails, IP logs, financial transactions, or social media accounts stored on foreign servers. However, data sovereignty laws restrict how this information can be accessed.

📌 **Major Data Privacy Regulations Affecting Cyber Investigations:**

☐ **EU GDPR** – Limits how personal data can be transferred outside Europe.
☐ **U.S. CLOUD Act** – Allows U.S. authorities to request data from global companies.
☐ **China's Cybersecurity Law** – Requires companies to store user data within China.

◆ **Problem for Investigators:**

✗ OSINT analysts may be unable to access crucial data due to legal barriers.

✗ Law enforcement agencies need lengthy legal procedures (e.g., MLATs) to obtain data.

✗ Companies (Google, Meta, Microsoft) must balance compliance with multiple laws.

✅ Best Practice:

- Use legal data-sharing agreements (e.g., MLATs, CLOUD Act requests).
- Work with data hosting companies to obtain logs legally.
- Respect local privacy laws to avoid legal violations.

5. International Cooperation in Cybercrime Investigations

5.1 How Global Law Enforcement Agencies Collaborate

Despite jurisdictional challenges, international agencies coordinate efforts to track and arrest cybercriminals. Organizations like INTERPOL, Europol, and the FBI play key roles in cross-border investigations.

📌 **Key International Cybercrime Cooperation Networks:**

☐ **INTERPOL Cybercrime Directorate** – Facilitates global intelligence sharing.
☐ **Europol EC3 (European Cybercrime Centre)** – Focuses on EU-wide cyber threats.
☐ **The Budapest Convention on Cybercrime** – The only legally binding treaty on international cybercrime cooperation.

◆ **Case Study: Operation Onymous (2014)**

☐ Europol, FBI, and U.S. Homeland Security coordinated to take down Silk Road 2.0, a major dark web marketplace.
☐ Cooperation between agencies led to multiple arrests across different countries.

✔ **Best Practice:**

- Engage with trusted law enforcement agencies when conducting OSINT investigations.
- Share intelligence legally through official channels (e.g., Europol, INTERPOL).
- Follow international treaties and agreements to ensure lawful investigations.

6. Best Practices for OSINT Analysts Investigating Cybercrime Across Jurisdictions

To avoid legal risks and jurisdictional conflicts, cybercrime investigators should follow these guidelines:

✔ Understand the cyber laws of the countries involved in an investigation.

✔ Use open-source intelligence (OSINT) legally without violating data protection laws.

✔ Avoid direct interactions with cybercriminals that could cross legal lines.

✔ Cooperate with international agencies instead of acting independently.

✔ Document findings carefully to ensure evidence is admissible in court.

★ Example Ethical Approach:

An OSINT analyst tracking ransomware groups should only use public blockchain explorers to trace payments rather than attempting to hack criminal wallets.

Conclusion: The Need for Global Cybercrime Policies

Jurisdictional challenges make cybercrime investigations complex and legally sensitive. As cybercriminals exploit legal loopholes and international borders, law enforcement and OSINT analysts must navigate these obstacles carefully.

◆ Key Takeaways:

✓ Jurisdictional conflicts slow down cybercrime investigations and arrests.

✓ Data sovereignty laws impact how investigators access and use information.

✓ International cooperation is essential to combat cyber threats effectively.

🚀 Final Thought:

As cybercrime evolves, global collaboration and standardized cyber laws will be crucial in overcoming jurisdictional barriers and bringing cybercriminals to justice.

12.3 Ethics of Engaging with Dark Web Forums & Actors

Investigating the dark web presents unique ethical challenges. While OSINT analysts, cybersecurity professionals, and law enforcement officers often monitor cybercriminal activities in forums, marketplaces, and encrypted chat groups, engaging with these actors raises legal, moral, and operational risks. The line between passive observation and active participation can be blurry, and crossing it can lead to legal consequences, ethical violations, and even personal danger.

This chapter explores the ethical considerations of engaging with dark web communities, including the risks of direct communication, infiltration techniques, and best practices for ethical OSINT investigations.

1. The Ethical Dilemma of Dark Web Investigations

1.1 Passive Monitoring vs. Active Engagement

OSINT investigations on the dark web typically fall into two categories:

1☐ **Passive Monitoring** – Observing forums, marketplaces, and discussions without interaction.
2☐ **Active Engagement** – Creating accounts, interacting with users, or attempting to establish credibility within cybercriminal communities.

📌 **Ethical Question**: At what point does an investigation turn into active participation in criminal activities?

◆ **Passive Monitoring – Ethical & Legal** ✅

✓☐ Viewing publicly available posts on marketplaces or forums.
✓☐ Using OSINT tools to track transactions and leaked data.
✓☐ Monitoring forums for threat intelligence and cybersecurity research.

◆ **Active Engagement – High-Risk & Ethically Complex** ⚠☐

✗ Creating fake identities to pose as cybercriminals.

✗ Engaging in private chats with threat actors under false pretenses.

✗ Pretending to purchase illegal goods or services to gather intelligence.

✅ **Best Practice:**

- Limit engagement to passive observation unless working within a law enforcement operation with proper legal authorization.
- Follow strict ethical guidelines set by your organization or legal team.

2. Legal Boundaries: What is Permissible in OSINT Investigations?

2.1 The Risk of Entrapment & Legal Violations

One of the biggest risks in engaging with dark web actors is accidentally crossing legal boundaries. Some activities that may seem harmless can be interpreted as facilitation of criminal activity or entrapment.

📌 **Legal Risks for OSINT Analysts & Investigators**

🔒 **Accessing Dark Web Sites** – Simply visiting certain dark web sites may violate laws in some countries.

🔒 **Participating in Transactions** – Even pretending to buy illicit goods could lead to legal repercussions.

🔒 **Downloading Illegal Materials** – Storing stolen credentials, malware samples, or illicit files can breach data protection laws.

🔒 **Entrapment Risks** – Law enforcement must ensure they do not induce a crime that would not have happened otherwise.

◆ **Case Example: The FBI's AlphaBay Operation (2017)**

The FBI seized control of AlphaBay, a massive dark web marketplace, and posed as administrators for weeks to track cybercriminals. This was a legally sanctioned undercover operation, but if an OSINT analyst attempted something similar without authorization, it could be illegal and unethical.

✅ **Best Practice:**

- Do not engage in private communications with cybercriminals unless you have law enforcement clearance.
- Do not make purchases or participate in transactions, even for intelligence-gathering purposes.
- Always consult with legal professionals before conducting dark web investigations.

3. Ethical Concerns When Engaging with Dark Web Actors

3.1 The "Slippery Slope" of Deep Cover Investigations

Engaging with cybercriminals can create ethical dilemmas. Some investigators justify going undercover to collect intelligence, but where should the line be drawn?

📌 **Potential Ethical Risks:**

🔒 **Creating Fake Identities** – Posing as a hacker or criminal may be seen as deceptive and unethical.

🏛 **Gaining Trust of Criminals** – Becoming part of a community could lead to moral conflicts.

🏛 **Risking Unintended Harm** – Actions taken during an investigation could escalate criminal activity instead of stopping it.

◆ **Case Example: An OSINT Analyst in a Ransomware Forum**

An analyst joins a dark web ransomware forum and interacts with a threat actor to gather intelligence. The cybercriminal later shares stolen medical records, putting the analyst in possession of illegally obtained sensitive data.

✅ **Ethical Approach:**

- Use OSINT techniques to collect publicly available information instead of engaging in deceptive tactics.
- Set clear ethical boundaries—never contribute to or encourage illegal activities.
- Report findings to law enforcement rather than taking action independently.

4. Best Practices for Ethical OSINT Investigations on the Dark Web

4.1 How to Conduct Ethical Dark Web Investigations

To avoid legal and ethical pitfalls, OSINT analysts should adhere to the following guidelines:

✅ **Follow Legal and Ethical Frameworks**

- Research and comply with local, national, and international laws.
- Work within the policies set by cybersecurity firms, intelligence agencies, or academic institutions.

✅ **Use Passive OSINT Methods**

- Collect publicly available intelligence without direct engagement.
- Use dark web monitoring tools rather than infiltrating criminal forums.
- Monitor cryptocurrency transactions without interacting with criminals.

✅ **Avoid Direct Contact with Cybercriminals**

- Do not engage in private communications unless you have law enforcement authorization.
- Never pose as a buyer or seller to gather intelligence.
- If accidental contact occurs, document the interaction and report it immediately.

✅ Maintain Transparency & Ethical Standards

- Be clear about the purpose of the investigation—intelligence gathering, cybersecurity defense, or academic research.
- Ensure that findings are used for legitimate cybersecurity and law enforcement purposes.
- Do not manipulate or entrap individuals into committing crimes.

✅ Report Criminal Activities to Authorities

- If you come across evidence of ongoing cybercrime, report it to law enforcement or relevant organizations.
- Avoid attempting to take down criminal networks alone, as this can have legal and personal risks.

5. Case Study: Ethical Dark Web Investigations in Action

Case: Investigating a Dark Web Phishing Kit Marketplace

🔍 Scenario:

A cybersecurity firm discovers a dark web marketplace selling phishing kits used for bank fraud and credential theft. The firm wants to investigate without violating ethical and legal boundaries.

Ethical OSINT Approach:

✅ Passive Monitoring:

- Analysts track phishing kit vendors and document their activity.
- They collect publicly available advertisements, forum discussions, and sample kits.

✅ OSINT Research:

- Analysts cross-reference the phishing kits with real-world phishing campaigns.
- They analyze domain registrations, WHOIS data, and leaked credentials.

✅ Reporting & Action:

- The firm compiles an intelligence report and shares it with law enforcement.
- The phishing kits are flagged, and major cybersecurity vendors add them to blocklists.

◆ Outcome:

By using ethical OSINT techniques, the firm successfully gathered intelligence, disrupted phishing operations, and avoided engaging with criminals directly.

Conclusion: Balancing Ethics & Effectiveness in Dark Web Investigations

Investigating dark web forums and actors requires a delicate balance between intelligence gathering, legality, and ethical responsibility. While OSINT analysts play a crucial role in tracking cybercriminals and preventing attacks, they must operate within legal and ethical boundaries to avoid unintended consequences.

◆ **Key Takeaways:**

✅ Passive monitoring is ethical—active engagement is risky.

✅ Direct communication with criminals can lead to legal issues.

✅ OSINT should be used for intelligence gathering, not entrapment.

✅ Always report criminal activity through proper channels.

🚀 **Final Thought:**

The dark web is a valuable source of intelligence, but ethical OSINT practices must be the foundation of every investigation. Responsible, lawful, and ethical approaches will ensure that investigators protect themselves while contributing to cybersecurity efforts.

12.4 How to Safely Collect & Report Dark Web Intelligence

The dark web is a critical intelligence source for OSINT analysts, cybersecurity professionals, and law enforcement agencies. It hosts criminal marketplaces, hacking forums, ransomware leaks, and stolen data repositories, making it essential for tracking cyber threats. However, safely collecting and reporting intelligence from the dark web requires strong operational security (OPSEC), legal compliance, and ethical responsibility.

In this chapter, we will cover:

- Safe methods for accessing and collecting dark web intelligence.
- OPSEC measures to avoid exposure and legal risks.
- Best practices for analyzing and storing intelligence.
- How to report findings to law enforcement or private-sector security teams.

1. Safe Access Methods for Dark Web Investigations

Before collecting intelligence, it's crucial to establish a secure and anonymous working environment. Directly accessing dark web sites without proper precautions can compromise an investigation, expose personal data, or even violate laws.

1.1 Using Secure and Isolated Environments

To minimize risks, investigators should use:

Dedicated Machines & Virtual Machines (VMs)

- Use a separate computer or virtual machine (VM) for dark web investigations.
- Never use your personal or work devices for direct dark web access.

Tails OS or Whonix for Anonymous Browsing

- Tails OS (a live operating system that leaves no traces) or Whonix (a secure VM system) provides better anonymity than using Tor alone.
- These systems prevent IP leaks and data tracking.

Tor, I2P, and VPNs for Secure Connectivity

- Tor Browser is the primary tool for accessing .onion sites, but it should always be used with a VPN.
- I2P (Invisible Internet Project) can be used for additional layers of anonymity.

No Personal Accounts or Identifiable Information

- Never use personal or work emails to register on dark web forums.
- Create burner accounts with randomly generated usernames and emails.

1.2 Avoiding Malicious Content & Tracking

The dark web is filled with malicious content that can compromise investigators.

Common Risks:

- **Drive-by downloads** – Some sites automatically download malware.
- **Tracking scripts** – JavaScript-based tracking can reveal IPs.
- **Booby-trapped files** – Downloaded documents may contain malware or tracking beacons.

Best Practices:

- Disable JavaScript in the Tor browser for better security.
- Never download files from unknown dark web sources.
- Use sandbox environments if file analysis is required.

2. Collecting Dark Web Intelligence Ethically & Legally

2.1 Identifying Valuable OSINT from Dark Web Sources

Not all dark web information is useful. Investigators should focus on:

Threat Intelligence:

- Leaked databases (credentials, PII, financial data).
- Hacking forums discussing exploits, tools, and vulnerabilities.
- Ransomware sites listing victims and stolen data.
- Underground marketplaces selling stolen assets.

Indicators of Compromise (IoCs):

- Email addresses and usernames linked to breaches.
- Cryptocurrency wallet addresses used in illicit transactions.
- Malware hashes and phishing domains.

Actor Profiling:

- Identifying threat actors, hacker groups, or ransomware gangs.
- Mapping communication patterns and alliances.
- Tracking social engineering techniques and attack methods.

2.2 Collecting Data Without Breaking Laws

Investigators must adhere to legal and ethical standards when collecting intelligence.

Legal Methods for Data Collection:

- **Publicly accessible data** – Any information that can be accessed without login credentials.
- **Threat intelligence feeds** – Many cybersecurity firms legally monitor dark web leaks.
- **Dark web search engines (e.g., Ahmia)** – Provide indexed .onion sites.
- **Passive monitoring** – Observing discussions without engaging in criminal activity.

Illegal & High-Risk Methods:

- Creating fake accounts to pose as criminals (unless law enforcement-approved).
- Attempting to purchase stolen data or illicit goods.
- Accessing forums that require proving criminal intent.

Case Example: Analyzing a Ransomware Data Leak

An OSINT investigator finds a ransomware group's leak site listing stolen corporate files. Instead of downloading illegal data, they:

- Document metadata (file names, sizes, timestamps).
- Capture screenshot evidence (without exposing victims' PII).
- Cross-check leaked data against public breach notification services.

This method avoids legal risks while still gathering actionable intelligence.

3. Secure Storage & Analysis of Dark Web Intelligence

Once intelligence is collected, it must be securely stored and analyzed to prevent data leaks and maintain chain-of-custody integrity.

3.1 Safe Storage & Documentation

Encrypted Storage Solutions:

- Use encrypted storage (e.g., VeraCrypt, BitLocker) for sensitive data.
- Store collected evidence separately from personal or work files.

Metadata & Context Preservation:

- Record URLs, timestamps, and site descriptions.
- Use screenshots instead of downloading illegal data.
- Log forum discussions and dark web trends for analysis.

3.2 Data Correlation & Threat Analysis

Cross-Referencing Dark Web Data with OSINT

- Compare leaked credentials with Have I Been Pwned?.
- Check cryptocurrency wallets with blockchain explorers.
- Use domain intelligence tools to track phishing and malware sites.

Dark Web Data Enrichment

- Identify threat actors' aliases across different platforms.
- Use linguistic analysis to track writing styles.
- Map connections between different cybercrime groups.

4. Reporting Dark Web Intelligence to the Right Authorities

4.1 Who Should Receive Reports?

OSINT findings should be reported to:

Law Enforcement – FBI Cyber Division, Europol, INTERPOL.

Corporate Security Teams – To protect their compromised data.
Cyber Threat Intelligence (CTI) Teams – To strengthen defense strategies.
Breach Notification Platforms – Such as Have I Been Pwned.

4.2 Structuring an Effective Intelligence Report

A well-organized report helps authorities act quickly on threats.

Key Sections of a Dark Web Intelligence Report:

- **Summary**: Overview of the investigation.
- **Threat Source**: Where the data was found (forum, marketplace, ransomware site).
- **Collected Evidence**: Screenshots, metadata (no illegal downloads).
- **Indicators of Compromise (IoCs):** Emails, IPs, domains, crypto wallets.
- **Risk Assessment**: How this intelligence impacts security.
- **Recommendations**: Mitigation steps for affected parties.

◆ Example: Reporting a Dark Web Data Breach

An OSINT analyst finds stolen login credentials for a major corporation on a hacker forum. Instead of downloading files, they:

- Collect screenshots and metadata.
- Cross-check credentials with known breach databases.
- Alert the company's security team and law enforcement.

Conclusion: The Balance Between Intelligence & Security

Dark web intelligence is invaluable for cybersecurity and OSINT, but it must be collected safely, legally, and ethically.

Key Takeaways:

- Use secure environments (VMs, Tails OS, VPNs) to access the dark web.
- Passively monitor forums—do not engage with cybercriminals.
- Store intelligence securely and avoid illegal downloads.
- Report findings to the appropriate cybersecurity teams and law enforcement.

Final Thought:

The dark web is a powerful OSINT resource, but only when handled with strong security, ethical responsibility, and legal caution.

12.5 The Future of OSINT in Combating Dark Web Crime

The dark web remains a haven for cybercriminals, facilitating data breaches, ransomware operations, illicit marketplaces, and underground forums. As digital threats evolve, so must the methodologies used to track and dismantle cybercrime networks. Open-Source Intelligence (OSINT) plays a pivotal role in uncovering hidden connections, tracking cryptocurrency flows, monitoring criminal activity, and aiding law enforcement efforts.

This chapter explores the future of OSINT in dark web investigations, covering:

- Emerging technologies that enhance OSINT capabilities.
- Challenges in investigating encrypted and decentralized networks.
- The role of AI, automation, and blockchain analytics in cybercrime tracking.
- The growing collaboration between public and private sectors in fighting dark web threats.

1. Emerging OSINT Technologies for Dark Web Investigations

The next generation of OSINT tools will significantly improve how analysts track criminal activities on the dark web.

1.1 AI-Powered Threat Detection & Deep Web Crawlers

Artificial Intelligence (AI) & Machine Learning (ML)

- AI can analyze massive amounts of dark web data to detect patterns, keywords, and emerging threats.
- Natural Language Processing (NLP) helps in deciphering slang, criminal jargon, and coded messages used on cybercrime forums.

Dark Web Crawlers & Automated Monitoring

- Future OSINT crawlers will be capable of indexing hidden forums, black markets, and encrypted chatrooms more efficiently.
- AI-driven automation will allow real-time threat alerts for stolen credentials, ransomware leaks, and cybercriminal discussions.

Example: An AI-powered crawler detects a new ransomware leak site before law enforcement becomes aware, allowing early intervention.

1.2 Blockchain & Cryptocurrency Tracking Advancements

As cybercriminals rely on cryptocurrencies for payments, OSINT will increasingly focus on crypto-tracing techniques.

Advanced Blockchain Forensics

- AI-based blockchain analytics will help de-anonymize cryptocurrency transactions.
- Pattern recognition tools can link crypto wallets to known cybercriminal networks.

Defeating Mixing Services & Privacy Coins

New de-anonymization methods will make it harder for criminals to use Bitcoin mixers, Monero (XMR), or other privacy-focused coins to launder money.

Example: A blockchain forensics team successfully traces ransom payments to a hacker group's real-world identity.

2. Challenges in Future Dark Web Investigations

Despite advances in OSINT, cybercriminals continuously adapt. Investigators face growing obstacles:

2.1 The Rise of Decentralized & Encrypted Networks

Decentralized Marketplaces & Forums

- Dark web criminals are shifting from centralized forums (e.g., darknet marketplaces) to decentralized platforms.
- Peer-to-peer (P2P) networks, blockchain-based messaging apps, and encrypted communities make it harder to track illegal activity.

End-to-End Encryption (E2EE) & Private Messaging Apps

- Signal, Telegram, Session, and Tox are replacing traditional dark web forums for cybercriminal communications.

- AI-powered metadata analysis will be key in identifying patterns in encrypted conversations.

2.2 The Evolving Tactics of Cybercriminals

More Sophisticated Operational Security (OPSEC)

- Threat actors are using multiple aliases, burner devices, and multi-layered encryption to evade detection.
- AI-driven deception tactics (e.g., deepfake voices and AI-generated fake identities) complicate investigations.

Example: A ransomware gang uses deepfake-generated videos to mislead OSINT analysts about their location.

2.3 Legal & Ethical Challenges

Jurisdictional Issues in Dark Web Crime

- Many cybercriminals operate in countries with weak cybercrime laws.
- Cross-border investigations require international cooperation, which is often slow and bureaucratic.

Balancing Privacy & Surveillance

- Ethical concerns will grow as OSINT tools become more invasive.
- Striking the right balance between law enforcement needs and digital privacy rights will be a major debate in the future.

3. AI, Automation & The Future of OSINT Tools

As OSINT evolves, expect greater automation, real-time tracking, and AI-driven intelligence.

3.1 Real-Time OSINT Dashboards & Automated Alerts

Live Threat Intelligence Feeds

- Future OSINT platforms will offer real-time alerts for compromised credentials, stolen credit card data, or cybercrime discussions.

- Integration with law enforcement databases will allow instant cross-referencing of cybercriminal activities.

AI-Driven Predictive Analytics

- AI will analyze cybercriminal patterns to predict future attacks and emerging threats.
- Dark web sentiment analysis will help forecast which companies or industries might be targeted next.

3.2 Using Deepfake Detection & Behavioral Analysis

Deepfake & AI-Generated Content Tracking

- As cybercriminals use deepfake voices, videos, and AI-generated personas, OSINT tools will evolve to detect synthetic identities.
- Behavioral analytics will play a key role in identifying deception tactics used in dark web scams.

Example: An AI-powered tool identifies that a hacker group's "leader" is actually an AI-generated persona used to throw off investigators.

4. The Role of Public-Private Collaboration

Combating dark web crime will require stronger collaboration between:

- Government agencies (FBI, Europol, INTERPOL)
- Private cybersecurity firms (CrowdStrike, Recorded Future, Mandiant, Chainalysis)
- Academic researchers and ethical hackers

4.1 Cybersecurity Firms & OSINT Intelligence Sharing

Dark Web Intelligence Feeds

- Security firms will provide live feeds of dark web threats, helping businesses protect against data breaches and ransomware.
- Threat-sharing platforms will improve global cybersecurity collaboration.

Joint Task Forces & AI-Based Threat Hunting

- Public and private sectors will share AI-driven insights on cybercrime trends.
- AI-powered crime prediction models will help law enforcement disrupt criminal operations before they escalate.

5. The Future of OSINT Ethics & Regulations

As OSINT becomes more powerful, ethical and legal frameworks must evolve to prevent misuse.

Key Ethical Questions for the Future:

- Should AI-powered OSINT tools be used for mass surveillance?
- How can we prevent bias and false positives in AI-driven investigations?
- Should OSINT tools be restricted to government agencies only, or available to private companies?

Future Cyber Laws & Dark Web OSINT Regulations

- Governments will likely introduce stricter laws on OSINT data collection to protect privacy.
- Ethical AI development will become a major focus to prevent misuse.

Conclusion: The Road Ahead for OSINT in Dark Web Investigations

OSINT is entering a new era of AI, automation, and advanced threat intelligence. While these advancements will revolutionize how investigators track cybercriminals, challenges remain, including decentralized networks, encrypted platforms, and evolving OPSEC tactics.

Key Takeaways for the Future of Dark Web OSINT:

- AI & machine learning will enhance dark web monitoring.
- Blockchain forensics will improve cryptocurrency tracking.
- Decentralized marketplaces will make investigations harder.
- Stronger public-private collaboration will be essential for cybercrime prevention.
- Ethical and legal frameworks must evolve alongside OSINT capabilities.

Final Thought:

The future of OSINT in combating dark web crime is both exciting and challenging. As cybercriminals adapt, so must investigators—leveraging AI, automation, and global intelligence-sharing to stay ahead of the threat.

12.6 Case Study: When OSINT Crossed Legal & Ethical Boundaries

Open-Source Intelligence (OSINT) is a powerful tool for cyber investigations, dark web monitoring, and law enforcement operations. However, there is a fine line between ethical intelligence gathering and privacy violations, entrapment, or even illegal surveillance.

This case study examines a real-world incident where OSINT analysts crossed ethical and legal boundaries, leading to controversy, legal consequences, and debates over privacy rights. It highlights the risks of unregulated OSINT practices and the importance of legal compliance and ethical considerations in cyber investigations.

Background: The Targeted Investigation

In 2021, an independent cybersecurity research group launched an OSINT investigation into a suspected cybercriminal group operating on the dark web. The group was allegedly responsible for:

- Selling stolen credentials from corporate data breaches
- Offering ransomware-as-a-service (RaaS) kits
- Running a marketplace for illegal hacking tools

The OSINT researchers, who were not law enforcement officers, took it upon themselves to track, infiltrate, and expose the group. Their goal was to publicly dox the cybercriminals and hand over their findings to authorities. However, their methods blurred the lines between ethical OSINT and illegal activities.

Phase 1: Infiltrating Dark Web Forums

What They Did:

- Created fake hacker personas to gain the trust of forum members.
- Used social engineering tactics to extract personal details from suspected criminals.

- Purchased stolen data to verify its authenticity.

The Ethical & Legal Issues:

- **Impersonation & Deception**: While common in law enforcement operations, private researchers using fake identities raised ethical concerns.
- **Handling Stolen Data**: Buying stolen credentials—even for investigative purposes—violated multiple cybersecurity laws.

Example: One of the researchers used an alias to purchase a leaked database of corporate logins, which was later deemed illegal possession of stolen property.

Phase 2: Cross-Referencing Identities & Doxxing

What They Did:

- Collected dark web usernames, Bitcoin wallets, and email addresses.
- Used OSINT tools to link these identities to real-world individuals on social media, LinkedIn, and corporate websites.
- Publicly posted the alleged cybercriminals' names, addresses, and workplaces.

The Ethical & Legal Issues:

- **Privacy Violations**: Some of the doxxed individuals were wrongly identified, leading to harassment of innocent people.
- **Defamation Risks**: Publicly accusing individuals without solid legal evidence created risks of lawsuits for libel and defamation.
- **Interference with Law Enforcement**: By prematurely exposing suspects, the researchers compromised ongoing investigations, making it harder for authorities to prosecute.

Example: One falsely accused individual received death threats after their personal details were leaked. They later sued the OSINT group for defamation.

Phase 3: Hacking & Unauthorized Access

What They Did:

- Attempted to gain access to private dark web marketplaces by exploiting security flaws.

- Used phishing techniques to trick cybercriminals into revealing login credentials.
- Gained access to a Telegram group used for illicit activities by social engineering an admin.

The Ethical & Legal Issues:

- Unauthorized Access (Hacking): Even if done with good intentions, gaining access to private systems without consent violated hacking laws (e.g., the Computer Fraud and Abuse Act [CFAA] in the U.S.).
- Entrapment Concerns: Some researchers posed as buyers of illegal goods, raising legal questions about whether they were encouraging criminal activity.

Example: The OSINT researchers tricked a dark web vendor into revealing their IP address, but since they used social engineering and hacking, their evidence was not legally admissible in court.

The Consequences

Legal Repercussions:

- Several researchers faced criminal charges for hacking and unauthorized access.
- The cybersecurity firm funding the investigation was sued for privacy violations and defamation.

Reputational Damage:

- The incident damaged the credibility of OSINT researchers, raising concerns about vigilante justice in cybersecurity.
- Law enforcement agencies distanced themselves from the investigation, stating that proper legal procedures were not followed.

Lessons Learned:

- **OSINT has limits** – even public data collection must follow privacy laws.
- **Doxxing can backfire** – wrongly identifying a suspect can lead to harassment, lawsuits, and ethical concerns.
- **Unauthorized access is illegal** – OSINT should be passive intelligence gathering, not hacking.
- **Cooperation with law enforcement is key** – instead of taking matters into their own hands, researchers should work within legal frameworks.

Conclusion: The Fine Line Between OSINT & Cybercrime

This case study serves as a warning about how OSINT investigations can cross ethical and legal boundaries when not handled properly. While OSINT is a powerful tool for cybersecurity and dark web investigations, it must always be used ethically, legally, and responsibly.

Key Takeaways:

✓☐ Always follow privacy laws & ethical guidelines when conducting OSINT.

✓☐ Avoid unauthorized access, hacking, or deception.

✓☐ Work with law enforcement, rather than acting as a vigilante.

✓☐ Verify all intelligence before public exposure to prevent doxxing innocent individuals.

Final Thought:

OSINT is a double-edged sword—when used ethically, it helps fight cybercrime, but when misused, it can turn researchers into criminals themselves. Responsible OSINT practices ensure that investigations stay on the right side of the law while still exposing cyber threats effectively.

Emails serve as a primary method of communication in both personal and professional settings, but they are also key sources of intelligence in cyber investigations. From tracking cybercriminal activities to uncovering data breaches, email intelligence plays a crucial role in OSINT. Similarly, the dark web—a hidden layer of the internet—harbors illicit markets, leaked data, and cybercrime discussions, making it a valuable but complex landscape for intelligence gathering.

Email & Dark Web Investigations: Tracking Leaks & Breaches equips you with advanced techniques to analyze email addresses, trace digital footprints, and investigate data breaches. It also provides a structured approach to safely navigating and investigating dark web sources to uncover cyber threats, leaked credentials, and hidden criminal activities.

What You'll Learn in This Book

- **Email OSINT Fundamentals**: Learn how email addresses create digital footprints and what information can be extracted.
- **Email Header Analysis**: Decode email metadata to trace IP addresses, servers, and sender information.
- **Reverse Email Lookup**: Use open-source tools to track emails across social media, forums, and data leaks.
- **Breach Data Investigations**: Learn how to check if an email address has been compromised in a data breach.
- **Dark Web Basics & Structure**: Understand how the dark web operates, from Tor networks to hidden marketplaces.
- **Investigating Data Leaks**: Find and analyze leaked credentials, databases, and financial data on underground forums.
- **Tracking Threat Actors on the Dark Web**: Learn techniques for monitoring cybercriminal activities and threat groups.
- **Using Dark Web Search Engines**: Explore tools like Ahmia, DarkSearch, and other indexing services for dark web investigations.
- **Operational Security & Anonymity**: Learn how to conduct dark web investigations safely while protecting your identity.
- **Ethical & Legal Considerations**: Understand the boundaries of lawful investigations and responsible OSINT practices.

With real-world case studies, practical exercises, and hands-on tutorials, Email & Dark Web Investigations provides essential knowledge for cybersecurity professionals, law enforcement, journalists, and intelligence analysts. Whether you're tracking a scammer, investigating a breach, or monitoring cyber threats, this book will guide you through the advanced methods of email and dark web intelligence.

Thank you for exploring **Email & Dark Web Investigations: Tracking Leaks & Breaches**. In an era where cyber threats and data breaches are increasing, the ability to investigate emails and the dark web is a crucial skill. Your dedication to learning these techniques strengthens the global effort to combat cybercrime, protect individuals, and uncover hidden threats.

As always, we emphasize ethical responsibility when using OSINT skills. Investigating email data and the dark web must be done with caution, legality, and respect for privacy. These techniques should be used for security, research, and investigative purposes—not for malicious intent.

We deeply appreciate your time and curiosity in studying this field. If you found this book helpful, we'd love to hear from you! Your feedback allows us to refine future editions and continue providing valuable intelligence resources.

Stay secure, stay ethical, and keep investigating.

Continue Your OSINT Journey

Expand your skills with the rest of The **OSINT Analyst Series**:

- **OSINT Foundations**: The Beginner's Guide to Open-Source Intelligence
- **The OSINT Search Mastery**: Hacking Search Engines for Intelligence
- **OSINT People Finder**: Advanced Techniques for Online Investigations
- **Social Media OSINT**: Tracking Digital Footprints
- **Image & Geolocation Intelligence**: Reverse Searching and Mapping
- **Domain, Website & Cyber Investigations with OSINT**
- **OSINT Threat Intel**: Investigating Hackers, Breaches, and Cyber Risks
- **Corporate OSINT**: Business Intelligence & Competitive Analysis
- **Investigating Disinformation & Fake News with OSINT**
- **OSINT for Deep & Dark Web**: Techniques for Cybercrime Investigations
- **OSINT Automation**: Python & APIs for Intelligence Gathering
- **OSINT Detective**: Digital Tools & Techniques for Criminal Investigations
- **Advanced OSINT Case Studies**: Real-World Investigations
- **The Ethical OSINT Investigator**: Privacy, Legal Risks & Best Practices

We look forward to seeing you in the next book!

Happy investigating!